SECOND EDITION

Becoming a Language Teacher

A Practical Guide to Second Language Learning and Teaching

Elaine Kolker Horwitz
The University of Texas at Austin

PEARSON

Boston   Columbus   Indianapolis   New York   San Francisco   Upper Saddle River   Amsterdam
Cape Town   Dubai   London   Madrid   Milan   Munich   Paris   Montreal   Toronto
Delhi   Mexico City   São Paulo   Sydney   Hong Kong   Seoul   Singapore   Taipei   Tokyo

To: Michael and Phil

Vice President and Editor-in-Chief: *Aurora Martínez Ramos*
Editor: *Erin Grelak*
Editorial Assistant: *Michelle Hochberg*
Executive Marketing Manager: *Krista Clark*
Production Editor: *Janet Domingo*
Project Coordination, Editorial Services, and Text Design: *Electronic Publishing Services Inc., NYC*
Manufacturing Buyer: *Megan Cochran*
Art Rendering and Electronic Page Makeup: *Jouve*
Cover Designer: *Diane Lorenzo*

Credits and acknowledgments borrowed from other sources and reproduced, with permission, in this textbook appear on the appropriate page within text.

Many of the designations by manufacturers and sellers to distinguish their products are claimed as trademarks. Where those designations appear in this book, and the publisher was aware of a trademark claim, the designations have been printed in initial caps or all caps.

Library of Congress Cataloging-in-Publication Data

Horwitz, Elaine Kolker
    Becoming a language teacher : a practical guide to second language learning and teaching / Elaine Kolker Horwitz. — 2nd ed.
       p.   cm.
    Includes index.
    ISBN 978-0-13-248998-0
    1. Language and languages—Study and teaching.   2. Second language acquisition.
I. Title.
P51.H67 2012
418.0071—dc23

2011048462

10 9 8 7 6 5 4 3 2 1

PEARSON

www.pearsonhighered.com

ISBN-13: 978-0-13-248998-0
ISBN-10: 0-13-248998-8

ABOUT THE AUTHOR

Elaine Horwitz is Professor of Curriculum and Instruction and Director of the Graduate Program in Foreign Language Education at the University of Texas at Austin. She was born in Washington, DC, and attended the Montgomery County, MD, public schools where she studied French and Spanish. She began her language teaching career in seventh grade when other students would ask her to explain what her teacher was saying.

Professor Horwitz earned her BA at the University of Maryland at College Park and her MA and PhD in Second Language Learning and Teaching at the University of Illinois at Urbana–Champaign. While at Illinois, she was a Title VII Bilingual Education Fellow and supervised foreign language, ESL, and bilingual student teachers.

She first taught French, Spanish, and English in the Prince George's County, MD, public schools and later went on to teach at University High School in Urbana, IL, and as a Graduate Assistant at the University of Illinois. Before moving to the University of Texas, she taught courses in French, language teaching methodology, and bilingual education at the State University College of New York at Buffalo.

At the University of Texas, Professor Horwitz teaches courses in language teaching methodology, second language acquisition, language testing, and second language research methods. She is well-known for her research on language anxiety and student and teacher beliefs about language learning. In addition to numerous scholarly articles and chapters, she is the coeditor with Dolly Young of *Language Anxiety: From Theory and Practice to Classroom Implications*. Her assessment tools, the Foreign Language Classroom Anxiety Scale and the Beliefs about Language Learning Inventory, are widely used to help teachers and researchers better understand the needs of second language learners. She has been an invited lecturer and consultant on improving language teaching throughout the world.

Professor Horwitz would love to hear from any readers of this book, especially from those who have started a BLT club (see Chapter 11). You can contact her via e-mail at horwitz@mail.utexas.edu.

CONTENTS

Preface   ix
Acknowledgments   xvii

PART ONE   What Do Language Teachers Think About?   1

1 What Should I Know About Language Learners and
Language Teaching Settings?   3

    Types of Language Learning Settings   4

    Learner Characteristics   7

    Younger Learners and Stages of Cognitive Development   18

    Identity and Language Learning   20

2 What Should I Know About Second Language
Acquisition?   25

    Theories of Second Language Acquisition   26

    The Critical Period Hypothesis   47

    How the Theories Differ on Important Language Teaching Issues   48

    Implications for Language Teaching   55

3 What Should I Know About Language Teaching
Methodologies?   60

    Language Teaching Methods   60

    What Is the Best Language Teaching Method?   71

    **Content-Based, Sheltered Instruction, Learner-Centered, and Task-Based
Approaches to Language Teaching**   72

    From Teacher-Centered to Learner-Centered Approaches   76

PART TWO   How Do You Teach a Language?   83

4   What Should I Know About Teaching Listening?   85

The Importance of Listening Comprehension   86

The Listening Process   91

Some Guidelines for Developing Listening Activities   95

Activity Ideas   97

Assessing Listening Comprehension   103

5   What Should I Know About Teaching Speaking?   109

The Importance of True Communication in the Language Classroom   110

Obstacles to Teaching Speaking   112

The Development of Speaking Ability   117

Some Guidelines for Developing Speaking Activities   120

Activity Ideas   123

Assessing Speaking   128

6   What Should I Know About Teaching Reading?   134

The Importance of Reading   135

The Reading Process   135

Types of Second Language Reading   136

Learning to Read in a Second Language   137

Types of Reading Materials   138

Helping Students Develop Effective Reading Strategies   139

ESL Teachers and Content Reading   141

Some Guidelines for Teaching Reading   142

Activity Ideas   144

Assessing Reading Comprehension   149

7 What Should I Know About Teaching Writing? 156

The Writing Process 157

Types of Second Language Writing 158

Helping Students Develop Effective Writing Strategies 163

Some Guidelines for Teaching Writing 167

Activity Ideas 169

Assessing Writing 173

8 What Should I Know About Teaching Academic English in Content Classes? 179

The Development of Academic Language 181

Generation 1.5 and Transnational Students 183

Scaffolding, Contextualized Input, and Thematic Units 184

Promoting Second Language Development in Content Classes 185

Academic Literacy 188

Integrating Language Skills Using Thematic Units and Task-Based Activities 192

Some Guidelines for Teaching Language Through Content 193

Activity Ideas 195

The Cognitive Academic Language Learning Approach (CALLA) 197

Assessing Language in Content Classes 199

PART THREE How Do I Know What to Teach? 207

9 How Do I Assess Language Learning? 209

Standards 210

Issues in Language Testing 214

Testing Approaches 217

Testing for a Variety of Purposes 220

Testing the Standards   220

The TOEFL, the ACTFL OPI, the TOEIC, and the IELTS   223

10 How Do I Plan My Classes?   229

Planning for *Your* Students   232

Common Language Teaching Activities   237

Differentiating Instruction and Supporting Learner Autonomy   241

PART FOUR   Where Do I Go from Here?   247

11 So, Am I Now a Language Teacher?   249

Thinking of Yourself as a Language Teacher   249

Becoming Open to New Ideas About Language and Language Teaching   250

Becoming a Better Language Teacher   251

Your Future as a Language Teacher   255

Beginning Your Journey as a Language Teacher   256

Appendix A: The Beliefs About Language Learning Inventory (BALLI): ESL Version 2.0   261

Appendix B: Foreign Language Classroom Anxiety Scale (FLCAS)   264

Appendix C: Teacher Foreign Language Anxiety Scale (TFLAS)   266

Glossary   268

Index   282

A Word to the New Language Teacher

- Why do you want to become a language teacher?
- How does teaching a language differ from other kinds of teaching?
- What do you want to remember about your own learning experiences when you become a language teacher?
- What experiences and personal strengths do you bring to language teaching?
- What kind of language teacher do you want to be?

Welcome to the Language Teaching Profession!

You are beginning a wonderful and exciting journey toward becoming a language teacher. Maybe you are preparing to teach English or another language or to become an elementary or high school teacher who will have English learners in your classes. Or you are an experienced teacher who is learning how to better help the English learners in your classroom. In any case, this book is designed to help you in your journey as a language teacher as well as to help you guide your students on their journeys as language learners. Its goal is to help you become the creative, competent, supportive, and up-to-date language teacher that you want to be and that your students deserve.

The concept of a journey is especially appropriate for language teachers. Many language teachers have themselves experienced the journey of language learning, and even language teachers who have never traveled abroad or learned a second language vicariously, experience the language learning journeys of their students and usually acquire some of their students' languages and cultures in the process. Language teachers are also guides in their students' language learning journeys. It would be very difficult for someone to learn a new language without the help of a teacher or at least a friend who speaks that language. Language teachers direct their students' attention to useful structures and vocabulary, interesting and appropriate materials, and helpful language learning approaches. Language teachers also help interpret the new language and culture for their students.

You are also undertaking the journey of your personal development as a language teacher. This book includes all the topics that language teaching methodology books typically cover but unlike most methods books, it also addresses the more practical questions that language teachers want to ask, such as: How do I plan a lesson? How will I know if the students are learning? How do I teach language when I am also teaching content material? This volume recognizes that you will have many questions and a range of emotional reactions as you pursue your journey as a language teacher. The advice that I give you along the way is the same advice I would give and have given to language teachers under my own supervision. I try to explain as clearly and as nontechnically as possible the information you will need to put current and effective language teaching methods into practice in your own teaching situation.

Although I personally believe that language instruction should be based on spontaneous communication, real-life language materials, the development of academic literacy, a caring relationship with learners, and the encouragement of learner autonomy, the message throughout this book will be that you are a competent and caring individual and that as the person most familiar with your students, their language needs, and your specific teaching situation, you are the best person to make instructional decisions. Throughout the book, you will be given practical guidelines for making decisions and specific teaching situations to think about to help you become comfortable with the process of thinking about language instruction. This book also includes many activities that you can use when you are teaching, and a glossary at the end of the book for all the terms appearing in **bold** type. The Finding Your Way section at the end of each chapter includes a checklist to help you remember important concepts from each chapter when you plan your classes. I hope that you will consult them as you prepare your classes.

This volume has another strong theme. Specifically, it maintains the perspective that both language learning and language teaching are dynamic processes that demand ongoing attention and adjustment. There is no one right way of going about language learning or language teaching for that matter. I believe that your approach to language teaching will evolve as you learn more about your students, yourself as a teacher, and the teaching approaches available to language teachers. In the same way, I believe that your students will also change as they learn more about their new language and culture, themselves as language learners, and even you as their language teacher. I also believe that the best way to become a language teacher is to learn to observe your students and yourself and reflect on these observations.

This book has several special features to help you create your personal approach to language teaching. There are reflection questions at the beginning of each chapter and Finding Your Way sections at the end of each chapter to help you think about your goals as a language teacher and make plans for your language teaching. I hope that you will keep a record of your answers to these questions and consult your responses from time to time during your teaching career to remind yourself where you started and to keep track of your progress in your journey as a language teacher.

Language teaching is an exciting, rewarding, and challenging profession. Welcome!

Looking Ahead

Becoming a Language Teacher offers both the knowledge and the practical skills you will need to construct a personal approach to language teaching. In addition to the basics of language teaching in any setting, it specifically considers approaches to the teaching and assessment of English in content classes. This book contains eleven chapters divided into four parts. The first part, "What Do Language Teachers Think About?" focuses on the foundations of language teaching. It includes the topics of learner characteristics and language teaching settings, second language acquisition theories, and language teaching methodologies. This part gives you the background knowledge you will need in your work as a professional language teacher. Chapter 1 is devoted to important learner characteristics that have been found to facilitate or hamper language learning, important terms used by language teachers, and differences in language teaching settings. It also discusses differences in younger and older language learners and how you can provide for these differences. This chapter will help you reach each of the language learners in your classes. Chapter 2 discusses major theories of second language acquisition and how they explain important questions about language learning, such as Do children and adults learn second languages differently? Why are some learners more successful than others? and How should learner errors be handled? Chapter 3 describes major language teaching methodologies and how they are applied in the classroom. It will help you decide which approaches might be most appropriate for you and your students.

Part II, "How Do You Teach a Language?" describes teaching approaches that will help you promote and assess your students' listening, speaking, reading, and writing abilities as well as their academic literacy. Chapter 4 discusses the educational principles and approaches associated with developing students' listening comprehension abilities, and Chapter 5 discusses the teaching of speaking. Chapters 6 and 7 consider the development of second language reading and writing, the essential components of second language literacy. Chapter 8 specifically considers language learning and teaching through tasked-based instruction and content learning. Each of these chapters includes testing and assessment approaches for listening, speaking, reading, writing, and academic English in content classes. I have chosen not to include a separate chapter on how to teach culture, since culture permeates all aspects of language learning and use. Instead, I have integrated ideas about culture and sociocultural influences on language learning throughout the book.

Part III, "How Do I Know What to Teach?" concentrates on adapting teaching practices to specific teaching settings. Chapter 9 discusses curriculum standards in English as a second language (ESL) and world languages and addresses the essential areas of language assessment and testing. It will help you determine if your students are learning what they need to know. Chapter 10 describes what language teachers do every day, such as choosing appropriate materials, working to motivate students, and presenting the language. This chapter describes typical language class activities, short- and long-term planning, and goal setting to help you develop your day-to-day lesson plans.

Finally, Part IV, "Where Do I Go from Here?" helps you envision your future as a language teacher. Chapter 11 is devoted to you and your personal development as a language teacher. It discusses how to improve and maintain your skills as a language teacher, how to evaluate your own teaching through action research, and ultimately how to become the teacher you want to be. It also offers advice on surviving and even flourishing in your first assignments as a language teacher. This chapter ends with a look ahead to future trends in language teaching. Language classes of the future will doubtless be influenced by technological breakthroughs as well as social, political, and economic changes around the world. Although this book is designed to help you become a confident, creative, and effective language teacher in today's classrooms, it is also important to think about your future as a language teacher.

A Word About the Second Edition

The second edition of *Becoming a Language Teacher* builds on the strengths of the original volume by speaking directly to new teachers in a clear and supportive voice while at the same time offering comprehensive and up-to-date information about language teaching in a variety of settings. It continues the image of a journey for new language teachers and asks readers to consider their own experiences as students and specifically as language learners to give them greater insight into what their own students must accomplish to attain language competence. The popular Teaching Checklists have been continued and expanded. Every chapter has been updated with the inclusion of new concepts, teaching scenarios, reflection activities, and references and suggestions for further readings. The second edition also includes the first publication of the long-awaited revision of the Beliefs about Language Learning Inventory.* The formatting in the second edition has been streamlined, and new terms and concepts have been added to the Glossary

Excitingly, there have been a number of important advances in language learning and teaching since the publication of the first-edition of this book. The major additions to the second edition of *Becoming a Language Teacher* are related to sociocultural approaches to second language acquisition and teaching, including the Output Hypothesis and sociocultural theories of SLA (introduced in Chapter 2 and integrated throughout the book). There is also expanded content (in Chapter 8 and throughout the book) focusing on the development of academic language and the development of language proficiency through content teaching. Both the SIOP Method (Chapter 3) and CALLA (Chapter 8) are included in this edition. An assessment for learning approach to student testing has also been added to Chapter 8. Finally, suggestions for using new technologies and digital media appear throughout the second edition.

Specific changes to each chapter include:

---

*Horwitz, E. K. (1988). The beliefs about language learning of beginning university foreign language students. *Modern Language Journal, 72*, 182–193.

Chapter 1

Chapter 1 includes a number of new terms that describe language learners, including **English learner, emergent bilingual, limited-English proficient** (as an obsolete term), **heritage learners**, and language learning programs including **dual language, world languages, sheltered English, newcomer centers,** and **self-access language learning centers**. The concepts of **willingness to communicate, language learner autonomy,** and the need for learners to develop a **second language identity** have been added to the material on learner characteristics. The first chapter has also been expanded to include conceptualizations of motivation beyond the Gardner and Lambert instrumental-integrative model traditionally used in second language teaching. The need for **differentiated instruction** is introduced in Chapter 1 and integrated throughout the second edition.

Chapter 2

The **Output Hypothesis** and **sociocultural theories of second language acquisition** join the **first language, experience,** and **social** theories of SLA in Chapter 2. This incorporation includes parallel tables summarizing the major premises of the new perspectives, how to implement them in the classroom, and their implications for major issues in second language acquisition. New concepts associated with the Output Hypothesis include **output, hypothesis testing, noticing, metatalk,** and **sociolinguistic competence**. The sociocultural theories of SLA add the Vygotskian notions of the **zone of proximal development, imitation, L2 internalization, mediation, private speech,** and **self-regulation** to the chapter. I have also relabeled the attention theories as cognitive learning theories; they are linked to the Cognitive Academic Language Learning Approach (CALLA) in Chapter 8. Finally, in addition to behavioral and cognitive learning theories, **constructivism** and **socio-constructivism** are introduced as are the concepts of **recasts** and **negative feedback**.

Chapter 3

A discussion of the **Sheltered Instruction Observation Protocol (SIOP)** appears in Chapter 3. The material on Sheltered Instruction has been expanded and the concept of differentiated instruction has been integrated into the discussion of there not being a single best method of language teaching. The choice of teaching approach needs to be compatible with learners' needs and characteristics and support their autonomy.

Chapters 4–7

As is the case with all the chapters, Chapters 4, 5, 6, and 7, have been updated with new questions, activities, and references. In addition to the perspectives offered by original SLA theories discussed in the first edition, listening, speaking, reading, and writing are interpreted through the new perspectives of the Output Hypothesis and sociocultural theories of SLA. Clearer relationships between and among the various language skills and the development of academic language and content skills have been drawn. Several new activity types have been added, including **information-gap activities**, **graded readers**, and **digital storytelling**. These chapters also give increased attention to advanced language learning.

Chapter 8

Chapter 8 focuses on the development of **academic literacy** through content learning. It describes Anna Chamot's **Cognitive Academic Language Learning Approach (CALLA)*** and ties **task-based** and **content-based** language learning to both SIOP and CALLA. The explanation of CALLA introduces a new SLA theory, called **socio-cognitive theory**, which is based on two types of knowledge: **procedural memory** and **declarative knowledge**. As noted earlier, socio-cognitive theory is also discussed in relation to the cognitive learning theory of SLA (Chapter 2).

Chapter 9

A number of new testing and evaluation concepts and their implications for language teaching have been added to Chapter 9. The new concepts include **alternative assessment**, **formative** and **summative evaluation**, and especially, **assessment for learning.** In addition to the tests described in the first edition, this chapter includes the **Common European Framework**, the **International English Language Testing System (IELTS),** and the **Test of English for International Communication (TOEIC)**. I also mention my personal image of what it means to know a second language: **authentic self-presentation**.

Chapters 10–11

Chapter 10 has been modified to give even greater emphasis to the development of academic language and the differentiation of instruction in lesson planning. In addition, consistent with the recommendations of SIOP and CALLA, it makes stronger recommendations about considering student background knowledge and including strategy instruction in lesson planning. Chapter 11 adds some suggestions for evaluating and implementing new technologies in language teaching.

How Do I Use This Book?

This book includes several special features to guide you in your journey as a language teacher. Each chapter begins with reflection questions and ends with a section entitled "Finding Your Way" designed to help you focus your thoughts and

---

*Chamot, A.U. (2009). *The CALLA handbook: Implementing the cognitive academic language learning approach* (2nd ed.). White Plains, NY: Pearson.

reflect on what you want to accomplish as a language teacher. I hope that you will use these sections as your personal language teaching planner. The "Projects" sections contain concrete tasks to help you translate the concepts in each chapter into effective language teaching practices, while the "Teaching Checklist" sections summarize important points from each chapter that you will want to remember when planning your own classes, either now or in the future. Finally, each "References and Suggestions for Further Reading" suggests sources for further understanding of each chapter's topics. These articles will help you advance your development as a language teacher. There is also a glossary at the end of the book that defines and illustrates essential terminology used by language teaching professionals.

I strongly hope that you will actually record your thoughts and ideas in the spaces provided in the "Finding Your Way" sections of this book. Think of these observations as notes to yourself. You might feel that you would never forget your wonderful teaching ideas, but being a teacher can be very stressful, and you will be glad that you already have some material to work with when you are developing your lesson plans. I also hope that you will look at these thoughts again after you have begun to establish yourself in your teaching career. The day-to-day demands of teaching may pull you away from your original goals and reviewing your early thoughts and ideas about language teaching might encourage you to return to some of your ideals. In fact, you might want to return to these materials from time to time during your teaching career to remember where you started as a language teacher, follow your progress, and chart where you want to go.

Being Open to New Ideas About Language Learning and Teaching

While you are reading this book, I hope that you will remain open to new ideas about language learning and teaching. Languages and language learning are the subject of a number of seemingly self-evident beliefs in many cultures, and it is not uncommon for language methods courses to do little to change teachers' preexisting beliefs about language teaching. Several years ago, at the end of one of my language teaching methods classes, one of my students came up to me and gushed, "That was a wonderful class! It reinforced *everything* I ever thought about language teaching!" Frankly, I did not know whether to be happy or sad. It was possible that she and I were kindred spirits when it came to thinking about language teaching, and that my class had indeed coincided with her thoughts about how to teach a language. On the other hand, it was also entirely possible that after picking and choosing selectively among the course concepts, she was able to find a group of ideas that supported her own preconceptions about language learning and teaching. Unfortunately, I was afraid that the latter possibility was closer to the truth.

Take for example the common beliefs that children are better language learners than adults and learn second languages instantly and effortlessly. Those beliefs are patently untrue. While children may have several advantages as language learners, adults also have a number of strengths. Even children who are immersed in the language typically take five or more years to fully achieve full literacy in the language, while adults tend to master the grammar of a language and develop reading ability relatively quickly. In addition, adults typically spend fewer hours engaged in language learning and must achieve a higher level of proficiency to be judged competent in the second language. Children only have to display the linguistic abilities of children.

Of course, the above paragraph is not a complete discussion of child language learning. Rather, it shows that issues surrounding language teaching and learning can be complicated. Although many beliefs about language learning may contain a grain of truth, they are not a sufficient basis for *professional* language teaching. It is likely that at least some of the material about language learning that you encounter in this book will conflict with the beliefs that you hold about language learning. The Beliefs about Language Learning Inventory (BALLI) (Appendix A) will help you become more aware of your own thoughts about language learning. I will ask you to reconsider your BALLI responses from time to time throughout the book. It is my sincere hope that this book will sensitize you to your own preconceptions about language learning and that you will accept my challenge to examine your assumptions about language learning and teaching as you develop as a language teacher.

CourseSmart eBook and other eBook Options Available

CourseSmart is an exciting new choice for purchasing this book. As an alternative to purchasing the printed book, you may purchase an electronic version of the same content via CourseSmart for reading on PC, Mac, as well as Android devices, iPad, iPhone, and iPod Touch with CourseSmart Apps. With a CourseSmart eBook, readers can search the text, make notes online, and bookmark important passages for later review. For more information or to purchase access to the CourseSmart eBook, visit http://www.coursesmart.com. Also look for availability of this book on a number of other eBook devices and platforms.

ACKNOWLEDGMENTS

As readers of the first edition of this book know, I must acknowledge Dr. Philip Redwine Donley above everyone else for his contributions to this book. Phil was my friend and collaborator in the original proposal for this book. We began it together, talked it through, examined the other language methods books, and decided how we could make *our* book special. But soon after we completed the prospectus, Phil became very ill. He passed away just after Aurora Martínez Ramos, our original editor at Allyn and Bacon, notified us that the project had been accepted. Phil was dedicated to helping language learners both as a scholar and as a language teacher, and I strongly recommend his publications to the readers of this volume. (These citations can be found in the *References and Suggestions for Further Reading* section of Chapter 1.)

I have many other friends, colleagues, and family members to thank as well. Melanie Bloom helped me prepare the manuscript for the first edition and contributed many good ideas throughout the book, and Alicia Thomas and Hayriye Kayi Aydar were very helpful with the second edition. Mary Petron was generous with her help on many issues but especially with her insights on heritage language learners. Hsi-chin Chu, Hsi-nan Yeh, Yuh-show Cheng, and Given Lee helped me understand the writing styles in their cultures, and Byung-kyoo Ahn helped me better understand the experiences of anxious language learners. I appreciate the generosity of my colleagues Zsuzsanna Abrams, David Birdsong, Carl Blyth, Rebecca Callahan, Tim Collins, Paul Garcia, Tom Garza, Lisa Green, Deb Palmer, Lia Plakans, Diana Pulido, Veronica Sardegna, Diane Schallert, Marilla Svinicki, and Keith Walters who were willing to discuss yet another issue whenever I asked. My summer 2011 SLA students helped me think about what an SLA book should look like. Special thanks to the reviewers who offered valuable feedback during the writing of this text: Anna Arlotta-Guerrero, University of Pittsburgh; N. Eleni Pappamihiel, University of North Carolina, Wilmington; Aixa Perez-Prado, Florida International University; and Nihat Polat, Duquesne University. I particularly want to thank Erin Grelak and Aurora Martínez Ramos who understood and understand the importance of a practical language methods book that speaks personally to teachers. I also want to thank my students, and especially my student teachers, who taught me what it means to become a language teacher. My deep love and appreciation to my children Jeremy and Deborah. Finally, I want to thank my own teachers—Bill DeLorenzo, Wilga Rivers, and Sandra Savignon— for helping me see that the learner can and must be the center of language teaching. My daughter Deborah is the talented artist of the drawing in Chapter 1.

—E.K.H.

PART ONE

What Do Language Teachers Think About?

1 What Should I Know About Language Learners and Language Teaching Settings?

- What difference does it make if you learn a language in a classroom or in the community where it is spoken?
- What kinds of help do people need to learn a new language?
- Why do you think that some people are more successful at language learning than others?

LANGUAGE LEARNERS AND LANGUAGE TEACHING SETTINGS

Language teachers work with many types of learners in a wide variety of settings. Some teachers work with learners who are surrounded by the language they are trying to learn (this is called a second language setting), while others teach a language that is only spoken by a distant community (a foreign language setting). Many teachers, such as history or fourth-grade teachers, do not immediately think of themselves as language teachers, but when some of their students are still learning English, they are also language teachers. Bilingual teachers have the triple objective of helping their students learn English and content subjects such as science or math while at the same time encouraging their first language development.

Teachers are especially interested in differences among language learners because they hope to find ways to help all of their students become more successful. Language learners differ with respect to emotions, language aptitude, learning styles, approaches to language learning, and, of course, their age. Although learner characteristics are difficult to change, teachers are sometimes able to help students develop more positive characteristics and become better language learners. Other times, teachers are able to adjust language teaching approaches for their particular students and teaching situation. Many educators feel that helping students become better language learners is essential so that they can become more autonomous and extend their language learning beyond the classroom.

Types of Language Learning Settings

The academic discipline called **second language acquisition** is the basis for the practices that all language teachers should employ. This field considers how people learn second languages and the factors that influence their learning. Second language acquisition includes learning a language where it is spoken—a **second language** setting—or learning a language that is spoken by a distant community—a **foreign language** setting. English learners in the United States are generally classified as second language learners because they are surrounded by English in school, in the media, and in the community. Many language teachers also distinguish the *acquisition* or unconscious development of a language through exposure from conscious *learning* through study and practice. (This distinction is associated with the input hypothesis, which will be explained in the next chapter.)

Despite these distinctions, second language acquisition is the general label for the academic field that studies language learning in all its variations: second language acquisition, second language learning, foreign language acquisition, and foreign language learning. The following descriptions of learners represent each of the four types of language development. Decide which terms best describe each of the learners.

VOICES FROM THE CLASSROOM

Although many people associate language acquisition with second language settings and language learning with foreign language settings, either process may be used in any learning context. Identify the setting and type of learning for each of the following people. The first answer is already filled in.

Xu is an international student from China studying biochemistry in the United States. He is sitting on a park bench practicing the pronunciation of some chemistry terms he needs to use in a presentation to the freshman chemistry class he is teaching.

Second Language Learning. Xu is <u>studying</u> *in an environment where English is spoken (second) and using* <u>conscious effort</u> *to improve his pronunciation of a list of terms (learning).*

Marina is an English learner in the third grade in the United States. She is listening and watching as her English-speaking teacher uses the blackboard to explain multiplication.

_____

_____

_____

_____

_____

Naciye is an English student in Turkey. She is watching the English version of the American situation comedy *Friends* on television.

_____

_____

_____

_____

_____

Tran is a high school student in the United States. He is studying a list of words for the weekly vocabulary quiz in his English class.

_____

_____

_____

_____

In addition to the differences between second and foreign language settings, there are several different types of language classes. **Stand-alone classes** are separate classes that students attend for at least part of the school day. This arrangement is typical in middle or high schools where students change classes and teachers on a regular basis. The typical stand-alone class is taught by a teacher who specializes in working with language learners, and the curriculum focuses primarily on language development. In the case of **English as a second language (ESL)** in the United States, stand-alone classes often include students of several first-language backgrounds and grade levels, and the teacher often devotes some class time to helping students with assignments from their other classes. Students in stand-alone classes may range from recent arrivals to the United States with very little or no English ability, to students who are almost ready to move to the regular **mainstream school program.** When there is a range of first languages, ages, and language proficiency levels, stand-alone teachers must **differentiate** instruction for each learner or group of learners in their classes. ESL teachers also consult with their students' other teachers so they can incorporate relevant content material into their lesson plans.

    Pull-out programs are more common at the elementary school level in the United States. In this arrangement, students leave their regular class for special language instruction. Pull-out classes tend to be smaller and more homogenous than stand-alone classes, with the teacher working with a single age group at a time. Since pull-out teachers work with the entire school population, they need to be prepared to work with learners ranging from early childhood—pre-K and kindergarten—to early adolescence. Pull-out teachers differentiate instruction for each age group, proficiency level, and so on, and they typically work closely with each child's classroom teacher to devise lessons that will complement the student's work in the regular classroom and to monitor their students' progress. At the middle and high school levels, a number of school districts have recently implemented **newcomer center** programs for newly arrived language learners. These programs offer both English and content instruction and other services in a single place. They are usually directed at learners who have had gaps in their schooling and/or low levels of literacy in their native language.

Students in **bilingual education** programs receive instruction in both their first and second languages to keep them from falling behind in their content learning and to encourage the development of their first language while they are learning English. The amount of ESL instruction within bilingual classes can vary greatly depending on the type of bilingual program, but typically a single teacher is responsible for teaching both the first and second language as well as the academic content. Bilingual teachers, thus, have the advantage of knowing their students' stage of first language development as well as how the learners will need to use both languages in their content learning. Bilingual teachers can, therefore, develop lesson plans that logically integrate their students' language and content learning needs. While most bilingual education programs only include **English learners** (ELs), **dual-language** programs are designed to teach a new language simultaneously to two groups of language learners. In the United States, these programs are typically composed of Spanish- and English-speaking students with approximately half of the instructional time in each language. In this way, the two groups of students have the experience of learning through both their first language and the new language, and they also have contact with peers from the other language group. Importantly, dual-language programs value and actively promote the development of learners' oral language proficiency and literacy in two languages.

In spite of the many possible ways of organizing English instruction, many English learners in the United States receive little if any special language instruction. Some states have mandated **English-only** instruction for ELs, while others have moved to an instructional model where all or most teachers have some ESL training. This approach makes regular classroom teachers rather than ESL specialists or bilingual teachers responsible for providing for the needs of ELs. In contrast, **sheltered English** refers to an approach where ELs are grouped together so that they do not have to compete with native English speakers while they are supported in their development of academic skills and competence in academic English. (Chapter 3 discusses the SIOP Model and other approaches to Sheltered Instruction; Chapter 8 is devoted to the topic of providing English language instruction through the mainstream content curriculum, including the CALLA approach.) Too often, however, ELs are left on their own to "sink or swim" in classes designed for native English speakers. Language educators use the pejorative term **submersion** when talking about putting ELs in regular classes with native English-speaking peers and giving them no extra support while they are learning English. Submersion contrasts sharply with the practices of language **immersion**, sheltered English, or bilingual education where students are put into a **target language** environment with the recognition that they are language learners and are given necessary assistance.

In addition to ESL and EL, it is important to mention a number of common terms and acronyms that language teachers use to distinguish various language learning settings. English as a second language **(ESL)** is often distinguished from **English as a foreign language (EFL),** and the letter *t* for teaching can be placed in front of both sets of initials to form TESL and TEFL. The term *TESOL*, standing for Teaching English to Speakers of Other Languages, is also commonly used. ESP and LSP translate to **English** or **languages for specific purposes** and refer to classes like English for Engineers or Spanish for Health Care Professionals. Similarly, EAP refers to English for academic purposes. These types of specialized classes recognize that learners have a range of learning needs and purposes.

Language teachers commonly use the terms English learner (EL) or English language learner (ELL), **English language learning** or **development (ELL/ELD), languages other than English (LOTE),** and **world languages** because the large number of non-English speakers in the United States has made the distinction between foreign and second languages unclear. For example, it would seem logical to classify English learners in the United States as second language learners, since they should have many opportunities to speak and listen to English; but if they live in segregated neighborhoods and remain with their peers in special English or bilingual classes in school, in some ways they are more similar to foreign language learners. In addition, world language students today have many more opportunities to interact with speakers of their target language than previously, and the use of the Internet and digital media further blurs the boundaries between second and foreign language learning. Moreover, world language classes often include **heritage learners** who have a family connection to that language and possibly some language proficiency. Some educators also worry that the use of either *second* or *foreign* puts an unnecessarily negative label on the learners. Similarly, the older term **limited-English proficient (LEP)** is seen as negative when compared to English learner. Language educators are increasingly using the term **emergent bilingual** to emphasize the importance of maintaining English learners' first language and to recognize that learners of world languages also possess their original language.

Learner Characteristics

In addition to being in different learning circumstances, language learners themselves differ in many important ways that can influence their language learning. Language teachers have generally been most concerned with three types of learner characteristics: **affective** (or emotional) **factors, cognitive factors,** and **metacognitive factors.**

Emotional factors include students' feelings about language learning and toward their particular target language and culture. Cognitive factors include the different ways that people process information and are considered to be less changeable than other learner differences. When people speak of language aptitude, they are usually speaking of different cognitive abilities that may help people learn languages. Finally, learners think about and control their language learning in different ways. Language learning strategies, study skills, and beliefs about language learning fall in this category and are referred to as metacognitive factors.

Language Learning Emotions

Attitudes and Motivation.   Language learners have very different goals for language learning. Older learners often have clearly defined goals involving earning a living, advanced schooling, helping their children with schoolwork, or understanding another culture, while younger learners do not think so much about learning a language but about wanting to fit in with the other students at school. Many scholars have found a strong relationship between motivation and language learning achievement. Of course, a relationship between motivation and achievement is not surprising; language learning requires a good deal of time and effort, and motivated students are more likely to expend effort as well as to seek out learning opportunities. In the 1970s, Gardner and Lambert (1972) identified two types of language learning motivation: **instrumental motivation** and **integrative motivation.** Instrumentally motivated learners have a pragmatic reason for learning a language, such as passing a high school exit examination or getting a better job, while integratively motivated learners want to learn the language so that they can get to know its people and culture. Naturally, it is possible to be both instrumentally and integratively motivated, as in the case of physicians who seek to work with Spanish-speaking communities. Although it was previously thought that integratively motivated learners would be more successful than instrumentally motivated ones, most scholars now think that the *degree* of motivation is more important than the *type* of motivation.

After Gardner and Lambert's original formulations (1972), Graham (1984) identified a third type of language learning motivation called **assimilative motivation.** Assimilative motivation goes beyond integrative motivation and refers to a desire to actually join the new culture. When teachers hope that school-age learners will want to become part of their peer group at school, they are hoping that their students will be assimilatively motivated. Assimilative motivation does not require learners to cut ties completely with their first language group, but they must desire to become functioning members of the new group. Thus, by its very definition, assimilative motivation is a particularly strong type of motivation.

Closely tied to the issue of motivation is the issue of learner attitudes toward the new language and culture. It is unfortunately true that many people have prejudices toward members of other groups, and it is almost trivial to say that people with negative attitudes toward a particular group, would be unlikely to learn that group's language successfully. Attitudes toward particular groups typically have a sociological basis, and most scholars believe that the attitudes and motivation of individual language learners or groups of learners cannot be understood outside of the particular social and political context where the language learning is taking place. Gardner (1985) reminds us that the learning environment has a strong influence on the actual attitudes and motivations that learners hold. In some learning situations, extreme motivation is required if the learner is going to achieve any ability in the new language. Many Americans interested in learning Swahili would not find classes readily available, while in many parts of the world, it is almost impossible to avoid English instruction.

While Gardner's social-psychological approach to motivation in second language learning has been very useful in understanding learners' perspectives on the target language and target culture, a number of scholars have called for language educators to think more broadly about motivation and to consider the ways motivation is more typically conceptualized in psychology and education. These theories recognize many learner-based and environmental influences on motivation beyond feelings about the particular language and culture. The concepts of **intrinsic** and **extrinsic** motivation are central to many motivational theories, and although instrumental and integrative motivation would seem to be related to the more general concepts of intrinsic and extrinsic motivation, the two approaches to motivation are clearly not identical. In addition, most recently, language educators have emphasized the importance of fostering **learner autonomy** in the development of language learning motivation. Learners who have more control of their learning goals and procedures are more likely to develop and maintain their individual language learning motivation. **Language learning self-access centers** are based on the premise that people who have control over their language learning are more effective.

Encouraging Positive Attitudes and Motivation.   Students will generally have some combination of instrumental, integrative, and possibly assimilative motivation as well as their own personal motivations for language learning. English learners in the United States are likely to have a particularly strong mix of motivations resulting from parental and peer pressure, the school environment, and their relationships with teachers. In order to understand students' motivations, it is necessary to consider the social and political circumstances surrounding their language learning. Spanish-speaking learners in the United States, for example, may be told that speaking English is the key to college and a successful career, but if they live in an entirely Spanish-speaking community, they will be less likely to recognize the instrumental value of learning English. By the same token, foreign language learners in the United States are often told of the usefulness of learning a second language for career purposes, but few career paths in the United States are actually closed to monolinguals.

Because of the strong societal forces involved, simply listing the advantages of language learning is not usually effective in changing students' attitudes and motivations toward language learning. Here are some more specific suggestions:

- Help students develop *personal goals* for language learning. Some students may not identify with the idea of going to college in the future, but want to participate in a school activity. World language students who are taking a language because of an academic requirement need help developing intrinsic reasons for learning the language.
- Discuss students' ideas about the language and culture. ELs are particularly vulnerable to developing stereotypes whenever they or someone they know has a negative interaction with English speakers.
- Help students make connections with members of the new community. Language buddies, field trips, and Twitter or Facebook exchanges are good ways

to put students in contact with the new culture (with appropriate supervision, of course!).

■ Give learners support before and after cultural contacts. Have students discuss their expectations, how to develop relationships with native speakers, and their previous cultural experiences. Help students better understand their experiences to avoid the development of new stereotypes.

■ Support autonomy by giving learners choices in materials, learning modalities, and activities.

Anxiety.   A number of studies have shown that learning and using a second language can make some people feel anxious. When our clothes or hairstyle are wrong, we worry that other people will perceive us as less stylish, intelligent, or "cool" than we really are. Similarly, language learners are often unable to display many of the personality traits that are important to their self-image. Kind people are unable to display their warmth and concern, funny people are unable to make jokes, and so forth. While *most* people accept these limitations as a natural consequence of being a learner, some language learners become anxious when they cannot "be themselves" when speaking in the new language. Listening can also make learners feel anxious. Some students think that they are supposed to understand everything and feel anxious whenever they miss a word. Although anxiety is usually associated with listening and speaking, studies have also found that some students feel anxious when they have to read or write the second language.

Students who have to function in the second culture may feel even more anxious. Adolescents are commonly worried about looking silly in front of their peers, and a new culture has different requirements for acting appropriately. Second language learners who must speak English in front of peers from their native culture group often feel that they are in a particularly uncomfortable situation. If they sound "American" enough to be accepted by English speakers, they might be perceived as disloyal by their native group.

Surveys have shown that many students (around one-third) feel moderately to strongly anxious about language learning, and a number of studies have found that students with higher levels of anxiety tend to do more poorly in their language classes. Interestingly, some cultural groups may have higher numbers of anxious learners than others. Korean learners of English seem to be somewhat more anxious than American foreign language learners, but Turkish- and Spanish-speaking English learners have been found to be somewhat less anxious than some other groups. However, Mejias, Applbaum, Applbaum, and Trotter (1991) studied bilingual Hispanic high school and college students, in the United States and found that these students felt uncomfortable when speaking *either* English or Spanish. The authors even speculated that anxiety contributes to high Hispanic drop-out rates.

MacIntyre (1991) suggests a different way to think about foreign language anxiety: he focuses on why or why not students choose to communicate in their new language when they have the opportunity. This idea called **willingness to communicate** (WTC) reminds language teachers that anxiety and motivation should be considered together. Perhaps not surprisingly, studies have found a strong relationship between WTC and foreign language anxiety; students with higher levels of anxiety are less willing to communicate in their new language. The Willingness to Communicate Model also identifies a number of social factors that can influence communication. For example, language learners are more willing to talk with conversational partners that they perceive to be helpful than judgmental partners.

VOICES FROM THE CLASSROOM

■ *Some students are very clear in expressing language anxiety. Consider these comments from learners in different settings. Have you encountered people who experience so much language anxiety?*

A middle school student confided to his ESL teacher, "I should make American friend, but the cafeteria is scary. I'm afraid to talk to anyone. I eat at 'foreign' table."

An American student offered the following comment about her college language class: "I feel like my French teacher is some kind of Martian death ray, and I never know when he is going to point at me."

■ *If students do not tell you about their anxiety, what are some nonverbal clues you could look for?*
■ *What can you do to help your students feel more comfortable communicating in their new language?*

Second language learners can be vulnerable to a particular type of anxiety called **culture shock.** Even students who do not have personal contact with members of the new culture can experience culture shock by watching TV or by hearing about difficulties that friends or family members have experienced. Culture shock refers to anxiety reactions resulting from difficulties people have when they have to function within the norms and requirements of a new culture. It occurs when people realize that their usual expectations of how things work and how people should act are not the same in the new culture. Ordinary behaviors such as greeting people, getting on a bus, or making a simple purchase are often difficult in the new culture, and simple misunderstandings can quickly lead to frustration and even anger. Although school-age children may not express their feelings, they may be the most susceptible to culture shock since they may spend many more hours each day dealing with the new culture than adults who have jobs that require little contact with English speakers.

Reducing Anxiety. Anxiety can be an important problem in language learning. As Mejias and his colleagues (1991) showed, in addition to making students feel uncomfortable, anxiety can have a negative impact on their academic success and career goals. While there is no way to eliminate anxiety entirely, there are several things that teachers can do to help their students feel more comfortable using the new language. Teacher support and understanding are particularly important. Pappamihiel (2002) found that middle school learners were more comfortable speaking English in their

ESL classes than in their mainstream content classes, suggesting that teachers may help reduce anxiety by creating a supportive classroom environment. The following approaches can also be used to help language learners feel less anxious in either their language or mainstream content classes:

- Acknowledge students' discomfort. Many students are relieved to learn that they are not the only ones experiencing anxiety.
- Acknowledge students' feelings of culture shock and offer opportunities for students to talk about their experiences.
- Use the Foreign Language Classroom Anxiety Scale (found in Appendix B) to help identify anxious learners and to start a discussion about anxiety.
- Help students develop more realistic expectations for language learning.
- Arrange contacts with more advanced students so that students see that people like them can learn the language.
- Correct errors gently.
- Use humor and games to distract attention away from individual speakers.
- Use small-group and pair activities rather than whole-class activities.
- Have students imagine becoming anxious while speaking and overcoming that anxiety.

Cognitive Factors: Language Aptitude, Learning Styles, and Stages of Cognitive Development

Language Aptitude.   Several tests of cognitive abilities have been developed that attempt to identify people who are likely to be successful language learners. The best-known of these tests is the *Modern Language Aptitude Test* (Carroll & Sapon, 1959), which examines learners in the areas of sound-symbol association, grammatical sensitivity, and the ability to memorize new vocabulary words. **Language aptitude tests** were first developed by the American military to identify personnel who would be able to develop new language skills and put them to use quickly. Aptitude tests have actually had limited success in identifying successful language learners in typical classroom situations, and today, most scholars have concluded that people with normal intelligence are capable of learning a second language, (and some scholars even reject that limitation). With the exception of the military and other specialized institutions, language aptitude tests are no longer commonly used except by second language acquisition researchers interested in understanding variation in second language achievement. Researchers interested in cognitive differences among language learners have turned their attention from language aptitude to learning styles, since language teachers must teach all their students and not just those who score well on language aptitude tests. Importantly, learning styles offer teachers the possibility of tailoring instruction to the learning strengths of different types of language learners.

Learning Styles.   **Learning styles** are persistent and instinctive ways that individuals process information when faced with a learning situation. The simplest example of a learning style is **sensory mode preference**. Some people are naturally visual learners while others are naturally auditory, tactile, or kinesthetic learners. Of course many people use a combination of sensory modalities. Even though it can be difficult to provide different instruction for a variety of learning preferences, an understanding of learning styles helps teachers recognize their students' learning strengths and difficulties. Visual learners, for example, are likely to have more difficulty listening than auditory learners.

The most widely studied learning style difference associated with language learning is called **field dependence–field independence (FD–FI).** (You may have already encountered FD–FI because it has been studied with respect to a great many types of learning.) FD–FI can be complicated to describe, but it may be thought of as asking whether learners tend to be influenced by the big picture or overall setting (called a field) or whether they are able to ignore the overall field and focus in on details. To adapt the old adage, field independent learners are better able to see the trees within the forest, while field dependent learners are better able to see the forest but not the individual trees. More field independent learners are better able to find hidden pictures disguised within a larger picture, such as those that appear in the magazine *Highlights for Children*. Of course, FD–FI is not an all or nothing proposition, but rather a continuum where some learners tend to the more field dependent (FD) side and others to the more field independent (FI) end. It is also important to point out that many educators object to the term *field dependence* since dependence often has a negative connotation in American culture. They prefer the term *field sensitivity* since FD learners have a number of positive attributes that stem from their ability to take in the whole field simultaneously.

VOICES FROM THE CLASSROOM

"If the teacher would only let me see what she is saying, I would understand."

A number of abilities have been associated with both FD and FI learners. FI learners are analytic and good at focusing in on details. Engineers tend to be more field independent. In contrast, more FD individuals are good at holistic tasks and seem to be particularly suited to "people" professions where perceiving interpersonal cues is important. From this description, it is natural to think that more FD people would be better language learners, but in fact, many studies have found that FI learners are the more successful language learners. This finding has been frustrating to many language teachers who feel intuitively that the ability to discern interpersonal cues should be a great advantage in learning to communicate effectively in a second language. Although scholars have not yet resolved this seeming contradiction, it is possible that the grammar focus and traditional language tests in many language classes favor the abilities associated with more FI learners. In addition, a number of scholars have suggested that Western schooling in general tends to be designed for FI learners.

Helping Students with Different Learning Styles.   Different learning styles would seem to imply that teachers should differentiate instruction based on students' individual styles. While this is an admirable goal, it is very hard to individualize instruction for every learning style in most language classes. In addition, second language acquisition research tells us that some language learning experiences are essential even if they clash with the learner's preferred style; for example, learners must listen to the language even if they are visual learners. Here are a few suggestions for helping students with different learning styles:

- Be aware of learning style differences and pay close attention when using an activity that is likely to be difficult for a particular type of learner. Visual learners may have difficulty with listening activities, for example, and field sensitive (dependent) learners will likely have difficulty focusing on grammatical concepts.
- Modify activities to make them more accessible to a wider range of learners. For example, listening activities could include written scripts.
- Include a variety of activity types that are appropriate for a range of learning styles. If you vary the activity type during your lessons, you will automatically include a wider range of learners.
- Change your teaching approach whenever you reteach material, since some students may not have understood a lesson the first time due to learning style conflicts. By changing your teaching approach, you give students a chance to learn in a different way.
- Pay close attention to learning styles when you work with individual students. You could vary the order of examples and generalizations, write your examples down, ask the student to listen, or have him or her act out new words. Over time, you will come to know which approaches work best with each of your students.

Metacognitive Factors: Beliefs About Language Learning and Language Learning Strategies

Educators have been concerned for a long time about the emotional and cognitive characteristics of learners, but recently they have begun to discuss the metacognitive aspects of learning. **Metacognition** refers to how and what learners think about the learning process. It is thinking about learning. Metacognitive factors describe differences in the ways learners approach language learning and include their beliefs, learning strategies, and any other "thinking" that they do about language learning.

Beliefs About Language Learning.   Although methods books, like this one, are designed to give language teachers an accurate and up-to-date understanding of second language acquisition, it is important to recognize that teachers are not the only ones with ideas about how languages are learned and how they should be taught. Language learners also have many beliefs about important issues in second language acquisition, such as how languages should be studied, how difficult it is to learn particular languages, who has language aptitude, and what makes a good language teacher! Some learner beliefs may be helpful while others can be counterproductive to language learning. In a study of beginning university language learners in the United States, for example, I found that over a third of the students thought that a language could be learned in two years or less by studying only one hour a day. Substantial numbers of students also believed that learning a second language primarily involved learning vocabulary words or grammatical rules (positions which will contrast strongly with the theories of second language acquisition described in the next chapter). Some American high school students I studied even believed that speakers of all languages across the world first formulated their thoughts in English and then translated their ideas into the particular language that was spoken in their countries. Besides showing great ethnocentrism, the students who believed that people of all other language groups first "thought" in English did not even consider that as language learners they were supposed to learn how to "think" in their new language, not merely to translate.

Misconceptions like these can lead to a number of important problems for language learners and their teachers. First of all, students tend to choose learning strategies (to be discussed in the next section) that are consistent with their beliefs about language learning. So learners who believe that language learning is synonymous with vocabulary learning are likely to spend their time memorizing words. Learners with unrealistic beliefs about language learning have also been found to be more anxious than other learners. Misconceptions about language learning become even more important when students are encouraged to become more **autonomous** and take greater responsibility for their own language learning.

Helping Students Develop a Realistic Understanding of Language Learning.   People are often surprised to learn that common beliefs about language learning they take for granted are actually the subject of lively debate among language teachers and scholars. The following are some suggestions for helping students develop more realistic expectations for language learning:

- Talk with your students about the process of language learning.
- Make discussions about language learning an important part of your classes. When looking for interesting discussion topics, language teachers often overlook the one topic that is relevant to everyone in the class: learning the new language!
- Determine your students' beliefs in order to explain the purpose of classroom activities more effectively.
- Use the Beliefs About Language Learning Inventory (BALLI) found in Appendix A to better understand your own and your students' beliefs and to encourage discussions about language learning.

Language Learning Strategies. **Language learning strategies (LLS)** are specific steps that learners take to increase their language learning. Although LLS are often associated with particular techniques or even tricks that learners use, such as flashcards or mnemonic devices, the term refers to a wide range of things that learners do to help themselves learn the language. Finding a quiet place to study, calming yourself when anxious, practicing how to order in a restaurant, or seeking out a conversational partner all fall under the heading of LLS. Some scholars believe that successful and less successful language learners use different strategies, and that less successful learners would benefit from learning the strategies of more successful students. Other scholars take a learning style approach, suggesting that teachers make students aware of a range of learning strategies and help them select the strategies that are most compatible with their learning styles. Many scholars emphasize **strategic learning** over the use of specific learning strategies. In strategic learning, the emphasis is on considering the specific learning task and developing approaches that are particularly suited to that task. Strategic learning involves analyzing the task, analyzing oneself as a learner, considering the resources that are available, and analyzing the learning situation. Strategic learning stresses flexibility and appropriateness in strategy use.

The well-known strategy researcher Rebecca Oxford (1990) differentiates direct and indirect LLS. **Direct strategies** involve actually using the language and include memory strategies (i.e., word associations and use of imagery), cognitive strategies (i.e., practicing and analyzing), and compensation strategies (i.e., guessing words and directing the conversation to a familiar topic). **Indirect strategies** support language learning without using the language directly. These include metacognitive strategies which help learners organize and plan their learning, affective strategies which help learners manage language learning emotions, and social strategies which involve interaction with other people. A number of specific strategies connected to various aspects of language learning, such as listening, reading, and learning vocabulary words, have also been identified (these strategies will be described in Chapters 4 through 8). The first graders in the following examples are using a number of different LLS. Decide which of the strategies are direct and which are indirect.

VOICES FROM THE CLASSROOM

Ms. Kelley observes her first graders using a number of language learning strategies. Classify each of the strategies as either direct or indirect and give a reason for your choice. Some of the strategies will have components of both types of strategies. The first answer is already filled in.

Reynaldo is in the cafeteria listening to another child getting lunch.

Direct Strategy. Reynaldo is listening to language. Reynaldo's approach also has elements of indirect strategies because it involves another person (social strategy) and possibly involves planning (metacognitive strategy) since Reynaldo may be listening to the other child order lunch so he can do the same thing when it is his turn.

David has made piles of English and Spanish books on his desk. He announces to Ms. Kelley that he is going to read an English book every time he finishes a Spanish book.

_____

_____

_____

_____

_____

Using self-invented spelling, Sonia writes the new English words she hears in a pretty flowered notebook. She usually draws a picture next to each word.

_____

_____

_____

_____

_____

Communication strategies are closely related to the "compensation" category of Oxford's direct strategies since they can be used to compensate for weaknesses in a learner's speaking ability. Communication strategies are the steps learners take to be as successful as possible when communicating in the new language. Teachers often remark that sometimes students with less language ability are better than others at achieving their communicative goals because they use their language skills to full advantage. Communication strategies include actions such as asking a conversational partner to repeat or talk more slowly, using gestures and pantomime, and repeating important words or phrases to encourage a partner to explain further.

Helping Students Develop Effective Language Learning Strategies.   Many language educators believe that language teachers should not only teach the language but also teach students how to learn the language. This practice is called **strategy training.** Students need indirect strategies such as setting aside time every day to review or seeking out conversational opportunities as well as direct strategies for specific tasks such as reading content material or listening to a classroom lecture. Many teachers see strategy training as most successful when students are encouraged to try learning approaches that are consistent with their individual learning styles, needs, and comfort levels. Here are some specific suggestions:

- Consult with students so that they are not left on their own to choose strategies.
- Suggest appropriate strategies whenever students encounter a new type of language learning task.
- Let students select some of their own learning materials and activities to encourage them to be more autonomous.
- Involve families in strategy training. Invite students and families to meetings or to drop-in homework sessions where you answer questions and model useful strategies.

Younger Learners and Stages of Cognitive Development

The characteristics discussed so far in this chapter can be found in learners of any age, but there are some important considerations to be especially aware of when working with younger learners. In addition to their many other differences, younger learners differ from older learners in terms of their level of **cognitive development.** (You may be familiar with Jean Piaget's cognitive development model.) Piaget describes a series of developmental stages that progress from babies' first cognitive efforts to differentiate themselves from their mothers to the culminating step of developing abstract reasoning abilities. Interestingly, the age associated with the development of abstract reasoning abilities, called the onset of **formal operations** in Piaget's theory, coincides with early adolescence, exactly the time that some researchers have associated with a loss of language learning ability. (This issue will be discussed further in Chapter 2.)

The achievement of formal operations is probably an important milestone in how people approach language learning. Since grammatical explanations are necessarily abstract, abstract reasoning ability is required for learners to be able to understand and manipulate grammatical rules. While there is great controversy over the usefulness of grammatical explanations and exercises with older learners, such practices are inappropriate for younger learners, at least those under the age of 11 or 12, since they will not have achieved the necessary level of cognitive development to be able to think about grammar abstractly. It is also important to note that not everyone reaches Piaget's highest level of cognitive development and that the achievement of formal operations is associated with formal schooling. It is possible, therefore, that older learners who have had irregular school attendance, such as refugees or migrant workers, may be similar to younger learners in their lack of readiness for abstract grammatical explanations.

VOICES FROM THE CLASSROOM

This true incident is from my own teaching. I had a second-year French class of twelve- and thirteen-year-olds that used a very grammar-heavy syllabus. (I did not design the syllabus!) One student in the class was never able to follow the grammatical explanations, even when I explained the concepts *in English* as simply as I could, so I would always give her grammatical charts to memorize. Her other teachers also complained that she had great difficulty with tasks that involved analysis and generalization. Several months into the school year, the student arrived to my class noticeably angry:

Student: Mrs. Horwitz, I'm so mad at you. You know that new verb you made me memorize last night? Well, it works like all these other verbs (she pointed to a section in her book). And you see these pronouns; well, these are like these other ones, and these ones all work the same! You've been making me memorize all this stuff when you could have just told me the rules!

Me: I'm so sorry, Esmerelda (this is a made-up name, of course), I promise that I will give you the explanations from now on.

Soon, her other teachers reported similar breakthroughs. We were all relieved; we believed that Esmerelda had achieved formal operations and that it would now be easier to teach her. And it was!

■ *Why do you think it was now easier to teach Esmerelda? Instead of waiting for her to reach formal operations, what else could I have done to help her learn French?*

Several scholars believe that the ability to use abstract grammatical rules accounts for the fact that adult language learners tend to make quicker early progress in learning a second language than children do. On the other hand, some speculate that the use of grammatical rules can actually impede language learning. Think of grammatical knowledge as a kind of filter between the learner and the language itself. Instead of absorbing language directly through listening or reading, learners analyze and categorize what they hear, looking for rules and contrasts and similarities with their first language. While this strategy can be useful at early stages of learning, ultimately, learners have to create and process language from an automatic, internalized system and not from the manipulation of explicit grammatical rules.

Identity and Language Learning

As humans mature, we develop in many ways, and many of these changes have implications for second language acquisition. As noted above, as learners progress in their cognitive development, they will have the possibility of approaching language learning in more analytic ways. A number of other psychological and social changes across the human lifespan also have important implications for language learning. (The role of social factors in SLA will be discussed further in Chapter 3.) Norton (2000) defines identity as *"how a person understands his or her relationship to the world because of power relations, how that relationship is constructed across time and space, and how that person understands possibilities for the future"* (p. 5). Learning a new language—and especially living in a new culture—can challenge our sense of our place in the world, of who we are, and of who we can be. Adolescent and adult students come to language learning with an already developed or at least developing sense of identity, and they can feel uncomfortable when interacting with people in the second language community because they do not receive the same type of responses they have come to expect in their first language. Norton rightly points out that developing language and cultural competence is not an abstract undertaking; language learners who have moved to another country are faced with creating a new life for themselves. Adult learners who have achieved some degree of status in their first language community become "learners" in the new culture and may even be treated as childlike or unintelligent. The new culture defines second language learners in many ways, and learners have little ability to control how they are perceived in the new environment. Norton's conceptualization of the roles of identity and power relationships in language learning reminds language teachers that learners are not simply composites of the characteristics described in this chapter and that language learning does not take place in a vacuum. We must always remember that our students are human beings with unique sets of life and language learning experiences and that language learning contexts are not neutral. Ultimately, neither second language learners nor second language learning can be understood outside the social context where the learning takes place.

FINDING YOUR WAY

REFLECTIONS

Which learner characteristics do you think are most important in successful second language learning? Do you think that different characteristics are helpful in different language learning settings?

_____

_____

_____

_____

_____

Is it possible to meet the needs of different types of learners in the same class?

_____

_____

_____

_____

PLANNING FOR YOUR CLASSES

How can you encourage your students' motivation for language learning?

_____

_____

_____

_____

In what ways do you think your students' beliefs about language learning will be compatible or incompatible with your own ideas about language teaching?

_____

_____

_____

_____

PROJECTS

- Complete the Beliefs About Language Learning Inventory (BALLI) in Appendix A and compare your answers with another person. What are your major areas of agreement and disagreement? What kinds of language learning beliefs do you think your students will have? Do you think they will have beliefs that could get in the way of their language learning?
- Find out the kinds of programs that your school district uses for ELs and world languages students. Are there different kinds of programs for ELs of different ages? At what age does instruction in world languages begin? Which world languages are taught in the school district? Does the district have dual-language programs?
- Interview a person who is trying to learn a language. What is his or her motivation for language learning? Is he or she anxious about it? What learning strategies does he or she use? (Ask about language learning tricks or how he or she studies, if your learner does not understand the idea of learning strategies.) Does your learner have any ideas about his or her learning style? What does your learner find relatively easy and difficult about language learning? If you were this person's language teacher, what

recommendations would you make for this person's language learning. Make specific recommendations based on the person's individual characteristics (motivation, learning style, etc.), not general recommendations that would be good for anyone.

IN YOUR JOURNAL

- What kind(s) of learning style(s) do you think you have? How has your learning style(s) helped or hindered you as a learner?
- Do you have any special language learning strategies?
- Were you or are you an anxious language learner? Teachers often do not realize that language anxiety is not limited to students. Several studies have found that some nonnative teachers are uncomfortable speaking in front of students and avoid classroom activities that require spontaneous speech. If you think you might be an anxious language teacher, you might want to read Horwitz (1996), "Even teachers get the blues: Recognizing and alleviating non-native teachers' feelings of foreign language anxiety", and complete the Teacher Foreign Language Anxiety Scale in Appendix C. Try to think about some things you can do to reduce your anxiety.
- Do you feel that you are *the same person* in all of the languages you speak? When you speak your second language, do you feel that people react to you in the same way that they do when you speak your first language? What accommodations do you have to make to function in the second culture?

TEACHING CHECKLIST

Yes	No	
☐	☐	I talk to my students about their language learning goals.
☐	☐	I encourage my students to see the new culture positively.
☐	☐	I acknowledge and attempt to reduce my students' anxiety.
☐	☐	I talk to my students about how to approach language learning.
☐	☐	I incorporate strategy training within my lessons.
☐	☐	I keep my students' learning styles in mind.
☐	☐	I do not use abstract grammatical explanations with younger learners.
☐	☐	I think about the opportunities and disadvantages that my teaching setting has for my students.
☐	☐	I encourage my students' learner autonomy.
☐	☐	I talk with my students about their feelings and thoughts about language learning.

REFERENCES AND SUGGESTIONS FOR FURTHER READING

Brown, A. (2009). Students' and teachers' perceptions of effective foreign language teaching: A comparison of ideals. *Modern Language Journal, 93*, 46–60.

Carroll, J. B., & Sapon, S. (1959). *The modern language aptitude test.* New York, NY: The Psychological Corporation.

Chamot, A. U. (1998). *Teaching learning strategies to language students*. Washington, DC: Center for Applied Linguistics.

Cohen, A., & Macaro, E. (Eds.). (2008). *Language learner strategies: 30 years of research and practice*. New York, NY: Oxford University Press.

Crookes, G. & Schmidt, R. (1991). Motivation: Reopening the research agenda. *Language Learning, 41*, 469–512.

Curtain, H. (1991). Methods in elementary school foreign language teaching. *Foreign Language Annals, 24*, 323–329.

Dickinson, L. (1995). Autonomy and motivation: A literature review. *System, 23*, 165–174.

DiFino, S. M., and Lombardino, L. J. (2004). Language learning disabilities: The ultimate foreign language challenge. *Foreign Language Annals, 37*, 390–400.

*Donley, P. R. (2002). Teaching languages to the blind or visually impaired: Problems and suggestions. *Canadian Modern Language Review, 59*, 302–305.

*Donley, P. R. (1999). Language anxiety and how to manage it: What educators need to know. *Mosaic, 6*, 3–9.

*Donley, P. R. (1997). Ten ways to cope with foreign language anxiety. *Mosaic, 4*, 17.

Dornyei, Z. (2005). *The psychology of the language learner*. Mahwah, NJ: Lawrence Erlbaum Associates.

Dornyei, Z. (2007). *Motivational strategies in the language classroom*. Cambridge, UK: Cambridge University Press.

Doughty, C. (1991). Second language instruction does make a difference. *Studies in Second Language Acquisition 13*, 341–469.

Ehrman, M. E., Leaver, B. L., & Oxford, R. L. (2003). A brief overview of individual differences in second language learning. *System, 31*, 313–330.

Erlam, R. (2005). Language aptitude and its relationship to instructional effectiveness in second language acquisition. *Language Teaching Research 9*, 147–171.

Escamilla, K. (2006). Semilingualism applied to the literacy behaviors of Spanish-speaking emerging bilinguals: Bi-illiteracy or emerging biliteracy? *Teachers College Record, 108*, 2329–2353.

Gardner, R. C. (1985). *Social psychology and second language learning: The role of attitudes and motivation*. London, UK: Edward Arnold.

Gardner, R. C., & Lambert, W. E. (1972). *Attitudes and motivation in second language learning*. Rowley, MA: Newbury House.

Genesee, F., Lindhom-Leary, K., Saunders, W., & Christian, D. (2009). English language learners in U.S. schools: An overview of research findings. *Journal of Education for Students Placed at Risk, 10*, 363–385.

Graham, C. R. (1984). Beyond integrative motivation: The development and influence of assimilative motivation. In P. Larson, E. L. Judd, & S. Messsersmitt (Eds.), *On TESOL '84: A brave new world for TESOL*. Washington, DC: TESOL.

Griffiths, C. (Ed.) (2008). Lessons from good language learners. Cambridge, UK: Cambridge University Press.

Horwitz, E. K. (1988). The beliefs about language learning of beginning university foreign language students. *Modern Language Journal, 72*, 182–193.

Horwitz, E. K. (1996). Even teachers get the blues: Recognizing and alleviating non-native teachers' feelings of foreign language anxiety. *Foreign Language Annals, 29*, 365–372.

Horwitz, E., Breslau, B., Dryden, M., Yu, J., & McClendon, M. (1997). A graduate course focusing on the second language learner. *Modern Language Journal, 81*, 518–526.

Horwitz, E. K., Horwitz, M. B., & Cope, J. A. (1986). Foreign language classroom anxiety. *Modern Language Journal, 70*, 125–132.

Horwitz, E. K., M. Tallon & H. Luo (2010). Foreign language anxiety. In J. C. Cassady (Ed.), *Anxiety in schools: The causes, consequences, and solutions for academic anxieties*. New York, NY: Peter Lang, 95–115.

Krashen, S., Tse, L., & McQuillan, J. (Eds.). (1998). *Heritage language development*. Culver City, CA: Language Education Associates.

Kubota, R., Austin, T. & Saito-Abbott, Y. (2003). Diversity and inclusion of sociopolitical issues in foreign language classrooms: An exploratory survey. *Foreign Language Annals, 36*, 12–24.

Liu, M. & Jackson, J. (2008). An exploration of Chinese EFL learners' unwillingness to communicate and foreign language anxiety. *Modern Language Journal, 92*, 71–86.

MacIntyre, P. D. (2007). Willingness to communicate in the second language: Understanding the decision to speak as a volitional process. *Modern Language Journal, 91*, 564–576.

McLaughlin, B. (1995). Fostering second language development in young children: Principles and practices. *Educational Practice Report 14* (Report No. ED386932). Santa Cruz, CA: National Center for Research on Cultural Diversity and Second Language Learning.

Mejias, H., Applbaum, R. L., Applbaum, S. J., & Trotter, R. T. (1991). Oral communication apprehension and Hispanics: An exploration of oral communication apprehension of Mexican American students in Texas. In E. K. Horwitz & D. J. Young (Eds.), *Language anxiety: From theory and research to classroom implications.* Englewood Cliffs, NJ: Prentice Hall.

Moore, Z. (2005). African-American students' opinions about foreign language study: An exploratory study of low enrollments at the college level. *Foreign Language Annals, 38*, 191–199.

Norton, B. (2000). *Identity and language learning: Gender, ethnicity and educational change.* London, UK: Longman.

Noels, K., Pelletier, L., Clément, R., & Vallerand, R. (2003). Why are you learning a second language? Motivation orientations and self-determination theory. *Language Learning, 53*, 33–64.

Oxford, R. (1990). Language learning strategies: What every teacher should know. New York, NY: Newbury House.

Oxford, R., & Green, J. M. (1996). Language learning histories: Learners and teachers helping each other understand learning styles and strategies. *TESOL Journal, 6*, 20–23.

Pappamihiel, N. E. (2002). English as a second language students and English language anxiety: Issues in the mainstream classroom language learning. *Research in Teaching English, 36*, 327–355.

Pavlenko, A. (2003). "I never knew I was a bilingual": Reimagining teacher identities in TESOL. *Journal of Language, Identity and Education, 2*, 251–268.

Peacock, M. (2001). Pre-service ESL teachers' beliefs about second language learning: A longitudinal study. *System, 29*, 177–195.

Piaget, J., & Inhelder, B. (1969, 2000). *The psychology of the child.* New York, NY: Basic Books.

Reid, J. M. (1995). *Learning styles in the ESL/EFL classroom.* Boston, MA: Heinle & Heinle.

Sandhu, K. (2000*). Reaching all students in an ESL class. Practitioner Research Briefs*, 1999–2000 Report Series (Report No. ED444395). Arlington, VA: Virginia Adult Education Research Network.

Singer, D. G., & Revenson, T. A. (1996). *A Piaget primer: How a child thinks* (revised ed.). Madison, CT: International Universities Press.

Sparks, R. (2006). Is there a "disability" for learning a foreign language? *Journal of Learning Disabilities 39*, 544–557.

Toohey, K. (2001). Disputes in child L2 learning. *TESOL Quarterly, 35*, 257–278.

Young, D. (1991). Creating a low-anxiety classroom environment: What does the anxiety research suggest? *Modern Language Journal 75*, 426–439.

Valdés, G. (2005). Bilingualism, heritage language learners, and SLA research: Opportunities lost or seized? *Modern Language Journal, 89*, 410–426.

Webb, J. B., & Miller, B. L. (Eds.). (2000). *Teaching heritage language learners: Voices from the language classroom.* Yonkers, NY: American Council on the Teaching of Foreign Languages.

Zuengler, J. (1988). Identity markers and L2 pronunciation. *Studies in Second Language Acquisition, 10*, 33–49.

*Publications by Philip Redwine Donley, my original collaborator on this book.

2 What Should I Know About Second Language Acquisition?

- Do you think that some languages are easier to learn than others?
- Does it matter whether you learn a language in a classroom or within a community where it is spoken?
- What kinds of practice are helpful in language learning?
- How much do students' first languages influence their second language learning?
- How do communities influence students' opportunities for language learning?
- How is learning a language different from learning other kinds of material?

SECOND LANGUAGE ACQUISITION AND LANGUAGE TEACHING METHODOLOGIES

This chapter and the next will discuss two essential topics for language teachers: second language acquisition theories and language teaching methodologies. Although there are many ways that these topics overlap, they generally discuss different issues and offer different kinds of advice for language teachers. Language teachers study the academic field of second language acquisition to understand how humans learn new languages so that they can plan activities and experiences for their students that are consistent with what scholars have discovered about the nature of language learning. Second language acquisition considers how people learn second languages and what factors influence their learning. It addresses questions such as Does the human brain "learn" second languages in the same way(s) it learns other things? What role does a learner's first language play in learning a second language? Why are some people more successful learning a second language than others? And do children and adults learn languages differently? Language teaching methodologies (the topic of Chapter 3) are much more specific about what language teachers should do in the classroom. They suggest specific types of activities and instructional sequences.

Theories of Second Language Acquisition

Second language acquisition (SLA) theories are descriptions of how people learn second languages and the factors that help or hinder language learning. To be useful to teachers, these theories should offer explanations of how languages are learned and why some learners are more successful than others. This chapter will describe five types of second language acquisition theories that have been most widely applied in language teaching and discuss how they can be applied in language teaching. They are first language theories, cognitive learning theories, experience theories, social theories, and sociocultural theories.

First Language Theories

The Contrastive Analysis Hypothesis: Some Important Concepts

Target Language	■ The language that the learner is trying to learn. Often referred to as second language and abbreviated as L2.
First Language	■ Usually the home language and the learner's strongest language. When learners grow up in a bilingual home, they can have more than one "first" language. Often abbreviated as L1.
Behavioral Psychology (Behaviorism)	■ A learning theory associated with B. F. Skinner which maintains that learning is achieved through practice and reinforcement.
Habit Formation	■ In behavioral psychology, behaviors can become habits when they are reinforced.
Reinforcement	■ A reward or other positive response to an action.
The Contrastive Analysis Hypothesis	■ An early SLA theory that maintained that the structure of the learner's first language either helped or hindered the learning of a second language.
Interference	■ When a grammatical structure or sound is different in the first language and the target language, the first language may intrude and cause difficulty in producing the new form. Also known as **negative transfer. Positive transfer** is the opposite process and occurs when there are similarities between the first language and the target language.
Fossilization	■ In the Contrastive Analysis Hypothesis, errors that are reinforced are believed to become permanent or at least *extremely* resistant to change.

First language theories view the learner's native language as a major source of difficulty in second language learning and advocate that students practice specific sounds and grammatical patterns in the target language to overcome potential errors. The degree of similarity between the first language and the target language is seen as very important in these theories. For example, first language theories would expect that it would be relatively easy for Spanish speakers to learn English but relatively difficult for Chinese speakers to do so since the grammar, vocabulary, and sound systems of Spanish and English are more similar than those of Chinese and English.

The **Contrastive Analysis Hypothesis (CAH)** is an early first language theory which emerged in the 1960s along with the **Audiolingual Method (ALM)** of language teaching (discussed in Chapter 3). Both the Contrastive Analysis Hypothesis and the Audiolingual Method are associated with the behavioral learning theories of the psychologist B. F. Skinner. Skinner believed that any human behavior followed by a reward would become *reinforced* and thus more likely to reoccur. With sufficient reinforcement, the behavior would become a *habit*. Language teachers thought of the sounds and grammatical structures of their target language as the behaviors they needed to reinforce. In the box below, Mrs. Ortega responds to Sara's question with a warm compliment and rewards her by agreeing to her *correctly* phrased request. In Skinnerian terms, Sara's request is the behavior and Mrs. Ortega's response is the reinforcement. By reinforcing Sara's grammatically correct English question the child should be more likely to use those same language forms correctly in the future.

VOICES FROM THE CLASSROOM

Sara: Can I get a book, please?

Mrs. Ortega: Wonderful, Sara! Of course, you can go get a book.

The CAH maintained that the learner's first language could either facilitate or hamper the learning of the sounds and the grammar of the new language and suggested that language teachers and textbook writers compare students' first languages with the specific target language to identify potential areas of difficulty. When the native language and the target language contrasted, it was believed that the first language would cause problems or **interfere** with the learning of the new language.

Based on a comparison of the learners' first languages with the target language, language drills could be developed to give students practice and reinforcement to overcome interference from their native language. Overcoming interference was seen as essential by the Contrastive Analysis Hypothesis because without correction interference errors would become fossilized, or permanent, and the learner would always speak the new language imperfectly. When the structures of the first language coincided with the structures of the target language, relatively little reinforcement would be needed to establish the new language habits, but when the structures of the second language differed from those of the first, much reinforcement would be needed to avoid **fossilization.** Carefully planned drills would also help learners take advantage of opportunities for **positive transfer** when their native language and the target language were similar.

The Contrastive Analysis Hypothesis had many impractical implications for language teaching, especially in **second language** settings where language classes often have students from a wide range of language backgrounds. Its stress on the specific pair of first and target languages required that language classes and learning materials be limited to students of the same first language background.

SLA Theories in the Classroom	*The Contrastive Analysis Hypothesis*
Helping Students Be More Successful	■ Give students practice in target language sounds and grammatical forms to overcome interference from their first language.
	■ Reinforce grammatically correct responses and native-like pronunciation.
	■ Provide practice based on students' native languages.

Universal Grammar Theory: Some Important Concepts

Universal Grammar Theory	■ A second language acquisition theory based on Chomsky's linguistic theory of language universals and marked features. In learning a new language, students must reset the parameters of their L1 to achieve the features of the new language.
Language Universals	■ Basic patterns or principles shared by all languages. For example, all languages have verbs.
Markedness	■ Language features that are more consistent with language universals are referred to as **unmarked** while those that differ from the universal are called **marked.**

Nativism	■ The perspective that the human brain contains language universals which direct the acquisition of language. This position contrasts with the behavioral view that all aspects of language are learned through practice and reinforcement.
Language Acquisition Device (LAD)	■ The human capacity for learning a first language. According to this view, all babies are born with the same language universals hardwired in their brains. Scholars differ as to whether and to what extent the LAD is available to second language learners.
Parameter (Re-) Setting	■ A child's brain selects the form of each universal feature (parameter) that corresponds to his or her L1 group. In the Universal Grammar Theory, second language learners reset their L1 parameters to those of the new language.
Critical Period	■ The idea that babies are born with the ability to learn language but that their innate language learning ability either decreases or is lost at a certain point or points in human development.

Based on the work of the famous linguist Noam Chomsky, the **Universal Grammar Theory** emerged in the 1980s and 1990s. Chomsky had observed that similarities and differences among languages were not quite as straightforward as linguists had previously thought. He noted that there were a number of aspects common to all languages across the world and called these commonalities **language universals.** Variation in human languages is accounted for by the way each language expresses the universal properties. For example, all languages have subjects, but the subject is expressed in different ways in different languages. In some languages the subject appears as a separate term in a sentence, while in others a verb ending functions as the subject. Features that are more consistent with language universals are referred to as **unmarked,** while those that differ from the universal are called **marked.** According to the Universal Grammar Theory of SLA, differences between the marked features in the learner's first and second languages as well as the degree of **markedness** (distance from the universal) could cause language learning difficulties.

Chomskyan scholars say that babies are born with the capacity for human language. By that they mean that the infant brain is prewired with the universal aspects of language. Babies are seen as having a **language acquisition device,** or

LAD, containing language universals which directs their acquisition of a first language. This position is often referred to as **nativist,** since language universals are believed to already reside in the human brain; it contrasts sharply with the behavioral position that all aspects of language are learned through practice and reinforcement. When applying the concept of language universals to second language acquisition, it is important to point out that the theory was originally based on first language acquisition, and since children develop their first language without being "taught," a number of scholars have reservations about its applicability to second language *teaching*.

If all children are born with the same language acquisition device, it is reasonable to ask why babies from around the world end up speaking languages with such different marked features. Scholars believe that the universal features contained in the LAD are not set linguistic features but rather a range of possible features. When children are born into a language community, their brains select the form of each universal feature that corresponds to the specific language they are being exposed to. This process, called **parameter setting,** is analogous to setting a station button on a car radio. At first you can access any of the possible stations. After you set the button, however, one specific station is fixed. From the perspective of second language learning, this means that learners will be starting out with parameters already preset for their native language.

Resetting first language parameters to achieve the marked features of the target language is currently the subject of much interest and controversy in second language acquisition research. Much current research is focusing on which, if any, parameters can be reset, how to reset them, whether instruction can have an effect on the resetting of parameters, and how age is related to the possibility of resetting parameters. The answers to these questions will likely have important implications for second language acquisition theories and language teaching methodologies in the future. Scholars are also trying to determine if there is a **critical period** for language learning after which the ability to learn language either decreases or changes. Difficulties resetting first language parameters after a particular age is consistent with the existence of a critical period for language learning. (The issue of a critical period for language learning is discussed later in this chapter.)

SLA Theories in the Classroom	
	Universal Grammar Theory
Helping Students Be More Successful	■ Language universals should transfer from the L1 to the L2.
	■ Students will have different needs and learning difficulties depending on their native language. For example, native speakers of Spanish and Korean will have different marked features to change when learning English.

Cognitive Learning Theories

Cognitive Learning Theories: Some Important Concepts

Meaningful Learning	■ Learning that involves the connection of new material to the learner's existing knowledge or schema.
Schema (Schemata)	■ Mental representations of knowledge.
Information Processing	■ How the human brain sorts and deals with the incoming information it receives at any given moment.
Focal Attention	■ Concerted attention; when a behavior needs so much attention that it is difficult to do anything else at the same time.
Peripheral Attention	■ Background attention; when a behavior is sufficiently automatic that the individual can focus on something else simultaneously.
Controlled Processing	■ Using language in a limited and conscious way before the learner is able to use it automatically.
Automatic Processing	■ Spontaneously using language without the conscious manipulation of rules.
Explicit Linguistic Knowledge	■ Knowledge about the language; being able to talk about the language.
Implicit Linguistic Knowledge	■ Linguistic knowledge that is automatically used when speaking or writing.

Just as Chomsky's ideas replaced **structural linguistics** in linguistics, in psychology, cognitive learning replaced behaviorism to explain how learning takes place. (There are, of course, other learning theories in addition to behaviorism and cognitive learning. **Constructivist** and **socio-constructivist** views are associated with the sociocultural SLA theories discussed later in this chapter.) Cognitive learning is associated with the work of the psychologist David Ausubel who distinguishes simple rote learning from **meaningful learning.** Meaningful learning involves the connection of new material to the learner's existing knowledge or **schema.** Behaviorism maintained that behaviors that are reinforced will be learned. So if learners practiced "He went to the store," "She went to the store," "They went to the store," enough times, and each recitation was reinforced by the teacher acting happy and saying, "Great," it was expected that learners would learn to produce the form "went" rather than "go" or "goed" when they spoke or wrote in English. Understanding of regular and irregular past tense formation was not seen as necessary or even helpful. Cognitive learning theories, in contrast, insist that understanding is required for the learning of complex material like language and that learners would be less likely to learn "went" if they did not explicitly understand what it meant and that it was an irregular verb.

Cognitive learning theories differ from many other second language acquisition theories in an important way. Many second language acquisition theories take a nativist approach and view language learning as different from other kinds of learning due to the language acquisition device. Cognitive learning theories, in contrast, view second language learning as very similar to learning other types of material such as mathematics or history. Thus, whatever is generally helpful in learning any subject matter should be helpful in language learning. Whether second language learning is the same as or different from other types of learning is an important on-going issue in second language acquisition research.

Cognitive learning theories of second language acquisition center around the concepts of attention and automatic control of the language. The two scholars most often associated with these theories are Barry McLaughlin and Ellen Bialystok. McLaughlin's approach, called **information processing,** is concerned with the way learners gain automatic control of the language and emphasizes the role of attention in the process. (The role of attention is so important in these theories that I called them attention theories in the first edition of this book.) At first, learners must pay close attention (**focal attention,** in McLaughlin's terms) as they produce the language, searching their memories for vocabulary words and remembering to use grammatical rules correctly. This concentration is called **controlled processing.** At this stage, learners' capacity to produce language is limited because the amount of information they must process exceeds their attention capacity. With practice, however, the use of many aspects of the language will become automatic and learners will not have to devote so much direct attention to producing sentences; for example, they will no longer have to search their memories for each word. This process is similar to the learning of other skills. When you first learn to knit, for example, you must pay close attention to putting the needle in the correct loop, properly wrapping the yarn around the needle, and so forth. Later the process becomes more automatic and you only need to use **peripheral attention** while knitting; you have sufficient attention capacity left over to be able to do other things at the same time, like talk or watch TV. With respect to language, at first the information processing load will be so great that learners will need to pay close attention (controlled processing) as they talk and will only be able to produce speech haltingly. As they gain automatic control of more sounds, words, and grammatical rules, they will be able to speak more easily (**automatic processing)**.

Similar to McLaughlin's distinction between automatic and controlled processing, Bialystok contrasts the concepts of **implicit** and **explicit linguistic knowledge.** Explicit knowledge refers to knowledge about the language that the learner is able to state, while implicit knowledge is the internalized knowledge that the learner can use to produce language automatically without thinking about grammatical rules. Unlike the Input Hypothesis, which will be discussed in the next section, Bialystok maintains that explicit linguistic knowledge can become implicit or automatic through practice.

SLA Theories in the Classroom

Helping Students Be More Successful

Cognitive Learning Theories

- Make practice meaningful.

- Draw students' attention to a grammatical structure **(consciousness-raising)** *before* they practice it.

- Activate students' background knowledge or schema related to the new material.

- Link new lessons to students' current understanding of the language.

- Give students substantial amounts of realistic language practice to help them increasingly gain automatic control over the language.

- Grammatical explanations are appropriate from the perspective of the cognitive learning theories because explicit discussion of the L2 should make language practice more meaningful for students.

Experience Theories

The Input Hypothesis: Some Important Concepts

Acquisition

- In the Input Hypothesis, acquisition refers to the unconscious development of a language through exposure. Acquisition results in true language proficiency. To use Bialystok's terms, acquisition results in implicit linguistic knowledge.

Learning

- In the Input Hypothesis, learning refers to conscious effort to develop the language through study and practice. Learning *only* results in the development of conscious knowledge about the language, which Stephen Krashen calls the *monitor* (see discussion below). In Bialystok's terms, learning *only* leads to explicit linguistic knowledge; it does *not* contribute to the development of implicit linguistic knowledge.

Input

- Material to listen to or read in the target language. The phrase "i + 1 input" refers to input that is neither too complex nor too simple for the learner's current language ability.

The Affective Filter

- The affective filter is made up of people's feelings about language learning and determines whether they acquire the language when they have the opportunity.

The Monitor

■ Similar to Bialystok's explicit linguistic knowledge, the monitor refers to the learner's knowledge *about* the target language. According to the Input Hypothesis, the monitor is the result of language *learning* rather than language *acquisition.*

The Input Hypothesis.   The **experience theories** hold that second languages are learned through direct experiences with the target language. That is, people learn second languages by using that language. Foremost among these theories is the **Input Hypothesis** of Stephen Krashen. The distinction between **second language acquisition** and **second language learning** explained in Chapter 1 is the core of this theory. Krashen views second language acquisition rather than learning as the basis of all true language development, and he therefore disagrees strongly with the cognitive learning theories that explicit linguistic knowledge and controlled processing can become automatic. Also unlike the cognitive learning theories, his theory maintains that second language learning is very different from other types of learning. He agrees with the Universal Grammar Theory's nativist assertion that children are born with a language acquisition device, but he believes that all learners regardless of age use the LAD when acquiring but *not* learning a new language.

Since language acquisition involves the LAD, it is similar to the way children develop their first language. It might best be explained as a result of successful listening or reading comprehension. For acquisition to take place, language learners must listen to or read material in the target language that is comprehensible to them. For example, when a language learner who has no background in Russian downloads a podcast from Radio Moscow, it is unlikely that language acquisition will occur because the learner will have no way to understand the Russian. But when students listen to their teacher speak in English and the teacher is careful to speak expressively, capitalize on vocabulary that is similar in the two languages, and use props and gestures, it is possible for students to *acquire* English. Language *learning* includes activities such as memorizing vocabulary, listening to grammatical explanations, and practicing grammatical structures. Although these activities are commonplace in many language classrooms across the world, according to the Input Hypothesis, true second language proficiency only results from second language *acquisition*. Language learning, in contrast, only leads to the development of a **monitor,** an accumulation of conscious knowledge *about* the language. Classrooms that follow the Input Hypothesis have an abundance of high-interest listening and reading materials to provide **input** for learners.

If contact with listening and reading material causes people to develop second language proficiency, it is natural to ask why people with the same amount of contact do not develop the same levels of language proficiency. According to Krashen's theory, learners have an **affective filter** which influences whether acquisition actually takes place. The affective filter is made up of the learner's feelings about language learning. Learners with low affective filters have positive dispositions toward the target language—high motivation, low anxiety, lack of negative stereotypes, and the like—and are therefore receptive to language input when they encounter it. Learners with high affective filters—low motivation, high anxiety, prejudice toward the target language group—are not open to target language listening and reading experiences, so they do not "take in" input even when they have the opportunity. Thus, for these learners input does not become **in-take.** It is also probable that less successful learners have not experienced comprehensible input at the appropriate level of complexity for them. In the Input Hypothesis, the optimal type of input—referred to as **i + 1**— is neither too complex nor too simple. As noted earlier, if the input is too complex, it is not comprehensible, but if the input is too simple, acquisition cannot progress.

SLA Theories in the Classroom	*Input Hypothesis*
Helping Students Be More Successful	■ Offer many opportunities for listening and reading interesting materials at an *appropriate* level of difficulty (complexity).
	■ Work to decrease the affective filter by fostering positive language learning emotions so that students will "take in" target language input.

Conversation Theories: Some Important Concepts

Scaffolding	■ When a more proficient speaker supports and maintains a conversation so that speakers with more limited linguistic resources are able to participate.
Feedback	■ A response which gives a conversational partner information about whether a previous comment has been understood and possibly offers suggestions for improvement.
Recast	■ A specific type of feedback where a conversational partner restates an ill-formed or difficult to understand utterance in clearer and/or more native-like language.
Negotiation of Meaning	■ Conversational partners collaborate to come to an agreement about the subject of their conversation. Conversation theories maintain that negotiation can assist the learner's linguistic development by pointing out connections between words and phrases and their meanings.

Conversation Theories.   A second type of experience theory emphasizes the importance of conversation in learning a new language. **Conversation theories** maintain that people learn to speak in a new language by participating in conversations. Although it might seem puzzling to think of people who do not speak the language as participating in conversations, there are many ways to participate in a conversation without actually talking. At first, a learner might simply look in the direction of the speaker and appear interested. Later, a learner might participate by interjecting a word or short phrase. In addition to oral practice, conversations offer comprehensible and interesting input which is probably more consistent with the individual's interests and needs than typical classroom input.

The most useful conversations include a process called **scaffolding,** where a better speaker, such as a native speaker, a teacher, or a more advanced language learner helps the learner participate in the conversation. Scaffolding includes paying close attention to the conversational partner, repeating the learner's words to indicate understanding, asking open-ended questions or making comments to encourage the learner to speak, and interpreting or expanding the learner's comments. Even speakers with limited linguistic resources can participate in conversations when there is a conversational partner who provides good scaffolding. In first language acquisition, it is common for parents to scaffold their children's conversational attempts. When a baby coos and the mother responds, "Oh you like your teddy," the mother is scaffolding a very early conversation for her child by putting the baby's coo and facial expression into words.

Consider the following conversation between Takahiro, a Japanese child learning English, and an English-speaking adult:

VOICES FROM THE CLASSROOM

Takahiro:	This broken
Adult:	Broken.
Takahiro:	broken
	This /ez/ broken.
	broken
Adult:	Upside down.
Takahiro:	upside down
	this broken
	upside down
	broken. (Peck, 1978, p. 385)

This conversation illustrates the benefits of scaffolded conversations as well as how conversational partners **negotiate** their understanding of a conversation. At the beginning of the conversation, the adult repeats the most important part of Takahiro's sentence, "broken." This repetition shows that she is listening to Takahiro and understands what he wants to talk about. It encourages Takahiro to continue to talk. It appears that Takahiro and the adult have now agreed that they are talking about something that is broken. In fact, Takahiro's next offering is considerably more complex, "broken. This /ez/ broken. broken." At this point, the adult finally understands what Takahiro is attempting to communicate by "broken" and intervenes. By saying that it was "broken," Takahiro had been trying to say that there was something wrong with the object he was describing, but he did not know the proper phrase. Fortunately, the adult was able to infer what Takahiro was trying to say and offered the correct phrase "upside down." Instead of being broken, Takahiro really meant that the object was upside down.

It is easy to see how scaffolded conversations could "teach" language. The adult in this example closely follows the child's utterances, determines his communicative intentions, gives **feedback** when she does not understand, and ultimately offers the needed English phrase. Takahiro had a specific communicative need; he wanted to communicate that the object he was talking about was upside down, but he did not know the phrase. The adult provided the exact English phrase that Takahiro needed at the exact moment that he needed it. The conversation "taught" Takahiro that the kind of "broken" that he was talking about is called "upside down." By creating a scaffold for the conversation, the adult was able to help clarify the child's thoughts and supply the specific vocabulary item he needed. A number of SLA scholars call the type of feedback offered by the adult in this conversation a recast. **Recasts** refer to the restatement of an unclear or poorly formed utterance in more native-like language.

SLA Theories in the Classroom

Helping Students Be More Successful

Conversation Theories

- Involve students in natural conversations and tasks that require negotiation of meaning.

- "Scaffold" students' conversations by listening carefully and rephrasing what they are trying to say. Ask questions and make comments to encourage students to talk.

- Do not require full-sentence responses. Allow students to participate in conversations in any way they are able (one-word responses, gestures, facial expressions, etc.).

The Output Hypothesis

The Output Hypothesis: Some Important Concepts

Output	■ Output is the language produced by the learner either orally or in written form. The Output Hypothesis emphasizes pushed or forced output so that learners are encouraged to produce increasingly complex and native-like language. Output should be perceived as a process that focuses the learner on refining their language rather than on its quality as a product.
Noticing	■ By speaking or writing (producing output), learners may become aware that they do not know how to communicate ideas or concepts that they want to communicate or that there are differences between how they produce the language and how the language is produced by proficient users of the language. Noticing may cause learners to consider how effective they are in communicating the *exact* ideas they want to. Producing output may also trigger learners to notice how their target language actually communicates that particular concept.
Sociolinguistic Competence	■ Language production must be both grammatically accurate *and* socially and culturally appropriate. Learners must follow cultural conventions for verbal and nonverbal behavior within interpersonal communication in areas such as suitability of topics, politeness, and turn-taking. Learners must also understand the cultural content of language and vary their productions according to the social context and their conversational partners.
Hypothesis Testing	■ Learners may use output to test their emerging ideas about how the target language functions.
Metatalk	■ A concept taken from sociocultural theory (see next section), metatalk refers to the learner's use of self-talk to think about the language. The learner reflects on how the language works and formulates new hypotheses to test. Metatalk may be silent or spoken.

In her **Output Hypothesis**—also referred to as the comprehensible or forced or pushed Output Hypothesis—Merrill Swain argues that simply listening to or reading the target language (processing input or acquisition in the terminology of the Input Hypothesis) is insufficient for learners to develop grammatical accuracy and cultural appropriateness in the second language. When learners produce language they become aware of difficulties expressing specific ideas or concepts. This **noticing** allows them to become aware of differences between their own language productions and the way the language is produced by native speakers and in formal writing. Importantly, noticing encourages learners to reflect on how the language functions. Pushed or forced output refers to the idea that learners should be put in situations where they *must* speak and write in the second language. The goal is for learners to produce language that is increasingly "precise, coherent, and appropriate" (Swain, 1985, p. 248). Thus, the goal of pushed output goes beyond simple negotiation of meaning; learners are not only expected to get their ideas across, they are expected to communicate in a way that ultimately matches the productions of excellent users of that language. While the cognitive learning theories maintain that learner production (meaningful language practice) can make controlled processing of the target language automatic and that understanding grammatical concepts helps students learn them, the Output Hypothesis gives a more important role to production. According to the Output Hypothesis, production focuses learners on differences between their language production and that of better users and encourages them to reflect on those differences and modify their output accordingly.

To a large extent, Swain formulated the Output Hypothesis in response to the Input Hypothesis and to her research on French immersion students in Canada. (These programs were not dual-language programs and generally included only English-speaking students.) Although the immersion students had been in an excellent language input environment (they had had years of exposure to comprehensible input and the immersion environment presumably contributed to a low affective filter), Swain observed that their spoken and written French remained different from the French of their native-speaking peers (French-speaking children in French-language programs). She concluded that input *alone* did not allow learners to develop precise and socially appropriate language fluency. In her view, output adds to language development, especially at higher levels of language proficiency.

In her examination of immersion students, Swain also observed that they spoke less frequently during the French portions of the school day than during the English portions and that teachers often did not require them to talk. Since several studies had found that students are more sensitive to conversational feedback offered by teachers than feedback offered by other students (nonnative peers), Swain concluded that productive language use as well as teacher feedback are essential to the development of high-level language competence.

Like the Social Distance Hypothesis (discussed in the next section), the Output Hypothesis stresses the importance of producing language that is culturally appropriate. Grammatically accurate and even complex language production is still not successful if it does not follow cultural and sociolinguistic requirements for language use. Specifically, appropriate language must follow target language conventions in areas such as politeness, nonverbal behavior, suitability of topics, turn-taking and silence, directness of speech, and so on. **Sociolinguistic competence** becomes even more important when students produce grammatically accurate speech because lack of attention to cultural requirements can make the speaker seem to have negative personality characteristics such as rudeness or insensitivity.

While most second language acquisition theories concentrate on the beginning stages of language learning, the Output Hypothesis offers an explanation as to how students can change communicative but imprecise language forms into more acceptable, native-like language. In the case of ELs, the Output Hypothesis may be useful in explaining how learners can move from everyday conversational language to the more formal varieties of language that are required for success in school.

SLA Theories in the Classroom

Output Hypothesis

Helping Students Be More Successful

- Put students in situations where they must produce oral and written language. These experiences should push learners to produce language that is increasingly "precise, accurate, and appropriate" (Swain, 1985, p. 248).

- Encourage students to reflect on differences between the way they produce the language and how it is used by highly proficient users of the language. Encourage them to think and talk about how the target language functions.

- Give students feedback about the accuracy *and* the appropriateness of their spoken and written language. Although feedback from other students is helpful, teacher feedback is especially helpful.

Social Theories

Social Theories: Some Important Concepts

Acculturation

- Refers to the process of learning to function appropriately and becoming comfortable functioning within the target language culture.

Psychological Distance

- Includes the learner's motivation, anxiety, feelings about the target language and culture, as well as other emotional traits. It is similar to the affective filter in the Input Hypothesis. High psychological distance is seen as an impediment to language learning.

Culture Shock

- A state of anxiety, tension, and/or disorientation resulting from being exposed to or living within a different culture.

Social Distance
- The relative dominance (economic, political, and social power) of the learning and target groups. The contact stance, degree of enclosure, degree of cohesiveness, size of the learning group, ethnic stereotypes, and amount of time the learning group intends to remain in the target language area contribute to the social distance between the learning and target groups. High social distance is seen as an impediment to language learning.

Social theories of second language acquisition explain second language learning from the multiple perspectives of the learner, the learner's first language group, and the target language group. First language, cognitive learning, and experience theories, in contrast, focus almost entirely on the individual who is doing the language learning and the type of language experiences provided by the language class or target language environment. If learners are not successful, it is because they started out with the "wrong" native language, did not get the right kind of practice, had a high affective filter, did not receive scaffolding, and so forth. In essence, either the language learner or the language teacher is blamed for any failure. Social theories, in contrast, view language learning within larger sociological and even political and economic contexts and are more likely to ask questions about why groups of learners are not motivated, or how state graduation exams might cause teachers to concentrate on grammatical analysis when they really prefer communicative teaching approaches. Social theories examine how societal forces such as cultural patterns, ethnic prejudices, access to schooling, and the global economy influence the outcome of language learning by both individuals and particular learning groups.

The most well-known social theory of SLA is John Schumann's **Social Distance Hypothesis,** also known as the **Acculturation Theory.** The social distance hypothesis is similar to Krashen's Input Hypothesis in how it views individual language learners. Learners are believed to be successful because of their emotional receptiveness to language learning. Good learners are motivated, empathic to native speakers, flexible, and experience relatively little culture shock. Thus, in terms of the Input Hypothesis, they have a low affective filter. The social distance hypothesis calls this openness to language learning low **psychological distance.**

Schumann points out, however, that in addition to individual traits, there are many social incentives and deterrents to language learning. For example, a learner may live in a society that values language learning or in a society that views second language learning as an assault against the native language and culture. Moreover, the willingness of the target language group to accept language learners of particular first language backgrounds is an essential component of this theory. Many people observe, for example, that English-speaking Americans seem to be more receptive to immigrants from some countries than from others. In addition, people are often receptive to small groups of immigrants from a particular country or first language background but become less welcoming when the number of immigrants from that country grows. Thus, according to the social distance hypothesis, a learner with low (positive) psychological distance may have difficulty obtaining good language learning experiences due to high social distance.

The relationship between the learning group and the target group in Schumann's theory is called **social distance,** and social distance determines in large part the learner's opportunities for acculturation. **Acculturation** refers to the process of becoming a functioning member of the target language culture. Contrary to the commonly perceived sequence in second language acquisition, when people learn to speak an L2 they will have opportunities for acculturation, Schumann maintains that people learn to speak the second language through the process of acculturation. That is, as learners have experiences in the target community, they will hear and have opportunities to use the target language. Ultimately, the degree of acculturation that learners attain will influence and even limit their levels of L2 development.

Schumann provides an interesting set of criteria for examining the amount of social distance between the learning group and the target language group. These characteristics help to explain why some groups tend to acculturate and achieve useful levels of language competence while others do not (Schumann, 1976). The characteristics that make up social distance include:

1. the relative dominance (economic, political, and social power) of the learning and target groups.
2. the "contact stance" of the learning group. That is, does the group wish to preserve its own culture entirely, adapt to the new culture to some extent, or assimilate entirely?
3. the degree of enclosure of the learning group. Does the learning group have separate schools, stores, churches, etc.?
4. the degree of cohesiveness of the learning group. How much do members of the learning group live, work, and socialize together?
5. the size of the learning group.
6. the degree to which the cultures of the two groups are similar (congruence).
7. the ethnic stereotypes by which the two groups either positively or negatively view each other.
8. the amount of time the learning group intends to remain in the target language area.

This list of characteristics includes a number of factors that would contribute to successful language learning and acculturation and a number that would work against them. Group size is a simple example. When the learning group is relatively small, the members would be more likely to learn the new language because their native language would have a relatively small amount of usefulness. Swedes, for example, are seen as highly successful language learners possibly because few people in the world speak Swedish, thus forcing them to learn other languages if they want to participate in world commerce. Spanish speakers, on the other hand, constitute a relatively large English-learning group in the United States. The size of the Spanish-speaking group makes possible the existence of many Spanish-speaking institutions such as stores and churches. From Schumann's perspective, the availability of Spanish-speaking services would result in less contact with English speakers and might make the learning of English seem less urgent. In addition, English-speakers (the target group) may feel threatened by such a large non-English–speaking group. Any negative perceptions on the part of either Spanish speakers or English speakers toward the other group would also discourage language learning.

Unique among second language acquisition theories, the social distance perspective recognizes that in addition to the prejudices and stereotypes the learning group might hold toward the target group, the responses of the target language group also play a critical role in successful language learning. For example, the degree of similarity between the two groups makes members of the target community either more or less eager to accept members of a particular learning group. The learning group might be extremely enthusiastic about language learning, but the target group may not be receptive to their learning attempts, and therefore their learning opportunities would be limited. Bonny Norton's conceptualization of **identity** negotiation (see Chapter 1) is relevant here. The target language group might not allow some language learners the opportunity to achieve a status in the L2 community that is consistent with their already developed self-concept.

In assessing the social distance between groups, it is important to note that Schumann composed his list of characteristics contributing to social distance before the Internet. It would seem that people who use digital media would have less social distance and increased opportunities for acculturation. Use of social media or participation in online groups can circumvent enclosure to some extent and give learners access to authentic discourse communities without necessarily identifying themselves as members of a particular language group. On the other hand, digital media also allow people to maintain contact with their L1 group and may decrease their need to interact with L2 speakers. In either case, use of digital and social media should probably be added to Schumann's list of factors used to represent social distance.

Although the social distance hypothesis appears to address language learning outside the classroom, it has important implications for language teaching. In the second language context, there are many social, economic, and political forces that affect the services that English learners receive and even the instructional approaches that teachers may employ. In the foreign language context, such forces clearly impact the languages schools offer and the languages students choose to study.

SLA Theories in the Classroom

Helping Students Be More Successful

Social Theories

- Decrease students' psychological distance by working to increase their motivation to learn the language and to decrease their anxiety and stereotypes of the new culture.

- Decrease students' social distance by arranging cultural experiences and opportunities to get to know members of the new culture.

- Help students to better understand the new culture. Give them opportunities to ask about the target culture and talk about their experiences with native speakers.

- Help students learn appropriate cultural behaviors so that they will be perceived positively when interacting with members of the target culture and therefore be given more opportunities to acculturate.

Sociocultural Perspectives on SLA

Sociocultural Theory: Some Important Concepts

Private Speech (Also Known as Inner Speech, Self-talk, or Metatalk)

- Speech—either spoken or internal in either the L1 or L2—that learners direct to themselves for the purpose of understanding the world and to solve problems. Private speech can also include imitations of other people's speech. James Lantolf goes so far as to say that private speech is itself language acquisition. (Private speech is a complex and important concept that cannot be discussed in a few sentences. See suggestions for further reading.)

Zone of Proximal Development (ZPD)

- Language learning is an inherently social act. The ZPD refers to the distance between the kind of language that learners are able to produce on their own and the language they can construct with the support of others through scaffolding.

Mediation	■ In sociocultural theory, language learning is said to be mediated. The human brain does not learn language directly by being exposed to language. Rather, humans use cultural tools such as books, computers, institutions, and other people to learn language. The language the learner has already developed also becomes a tool for learning more language and for other purposes such as problem solving and developing relationships.
Self-regulation	■ Learners reflect on, plan, and use various tools and strategies to control their learning. Self-regulation includes **metacognition,** or the learner's thinking about learning and the learning process.
L2 Internalization	■ When the second language is internalized, it becomes automatic and under the control of the learner. At that point, the language becomes a tool for self-regulation and thinking.
Imitation	■ A useful strategy where learners employ words and phrases that they have heard others use. Imitation may be combined with private speech to help the learner think about how the new language functions.

Sociocultural theories have commonalities with both experience and social theories of SLA since they focus on the learner's language experiences, the social and cultural factors that influence language learning, and the experiences that are available to the learner. In addition, like social theories, they recognize that language learning always takes place within larger cultural contexts. Interestingly, in that they take into consideration how much cognitive attention that production of the second language requires, they also have elements in common with cognitive learning theories. Perhaps the commonalities with other SLA theories are not surprising in that sociocultural theories attempt to be comprehensive and take into account both individual and social factors that influence language learning. But one important difference between sociocultural theories and other SLA theories is the strong emphasis that the sociocultural theories place on the purposefulness of the language learner. While the experience and social theories describe how language experiences facilitate language development, the sociocultural theories stress how learners manage these experiences for their own purposes.

Actually as Lantolf (2006) notes, second language scholars conceptualize sociocultural approaches to second language acquisition in two different but reasonably complementary ways. Originally, the term sociocultural theory was used to represent the application of the Russian psychologist Lev Vygotsky's developmental theories to second language learning, but the term sociocultural theory of SLA has also been used more broadly to stress the role of social and cultural factors in second language acquisition. In both cases, sociocultural theories are rooted in two related axioms: 1) all language is cultural, and 2) all language learning is cultural. From this perspective, internalizing a second language is the same thing as internalizing the new culture and vice versa.

There are several essential Vygotskian concepts that sociocultural theories apply to second language acquisition. (Of course, it is far beyond the scope of this chapter to summarize either Vygotskian theory or all its applications to second language learning. There are several good suggestions for further reading at the end of the chapter.) Vygotsky sees all learning as mediated and the result of social interaction. Mediation refers to the use of tools—both physical tools such as books and symbolic tools such as the use of language either itself—to develop language proficiency. Ortega (2009) notes language itself is a tool, and "as all tools, language is used to create thought but it also transforms thought and is the source of learning" (p. 219). Learners are able to choose from a range of tools offered by their specific social-cultural context. Computer use may be a common tool for learners in one cultural context while other learners may not even have access to print materials.

Second language learners interact purposefully with speakers of the new language within the zone of proximal development. That is, they seek out language experiences which will help them develop language that is within their reach. Sociocultural theories view language learners as active in seeking out and utilizing appropriate tools and experiences rather than passive recipients of the language learning opportunities that happen to come along. Language learners also practice self-regulation. They reflect on, plan, and use various tools and strategies to control their learning. The term metacognition is often associated with sociocultural theories because learners are seen as thinking about their learning and the new language.

While both conversation theories and sociocultural theories recognize the importance of scaffolding in second language learning, sociocultural theories emphasize the role of learners in encouraging scaffolding and directing the conversation to their learning needs within the zone of proximal development. As was the case in the Voices from the Classroom example of scaffolding, Takahiro and the adult can be seen as co-constructing the utterance about the broken object since they both contribute words and phrases. In my earlier discussion of this conversation, I emphasized how the adult "taught" the phrase "upside down" to Takahiro. From the perspective of sociocultural theory, the focus should be on the learner. By starting the conversation about the broken object, Takahiro is directing the conversation toward the element of language he wants to concentrate on. Rather than seeing the adult as offering scaffolding, Takahiro is eliciting the scaffolding. In addition, Takahiro's final utterance in the conversation

upside down
this broken
upside down
broken

could be interpreted as self-talk. Takahiro seems to be considering "upside down" and that it represents the kind of "broken" he wanted to talk about. This utterance seems more like self-talk than an informational comment he is offering to his conversational partner.

Sociocultural theories use the term internalization to refer to the point when the second language becomes automatic and under the control of the language learner. Although internalization is the ultimate goal of language learning, movement within the ZPD is uneven and depends on the mediation negotiated between learners and their partners. Thus, teachers should anticipate that language learning will evolve at different rates and stages for each learner. The concept of internalization can also explain the differences that teachers often observe between the kind of language that learners can produce socially and the language that they are able to use for problem solving and thinking. Lantolf (2006) notes, "The fact that speakers can use an L2 socially does not mean that they can use it to regulate cognitive activity because although it is derived from social speech, the psychological function of speech takes time for appropriate experiences to develop" (p. 74).

SLA Theories in the Classroom

Helping Students Be More Successful

Sociocultural Theories

- Recognize that learners are in control of their own learning and support their autonomy.
- Scaffold students' conversations being careful to pay attention to where the learner is leading.
- Help students access a variety of tools that they can use to mediate their language learning.
- Recognize that students may not have full control of any language they produce. Just because they can use the language orally does not mean that it is fully internalized so that it can be used for thinking, problem solving, or higher-level academic tasks.

The Critical Period Hypothesis

Strictly speaking, the critical period hypothesis is not a second language acquisition theory in the same way the previously discussed theories are. A **critical period** is a biological concept that states that there is a specific moment during the lifespan of many animals when a particular ability must be learned. For example, birds that have broken wings at the moment they are supposed to learn to fly remain flightless. The idea of a critical period for language learning was proposed first by W. Penfield and L. Roberts and later by Eric Lenneberg and has traditionally been associated with the onset of puberty. Lenneberg maintained that the human brain remains relatively plastic and flexible until puberty when **brain lateralization** takes place. Brain lateralization refers to the assignment of specific functions to the left or right hemisphere of the brain. For example, in right-handed people, language is assigned primarily to the left hemisphere. This loss of brain flexibility was believed to contribute to a loss of second language learning ability, especially in the area of accent.

There is great controversy among second language acquisition scholars as to whether a critical period exists for language learning, and if so, whether it exists for all areas of language. For example, more research studies have found evidence for a critical period for accent than for grammar. The current controversy centers primarily on the issue of accessibility to the language acquisition device and universal grammar. As noted earlier, the issue of age and the ability to reset parameters remains the subject of debate. If universal grammar remains available to older learners, there should not be a critical period. Older learners would still be able to learn a second language similarly to the way children learn their first language. Unfortunately, scholars differ greatly on both *if* and *when* children may lose their inborn language learning ability, with estimates for a loss of language learning ability ranging from birth, to six to nine months, to six years, to puberty. David Birdsong has argued that it is more appropriate to speak of age differences in general terms—younger being better—than a strict critical period or cutoff age for language learning ability. Other scholars, including Stephen Krashen, maintain that language learners of *all* ages have access to universal grammar and therefore there is not a critical period for language learning.

How the Theories Differ on Important Language Teaching Issues

Language teachers are often most interested in several practical questions about second language acquisition: Why are some language learners more successful than others? How should errors be handled? Why do children tend to be more successful language learners than adults? (In other words, Is there a critical period for language learning?) Not surprisingly, the various theories have different positions on each of these questions.

The First Language Theories

Many language learners and teachers are particularly interested in understanding why some learners are more successful than others. The first language theories see differences in individual achievement as resulting primarily from the learner's first language and how similar or different it is from the language being learned. Whether learners have had the practice they need to overcome the influence of their native language also helps these theories explain why some learners are more successful than others. Thus, the closer the learners' first and second languages and the more practice and reinforcement they have had, the more likely it is that they will be successful.

With respect to learner errors, the first language theories generally favor correction. These theories hypothesize that it would be very unlikely for learners to overcome their errors if they are allowed to practice incorrect utterances without feedback. Grammatical patterns or sounds influenced by their native language would be particularly difficult to change. Thus, language teachers are urged to have students produce error-free utterances whenever possible and to swiftly correct any errors.

The original Contrastive Analysis Hypothesis does not envision clear child-adult differences because all learners are believed to learn language through behavioral reinforcement. Thus, child and adult learners with the same first and second languages would have the same opportunities for positive transfer and would have to overcome the same instances of interference. It is possible, however, that children would need fewer practice opportunities and less reinforcement since their first language habits would be less well established due to their young age. In contrast, the Universal Grammar Theory recognizes the possibility of child-adult differences since unlike babies second language learners already have preset language parameters. But as already noted, scholars do not agree about whether or when children lose their access to universal grammar as they get older.

First Language Theories

Why are some learners more successful than others?	■ Learners are successful when their L1 is close to the target language, they practice new language patterns to overcome interference from their L1, and they are reinforced for correct language use.
Should errors be corrected?	■ Yes. To avoid fossilization and to help students become aware of differences between their native language and the target language.
Why do children tend to be more successful language learners than adults?	■ As children get older, they may lose their innate language learning ability, and their L1 patterns are pre-set.

Cognitive Learning Theories

The cognitive learning theories do not have as clear positions on these issues as other second language acquisition theories. Differences in success could be explained by people's different amounts of background knowledge (schema) and the quality of practice they have. Practice must be meaningful and relate to the learners' background knowledge. But cognitive learning theories also recognize that negative emotions could interfere with learning by taking up some of the learners' available attention.

With respect to learner errors, cognitive learning approaches clearly suggest feedback and correction. Learners need feedback so that they can correct any misconceptions in their explicit linguistic knowledge, and practice of incorrect forms could lead to the automatic production of incorrect forms. With respect to child-adult learning differences, the cognitive theories say children would have the advantages of fewer demands on their attention and the need to perform less complex language tasks, but adults would have more general background knowledge and more explicit knowledge about the language. It is also likely that children would have more opportunities for meaningful practice and be more willing to take advantage of those opportunities.

Cognitive Learning Theories

Why are some learners more successful than others?

- Learners are successful when they have meaningful practice opportunities so that their use of the language becomes automatic.
- Learners with more background knowledge about the language would also be expected to be more successful.

Should errors be corrected?

- Yes. So that misconceptions about the language can be corrected and so that learners do not practice incorrect forms.

Why do children tend to be more successful language learners than adults?

- Children have less complex language tasks to perform.
- Children have fewer demands on their attention.
- Children have more opportunities for meaningful practice and are willing to take advantage of those opportunities.

The Experience Theories

It is not surprising that the Input Hypothesis disagrees with the first language and cognitive learning theories with respect to these important issues. Since in this theory learners develop language proficiency through listening and reading, explicit error correction is seen as unnecessary. Errors will disappear naturally when students have acquired enough language. Error correction might actually have negative consequences from the perspective of the Input Hypothesis. If errors are strictly corrected, students may become fearful of speaking and increase their affective filters, thus interfering with further language acquisition. In addition, since error correction contributes to conscious learning, it may give learners the false impression that they should spend time *learning* rather than *acquiring* the target language.

The Output Hypothesis and the conversation theories take a different position on error correction. Error correction is seen as appropriate, even essential, for language learning, but the correction must focus on meaning and be tailored to the specific conversational context. In the conversation with Takahiro, the adult *corrected* Takahiro's use of the word "broken" and offered the phrase the child was trying to communicate, "upside down." The Output Hypothesis goes further to have feedback focus not simply on successful communication of ideas but also on the cultural appropriateness and precision of the language. The Input Hypothesis, the Output Hypothesis, and the conversation theories agree that learner errors are a natural part of language learning which should not be regarded with alarm by language teachers. Neither the Input Hypothesis nor the conversation theories are concerned that learners will develop fossilized errors. In contrast, the Output Hypothesis sees learner language as remaining imprecise and unnativelike if learners are allowed to speak (or write) without feedback, especially without teacher feedback.

The Input Hypothesis, the Output Hypothesis, and the conversation theories also differ with respect to why some learners are more successful than others. Krashen would attribute individual differences in language achievement to the student's amount of language acquisition. The amount of acquisition would, in turn, depend upon how much comprehensible target language input the learner has received through listening and reading as well as on the learner's affective filter. Conversation theories, in contrast, see individual differences as a result of the number and quality of the conversations the learner has participated in. Conversation theories would also attribute differences in success to the learner's own ability to manage conversations. Some learners concentrate more and are more talented at making conversations work than others. The Output Hypothesis would emphasize the range of language experiences and the quality of feedback that the learners have received.

In short, the experience theories would agree that child-adult differences result primarily from environmental differences. That is, children generally have greater access to comprehensible input and scaffolded conversations in school and playground settings than do adults in their daily lives. In addition, children likely have lower affective filters and are, thus, more receptive to input. They may also receive more and better feedback.

Experience Theories	*The Input Hypothesis*
Why are some learners more successful than others?	▪ More successful learners have received more comprehensible input and are more receptive to the available input because of their low affective filters.
Should errors be corrected?	▪ No. Errors will go away naturally as acquisition proceeds, and error correction may increase the affective filter.
Why do children tend to be more successful language learners than adults?	▪ Children receive more comprehensible input and have lower affective filters.

Experience Theories

Why are some learners more successful than others?

Should errors be corrected?

Why do children tend to be more successful language learners than adults?

Conversation Theory

- More successful learners have had access to more conversations and received better scaffolding when they participated in conversations.

- Yes. Errors should be corrected in the context of a conversation as the conversational participants negotiate the course of the conversation.

- Children have access to more and better conversations. Proficient second language speakers are more likely to offer scaffolding to children than to older learners.

Experience Theories

Why are some learners more successful than others?

Should errors be corrected?

Why do children tend to be more successful language learners than adults?

The Output Hypothesis

- In addition to other good language learning experiences, more successful learners have been pushed to produce "precise, accurate, and appropriate" language and given proper feedback (Swain, 1985, p. 248). They have been pushed to communicate at a high level.

- Yes. Allowing errors to go unnoticed will keep learners from refining their language.

- They may be required to produce more and more varied output. They may also elicit more feedback, especially from teachers.

Social Theories

Schumann's Social Distance model of SLA makes similar assumptions about error correction, individual differences, and child-adult differences to those of the experience theories. Specifically, error corrections within conversations might be useful *if* the learner has low psychological distance and *wants* to become acculturated into the second language community; individuals who are more motivated would seek out more language input and conversations, and children might be at an advantage for language learning because of their greater access to advantageous language learning settings. However, the social aspect of Schumann's theory points to an important additional consideration to these explanations: the receptiveness of the language learning environment. It is possible that learners of different ages or ethnic groups receive different types of error correction and have access to more or less comprehensible input and different kinds of conversations. Many scholars believe that children typically receive better input and more and better conversational opportunities than older learners. Thus, it is possible to view the children in any learning group as having less social distance than the adults from the same learning group. With respect to individual differences, both the learner's community and the target community must be considered in addition to the individual characteristics of the learner and differences in the language experiences the learner has had. That is, an individual learner might be very motivated to seek out excellent learning opportunities, but the target group may not wish to allow learners of that particular type (age, race, country of origin, etc.) to join its daily interactions. It is also possible that the target group would be more receptive to certain subgroups within the learner community, such as children or people of a higher social class, and that those people might get better learning opportunities than other members of the learning group. Moreover, the learner's own group might have predispositions against its members learning a particular language and as a result put up barriers to learning. Unfortunately, it was not uncommon during the Cold War for American students of Russian to have their patriotism questioned.

Social theories of SLA do not have a clear position on error correction, but to the extent that they are consistent with the experience models of SLA, natural error correction in the context of a meaningful conversation would be favored. In addition, if acculturation is the primary force for language learning, learners who wish to acculturate may seek out error correction or monitor their language output carefully and self-correct so that they can make their language as native-like as possible. More acculturated individuals would likely also have access to more sophisticated conversations where they would have the opportunity to communicate more complex ideas and receive feedback from individuals who are more invested in understanding them. Specifically, learners who are more acculturated are more likely to have conversations with friends, coworkers, or even family members in situations where successful negotiation of meaning is valued by all the participants in the conversation.

Experience Theories	*Social Theories*
Why are some learners more successful than others?	■ More successful learners have lower psychological and social distance.
Should errors be corrected?	■ Maybe. If errors are corrected, learners may be better able to acculturate.
Why do children tend to be more successful language learners than adults?	■ Children have access to more opportunities for acculturation. Some communities may be more receptive to child language learners than adult learners.

Sociocultural Theories

Since sociocultural theories have commonalities with both experience and social theories of SLA, they have somewhat similar positions on error correction, individual differences, and child-adult differences. On the other hand, since they emphasize self-regulation and the use of mediation (tools) in learning language, the agency of the learner and the role of the entire cultural context are much more central. Importantly, the emphasis is on the learner's management of conversations and other learning tools. From this perspective the idea of error correction would be seen more appropriately as **negotiation of meaning** or **co-construction of meaning**. The conversational participants negotiate what they are trying to communicate in the process of co-constructing their conversation. Scaffolding and feedback within the zone of proximal development would lead to language learning, but not necessarily **internalization** at this point. Learner "errors" may actually be strategic requests for feedback. Instead of thinking of a word like "broken" as an error, sociocultural theories would see it as an effort on the part of the learner to lead the conversation to needed information. Thus, sociocultural theories would favor natural error correction and direct feedback within the context of a conversation that is meaningful to the learner. More successful learners may elicit and/or receive more appropriate scaffolding and feedback, and conversational partners may be more likely to offer helpful scaffolding and feedback to children. In addition, children may employ the specific strategy of imitation more frequently than older learners. Imitation combined with reflection on the language through private speech (self-talk) is a particularly powerful approach to language learning.

Experience Theories	*Sociocultural Theories*
Why are some learners more successful than others?	■ More successful second language learners practice self-regulation and self-talk and may elicit more and better scaffolding within the zone of proximal development. They may also have access to more and better tools for language learning (mediation).
Should errors be corrected?	■ Both the terms "error" and "corrected" are problematic from the perspective of sociocultural theories. **Negative feedback** and **negotiation of meaning** are better terms, and feedback should be within the ZPD. Incorrect utterances may represent hypothesis testing by the learner and/or an indirect request for feedback.
Why do children tend to be more successful language learners than adults?	■ Imitation through private speech is integral to the internalization of a second language and children may be more willing and more frequent users of imitation and self-talk about language learning. They may also have access to more/better learning tools and scaffolded conversations.

Implications for Language Teaching

The array of second language acquisition theories and their disagreements about important language teaching issues can be very frustrating to teachers. It is clear that the first language theories, the cognitive learning theories, the experience theories, the social theories, and the sociocultural theories take very different positions on why learners are successful, how class time should be used, and how teachers should deal with errors. You should review the SLA Theories in the Classroom sections in this chapter for suggestions about how to help your students be more successful. In general, the first language theories emphasize the need for teachers to understand how a learner's first language might influence their language learning, and the cognitive learning theories stress the importance of meaningful language practice. The experience and social theories are more concerned with the learner's emotions and "natural" language experiences, while the sociocultural theories stress the role of culture in language learning, the learner's ownership of language learning, and their inclusion in the target language community.

Although the theories all offer very different explanations of how languages are learned, they also agree on a number of things that teachers can do to help their students. Teachers should pay attention to learners and their L1 backgrounds (first language theories), their knowledge about the new language (cognitive learning theories, the Output Hypothesis, and sociocultural theories, but *not* the Input Hypothesis), their feelings about language learning (experience, social, and sociocultural theories). In other words, the theories agree that how and what is taught should depend on the particular group of learners. The theories also agree that students must have as much contact with the new language as possible and that language learning activities should be realistic and meaningful. Students also need contact with a range of input and conversation types. The first language theories suggest practice focusing on specific sounds and grammatical forms; the cognitive learning theories encourage meaningful practice; the Input Hypothesis recommends listening and reading; the conversation theories require scaffolded conversations; and the social, conversation, and sociocultural theories emphasize high-quality interactions with speakers of the new language, including thoughtful feedback. In fact, most language teachers are **eclectic,** which means that they use approaches from more than one second language acquisition theory, and most language classes include all of these activities advocated by the various theories but in different amounts and proportions. The next chapter concerns language teaching methodologies, which are more specific and comprehensive about what teachers should do in the classroom. Some of the methodologies are closely associated with the second language acquisition theories described here, and some are not.

FINDING YOUR WAY

REFLECTIONS

How have your ideas about how people learn languages changed as a result of reading this chapter?

_____

_____

_____

_____

_____

Which SLA theory(ies) most closely coincides with your own beliefs about language learning?

_____

_____

_____

_____

_____

Does eclectic language teaching mean that language teachers should teach in any way they want?

_____

_____

_____

_____

_____

Which components of second language learning are under the teacher's control? The learner's control? What outside factors also influence language learning?

_____

_____

_____

_____

_____

What language learning resources/tools are available to learners in your setting?

_____

_____

_____

_____

_____

What questions do you still have about how people learn languages?

_____

_____

_____

_____

_____

PLANNING FOR YOUR CLASSES

What do you want to remember from this chapter to use in your own classroom?

_____

_____

_____

_____

_____

What social, economic, or political trends in your teaching setting might influence the way you will teach?

_____

_____

_____

_____

_____

PROJECTS

- Compare and contrast the SLA theories in this chapter with respect to their ability to explain how people learn second languages. In your opinion, which theory(ies) offers the most reasonable explanation?

- Complete the BALLI (Appendix A) again and compare your responses with your original responses. Have you changed your mind on any items?

IN YOUR JOURNAL

- What language learning experiences especially contributed to your personal second language development?
- What specific social, economic, and/or political factors influenced your own language learning?
- Do you experience interference from your first language when you speak in a second language? Is the interference in the area of **phonology** (sound) or **syntax** (grammar)?
- How has your understanding of the grammar of a second language contributed to your ability to speak or write that language?

TEACHING CHECKLIST

Yes No

☐ ☐ I think about SLA theories when I choose language teaching materials.

☐ ☐ I think about SLA theories when I choose teaching activities.

☐ ☐ I read about SLA. SLA journals include *TESOL Quarterly, International Journal of Bilingual Education and Bilingualism, Bilingual Research Journal, NABE* (National Association for Bilingual Education) *Journal of Research and Practice, Modern Language Journal, Foreign Language Annals, Applied Linguistics, Language Learning, Studies in Second Language Acquisition,* and *System.*

☐ ☐ I talk to other teachers about SLA.

☐ ☐ When I hear about new approaches to language teaching, I consider whether they are consistent with what I already know about second language acquisition.

☐ ☐ I recognize that the various SLA theories may give me conflicting advice about what to do in my classroom.

REFERENCES AND SUGGESTIONS FOR FURTHER READING

Ausubel, D. A. (1964). Adults vs. children in second language learning: Psychological considerations. *Modern Language Journal, 48,* 420–424.

Ausubel, D. A. (1968). *Educational psychology: A cognitive view.* New York, NY: Holt, Rinehart & Winston.

Bialystok, E. (1978). A theoretical model of second language learning. *Language Learning, 28,* 69–83.

Bialystok, E. (1982). On the relationship between knowing and using linguistic forms. *Applied Linguistics, 3,* 181–206.

Bialystok, E. , & Hakuta, K. (1994). *In other words: The science and psychology of second language acquisition.* New York, NY: Basic Books.

Birdsong, D. (1999). *Second language acquisition and the critical period hypothesis.* Mahwah, NJ: Lawrence Erlbaum Associates.

Cohen, A. (1990). *Language learning: Insights for learners, teachers, and researchers.* New York, NY: Newbury House.

Collier, V. (1995). *Promoting academic success for ESL students: Understanding second language acquisition for school.* Jersey City, NJ: NJTESOL-BE.

Cook, V. , & Newson, M. (1996). *Chomsky's universal grammar: An introduction* (2nd ed.). Oxford, UK: Blackwell.

Cross, R. (2010). Language teaching as sociocultural activity: Rethinking language teacher practice. *Modern Language Journal, 94,* 434–452.

Ellis, N. (1999). Cognitive approaches to SLA. *Annual Review of Applied Linguistics 19,* 22–42.

Ellis, R. (1990). *Instructed second language acquisition.* Oxford, UK: Basil Blackwell.

Ellis, R. (1996). SLA and language pedagogy. *Studies in Second Language Acquisition, 19,* 69–92.

Firth, A. , & Wagner, J. (2007). On discourse, communication, and (some) fundamental concepts in SLA research. *Modern Language Journal, 91,* 757–772.

Horwitz, E. K. (1986). Some language acquisition principles and their implications for second language teaching. *Hispania, 69,* 684–689.

Izumi, S. (2002). Output, input enhancement, and the noticing hypothesis: An experimental study on ESL relativization. *Studies in Second Language Acquisition 24,* 541–577.

Izumi, S. , & Bigelow, M. (2000). Does output promote noticing and second language acquisition? *TESOL Quarterly 34,* 239–278.

Krashen, S. (1985). *The input hypothesis: Issues and implications.* New York, NY: Longman.

Lantolf, J. (2006). Sociocultural theory and L2: State of the art. *Studies in Second Language Acquisition, 28,* 67–109.

Lantolf, J. & Beckett, T. (2009). Sociocultural theory and second language acquisition. *Language Teaching, 42,* 459–475.

Lenneberg, E. H. (1967). *The biological foundations of language.* New York, NY: John Wiley and Sons.

McLaughlin, B. (1987). *Theories of second language learning.* London, UK: Edward Arnold.

McLaughlin, B. , Rossman, T. , & Mcleod, B. (1983). Second language learning: An information-processing perspective. *Language Learning, 33,* 135–158.

Muñoz, C. & Singleton, D. (2011). A critical review of age-related research on L2 ultimate attainment. *Language Teaching, 44,* 1–35.

Nicholas, H., Lightbown, P. , & Spada, N. (2001). Recasts as feedback to language learners. *Language Learning, 51,* 719–758.

Ortega, L. (2009). *Understanding second language acquisition.* London, UK: Hodder Education.

Peck, S. (1978). Child-child discourse in second language acquisition. In E. Hatch (Ed.), *Second language acquisition: A book of readings* (pp. 383–400). Rowley, MA: Newbury House.

Penfield, W. , & Roberts, L. (1959). *Speech and brain mechanisms.* Princeton, NJ: Princeton University Press.

Rivers, W. M. (1964). *The psychologist and the foreign language teacher.* Chicago, IL: Chicago University Press.

Schmidt, R. (1993). Awareness and second language acquisition. *Annual Review of Applied Linguistics 11,* 206–226.

Schumann, J. H. (1976). Social distance as a factor in second language acquisition. *Language Learning, 26*(1), 135–143.

Schunk, D. H. (2012). *Learning theories: An educational perspective* (6th ed.). New York, NY: Pearson.

Sharwood Smith, M. (1993). Input enhancement in instructed SLA. *Studies in Second Language Acquisition 15,* 165–179.

Skinner, B. F. (1957). *Verbal behavior.* New York, NY: Appleton-Century-Crofts.

Swain, M. (1985). Communicative Competence: Some roles of comprehensible input and output in its development. In: S. Gass & C. Madden (Eds.), *Input in Second Language Acquisition* (235–253). Rowley, MA: Newbury House.

Swain, M. (1993). The output hypothesis: Just speaking and writing aren't enough. *Canadian Modern Language Review 50,* 158–164.

Swain, M. (2000). The output hypothesis and beyond: Mediating acquisition through collaborative dialogue. In: J. P. Lantolf (Ed.), *Sociocultural Theory and Second Language Learning* (97–114). Oxford, UK: Oxford University Press.

Swain, M. (2005). The output hypothesis: Theory and research. In: E. Hinkel (Ed.), *Handbook on Research in Second Language Teaching and Learning* (471–484). Mahwah, NJ: Lawrence Erlbaum.

Vygotsky, L. S. (1962). *Language and thought.* Cambridge, MA: Massachusetts Institute of Technology Press.

Vygotsky, L. S. (1978). *Mind in society: The development of higher psychological processes* (14th ed.). Cole, M., John-Steiner, V., Scribner, S., & Souberman, E. (Eds.). Cambridge, MA: Harvard University Press.

3 What Should I Know About Language Teaching Methodologies?

- Which second language acquisition theories would you like to apply as a language teacher?
- How should language teaching be different in second and foreign language settings?
- What have you liked and disliked about the language teaching methodologies that you have experienced?
- What are your students' specific language learning needs?

LANGUAGE TEACHING METHODOLOGIES

Although second language acquisition theories like the ones you read about in Chapter 2 provide the broad basis for language teaching, they focus on how languages are learned rather than on how they should be taught. In contrast, language teaching methodologies describe specific approaches for teaching second languages. Language teaching methodologies make assumptions about how languages are learned and vary with respect to how related they are to formal second language acquisition theories. It is not unusual for language teaching methods to remain in use even when new research in second language acquisition calls their assumptions into question. Major language teaching methods include the Audiolingual Method, Grammar Translation, Total Physical Response, the Natural Approach, Communicative Language Teaching, and Proficiency-Oriented Language Teaching. Content-Based Instruction, Sheltered Instruction, and Task-Based Language Instruction are recent approaches to language teaching. The Sheltered Instruction Observation Protocol (SIOP) Model is a recent approach specifically designed to integrate academic content with language development for English learners.

Language Teaching Methods

A language teaching method is a coherent and comprehensive approach to teaching second languages. Most methods include statements about how the language should be presented, the sequencing and amount of focus on the various language skills (listening, speaking, reading, writing, culture, vocabulary, pronunciation, grammar), and descriptions of specific learning activities. Typically, methods also suggest a syllabus or teaching sequence based either on grammatical complexity, communicative usefulness, or academic needs. Some language teaching methods include their own second language acquisition theory, and some, such as the Audiolingual Method, are closely aligned with a separate SLA theory.

Early Methods

Grammar Translation

Complementary SLA Theory	*Grammar Translation*
First Language Theories	■ Focuses primarily on reading and writing.
	■ Uses authentic texts.
Cognitive Learning Theories	■ Students have the same native language background.
	■ Encourages students to translate rather than "think" in the target language.
	■ Highlights grammar and vocabulary differences between the native and target languages.
	■ Class is conducted primarily in the students' native language.

Although the **Grammar Translation Method** is considered old-fashioned by many language teachers today, it is still commonly used across the world. (All three early methods described in this section are still used entirely or in part in many language classes.) Even teachers who believe strongly in more modern communication-centered approaches to language teaching sometimes use Grammar Translation activities to illustrate a particular grammatical point or to show the nuances of a word in a written text. Most people have experienced at least some Grammar Translation activities in their language learning experiences, and many nonlanguage teachers view translation as the commonsense way to learn and teach languages.

In the Grammar Translation approach, teachers emphasize understanding the target language and how it is put together. Typically, teachers have students read and translate **authentic** target language texts and then complete written exercises focusing on grammatical features that appeared in the text. Translations are used in both directions. Target language to first language translations ensure that students understand what they read, and first language to target language translations help learners develop the ability to articulate exact messages in the target language. Obviously, the Grammar Translation approach is better suited to developing reading ability than speaking ability in the second language. It is most appropriate for learners who require a very precise reading ability in their second language, such as people who use another language in their research or foreign language learners who must use textbooks written in another language (e.g., Chinese engineering students who use English-language textbooks). While most language teachers today view Grammar Translation as particularly inappropriate for beginning learners, many would concede a role for translation in advanced learners who need to develop the ability to express their ideas accurately and acceptably.

VOICES FROM THE *GRAMMAR TRANSLATION* CLASSROOM

What Teachers Do:

- Conduct class in the students' native language.
- Select readings that illustrate particular grammatical, historical, or literary concepts.
- Preview the cultural, literary, and historical background of the readings.
- Ask questions about the readings that draw students' attention to specific grammar constructions, vocabulary, and literary devices.
- Explain the grammar, vocabulary, and cultural contexts of the readings.
- Prepare written grammar and vocabulary exercises.

What Students Do:

- Read silently and aloud.
- Do written exercises.
- Prepare written translations.
- Listen to teacher explanations.
- Read texts aloud and translate.

The Audiolingual Method

Complementary SLA Theory	*Audiolingual Method (ALM)*
The Contrastive Analysis Hypothesis	■ Emphasizes listening and speaking.
	■ Focuses on oral language as it is used by target language speakers.
Behavioral Learning Theory	■ Sequences grammar according to similarities and differences with the first language (contrastive analysis).
	■ Uses memorized dialogues and pattern drills.
	■ Encourages students to internalize language patterns with little or no grammatical explanation.
	■ Requires well-pronounced, grammatically correct, full-sentence responses from students.

The **Audiolingual Method (ALM)** is one of the most well-known older language teaching methodologies. Like Grammar Translation, it is still in use in many language classrooms today. ALM was developed in the 1960s to take advantage of the insights into language learning offered by the **Contrastive Analysis Hypothesis.** Its two most prominent features are **structure drills (**also called **pattern drills)** and memorized **dialogues.** ALM language textbooks isolate target language patterns or structures and present drills so that learners can practice a pattern until they can use it automatically (habit-formation). Drills range from simple repetition of a verb conjugation (I go, He goes), to substitutions of verb forms (I eat, I am eating), to transformations of patterns (from the affirmative to the negative, for example). Dialogues, short conversations set within the new culture, give students practice with pronunciation and conversational phrases, as well as useful cultural information. ALM also has very specific ideas about the sequence of language teaching. Grammar should move from simple to complex, and learners are supposed to be able to understand and produce grammatical structures orally before they see them in writing.

At the time it was introduced, ALM was seen as a very modern teaching method since, unlike Grammar Translation, it emphasizes oral language and focuses on language as it is actually spoken by native speakers rather than on literary language. However, there were also two important criticisms directed toward ALM. First of all, teachers and students complained that it did not prepare learners for the spontaneity required by natural conversations.

The second criticism of ALM concerned its de-emphasis of explicit grammar teaching consistent with behavioral learning theory. ALM had students practice grammatical patterns and only later presented them with the **generalization** meant to summarize the rule for the pattern they were practicing. The emergence of cognitive learning theories made this practice particularly suspect, and some language teaching professionals advocated a new language teaching methodology called **Cognitive-Code** that was more consistent with cognitive learning theories of second language acquisition. Similar to the more recent **consciousness-raising** approach to grammar, the Cognitive-Code approach required grammatical explanations before language drills.

VOICES FROM THE *AUDIOLINGUAL* CLASSROOM

What Teachers Do:

- Conduct class in the target language.
- Lead class through drills focusing on grammatical concepts to avoid first language interference.
- Reinforce students for grammatically correct answers.
- Maintain a lively atmosphere to keep students' attention during drills and repetition.
- Require students to answer in full sentences.
- Lead students through oral practice of dialogues.
- Have students learn to pronounce target language forms correctly before they write them.

What Students Do:

- Repeat after the teacher.
- Memorize dialogues and, sometimes, act them out in front of the class. Use dialogue lines in new conversations.
- Practice dialogues with other students.
- Do oral and written grammar exercises.

The Direct Method

Complementary SLA Theory

The *Direct Method* predates the *Input Hypothesis,* but its emphasis on listening is consistent with that theory. Direct Method's emphasis on teacher questions and student responses has elements in common with *conversation and forced output theories.*

Direct Method

- Emphasizes listening and speaking.
- Focuses on oral language as it is used by native speakers.
- Conducts classes in the target language.
- Uses spontaneous conversations and explanations based on classroom objects and events.

The **Direct Method** is an early (1900s) oral and conversational method that is still in use today. Like ALM, the Direct Method concentrates on conversational speech and conducts lessons almost entirely in the target language. Direct Method teachers talk to students in the target language from the first day of class and work very hard to make students understand what they are saying. Students are also expected to speak only in the new language. Direct Method teachers are often dramatic and artistic, using their personal talents to act out what they are saying or employing elaborate props and pictures to help students understand. When you see a language teacher gesturing extravagantly in a movie, the teacher is probably using the Direct Method. Direct Method teachers who were asked to switch to ALM often complained that their job was no longer as fun and creative as when they were using the Direct Method.

A number of criticisms were also directed against the Direct Method. Since it focused primarily on listening and speaking, some educators felt that it neglected the literary and cultural reading that was associated with Grammar Translation teaching in favor of mundane, *nonacademic* conversations. The approach also had difficulty dealing with abstract topics. It was fairly easy for teachers to act out everyday actions like eating or sleeping, or to point to classroom objects, but it was very difficult to engage students in discussions of the future or of love. Some Direct Method teachers were seen as dogmatic in their avoidance of the native language, spending ten minutes trying to act out an abstract word like "truth" rather than simply giving the translation and moving on. The fact that the approach was so teacher-centered also required great effort on the part of the teacher. Many teachers simply did not have the language fluency, personality, or energy to be Direct Method teachers!

VOICES FROM THE *DIRECT METHOD* CLASSROOM

What Teachers Do:

- Conduct class in the target language.
- Use gestures, pictures, props, and dramatic flair.
- Engage students in conversation.
- Maintain a lively atmosphere.
- Encourage students to answer in full sentences.

What Students Do:

- Watch the teacher act out target language vocabulary and phrases and infer the teacher's meaning.
- Reply to the teacher's questions.
- Listen to the teacher's replies for feedback on their responses.

Although Grammar Translation, ALM, and Direct Method are still used today to a greater or lesser extent, since the 1970s, language teaching methodologies have been more influenced by the experience, social, and sociocultural theories of second language acquisition, which put much more emphasis on comprehensible input and participation in authentic conversations. Current language teaching methodologies also recognize the importance of culture in language learning and place a greater focus on the development of **cultural competence** and the use of authentic materials.

Input Methods: Natural Approach and Total Physical Response

Compatible SLA Theory

The Input Hypothesis and Asher's theory that physical actions reinforce language. The Output Hypothesis is consistent with TPR Storytelling.

Total Physical Response (TPR)

- Emphasizes listening and encourages a silent period.
- Teacher gives commands in the target language, and students act out the commands.
- In TPR Storytelling, students retell and act out stories they have already listened to.

The input methods include the **Natural Approach (NA),** developed by Tracy Terrell and Stephen Krashen, and **Total Physical Response (TPR),** developed by James Asher. Both approaches focus on the development of students' listening abilities based on the premise that listening comprehension is the basis of all language ability. Thus, these methods are consistent with the Input Hypothesis. Both methods allow a **silent period** where students are not required to talk to encourage the development of listening comprehension abilities. Both TPR and NA posit that just as babies learning their first language need time to listen before they start to talk, second language learners should be given time to acquire sufficient language before teachers ask them to speak or write.

The Natural Approach and Total Physical Response differ in the way they offer listening experiences to the learner and how much speaking is asked of the students. TPR uses a procedure similar to a "Simon Says" game. The teacher gives commands in the target language and models the actions required by the commands; students, in turn, follow the commands. The "total" of TPR refers to the fact that students do not simply listen to the commands, they actually carry them out with their "whole" bodies. Asher's theory maintains that physical action helps reinforce language learning because the body associates the command it hears with the action it is carrying out.

It can be difficult to imagine how a large amount of language can be presented through commands, but TPR teachers are resourceful and have come up with many inventive ways to present structures and vocabulary. Colors can be taught, for example, by asking students to "pick the red crayon" when many colors are available, and the conditional can be taught by commands such as, "If I drop the pen, then close your notebooks, but if I drop the pencil, then open your English textbook." Even so, until recently, many language teachers have seen TPR as an approach with limited usefulness after the beginning stages of language learning or for older learners who often find the commands silly. However, a recent TPR variation called TPR Storytelling has become very popular because it accommodates complex language in a more natural conversational context and is suitable for older language learners.

TPR Storytelling (TPRS) is used after students have begun to speak in the target language; that is, after the silent period. Typically, students are first introduced to new vocabulary words and expressions in the target language through pictures, actions, or gestures. Once the students have learned the actions that are represented by the vocabulary words, the teacher reads a short story in the target language containing the learned vocabulary and expressions. Students are encouraged to act out the story as the teacher tells it. As students progress in language acquisition, they offer their own versions of the story, combining the gestures they have learned with oral narration. When students are encouraged to retell the stories, TPRS is consistent with the Output Hypothesis of SLA.

VOICES FROM THE *TOTAL PHYSICAL RESPONSE* CLASSROOM

What Teachers Do:

- Give commands in the target language.
- Use gestures, pictures, props, and dramatic flair.
- Carefully prepare commands that illustrate vocabulary and grammatical concepts.
- Introduce new vocabulary and expressions and read stories for students to act out (in TPR Storytelling).

What Students Do:

- Act out the commands.
- Listen to the TPR stories.
- Infer meaning from commands and stories.
- Act out and retell the TPR stories.

The Natural Approach

Complementary SLA Theory

The Input Hypothesis. Allowing students to participate with any type of response (gesture, native language phrase, etc.) is consistent with conversation and sociocultural theories.

Natural Approach (NA)

- Emphasizes listening and reading as sources of second language acquisition.
- Encourages a silent period.
- Uses many means to offer comprehensible input, including TPR commands and pair and group work.
- Allows students to respond in any way that shows they have comprehended the input.
- Grammar is generally taught incidentally.

The **Natural Approach (NA)** is also associated with the Input Hypothesis, and like Total Physical Response, it emphasizes the development of listening comprehension. In fact, the Natural Approach employs TPR as one of its instructional strategies. NA also makes use of many of the same instructional practices as Direct Method classes. NA classes are oral and emphasize everyday, here-and-now conversation. They differ radically, however, in the kinds of oral responses expected of students. Where Direct Method classes insist that all responses be in the target language, preferably in a full sentence, NA classes allow students to respond in any way that shows they understand. For example, if a Spanish teacher asks a student, "*¿Cuántos hermanos y hermanas tienes?*" (How many brothers and sisters do you have?), NA students may answer in a variety of ways. They may, of course, answer with a complete sentence in Spanish, but they may also answer in their L1 or with a sentence fragment in Spanish. They could also show three fingers to indicate that they have three brothers and sisters, mix Spanish and English (dos sisters, un brother), or even take out a picture of their family and point. NA teachers believe that speaking *emerges* when the students are *ready,* which means when their silent period is over. When learners have processed enough comprehensible input they will, then, have internalized or acquired enough language to start talking. Even so, teachers do not expect NA students to offer fully formed sentences. Just as in many natural conversations, a gesture or a simple "yes" or "no" is seen as an appropriate response.

In NA classes, grammar is supplementary to communication and is taught according to communicative usefulness. That is, a relatively complicated grammar point such as the past tense may be taught early because most people find it difficult to talk if they cannot mention things that happened in the past. But grammar is not the main focus of instruction in NA classes, and NA textbooks are often organized so that the grammar is studied out of class so that class time can be spent in acquisition and communication activities. Instead of explaining or drilling grammar, an NA teacher is likely to ask at the beginning of a class if anyone had any questions about the previous evening's grammar assignment. Grammar discussions may be in the L1 so that grammatical topics can be disposed of quickly and the class can turn to the important tasks of listening, reading, and speaking.

VOICES FROM THE *NATURAL APPROACH* CLASSROOM

What Teachers Do:

- Conduct class primarily in the target language.
- Use gestures, pictures, props, and dramatic flair.
- Engage students in conversation.
- Maintain a lively atmosphere.
- Supply interesting and comprehensible input such as stories and jokes.
- Use small-group and role-play activities.
- Encourage students to answer in any way they can or want to.
- Explain grammar as students have questions.

What Students Do:

- Listen to and read the input.
- Participate in small-group and conversational activities.
- Study grammar related to communicative needs.

Communicative Language Teaching

Complementary SLA Theory	Communicative Language Teaching (CLT)
Conversation Theories	■ Encourages the development of listening comprehension.
The Input Hypothesis	■ Encourages target language responses.
	■ Uses pair and group work extensively.
The Output Hypothesis	■ Involves substantial use of negotiation of meaning tasks.
Sociocultural Theories	■ Corrects errors within conversational contexts.
	■ Emphasizes cultural appropriateness.
	■ Teaches grammar as needed for communication purposes.

Since the mid-1970s most language classes have included the term *communicative* in their descriptions. To a great extent, **Communicative Language Teaching (CLT)** is a reaction to the limited oral flexibility students developed in ALM courses. CLT classes emphasize **authentic communication** from the first day of class and are associated with Sandra Savignon's research on the development of second language **communicative competence.** In classes for beginning language learners, CLT courses look a great deal like Direct Method and NA classes. That is, the teacher speaks in the target language about here-and-now topics and encourages students to reply. Whole- and small-group discussions and problem solving and role-play activities are typical practices in CLT classrooms. Like NA classes, CLT classes employ substantial amounts of group work. CLT classes, however, differ from Direct Method and NA classes in several important ways. First of all, unlike NA teachers, CLT teachers urge students to communicate in the target language. They do not generally accept answers in the L1, but if the student offers a gesture or a phrase in the L1 as a response, the CLT teacher will help the student formulate that idea in the second language. Thus, CLT teachers do a lot of scaffolding. CLT classes also include a strong cultural component. Students are encouraged to employ proper greetings, gestures, and other nonverbal behaviors and participate in culturally appropriate scenarios.

Since scaffolded conversations and communication strategies are important parts of CLT classes, this approach is most consistent with the conversation and sociocultural theories. In addition to opportunities to teach structure and vocabulary, the scaffolded conversations make possible the fine-tuned, context-based corrections favored by conversation theory, Output Hypothesis, and sociocultural theory scholars. Grammar teaching is de-emphasized but not eliminated entirely in CLT classrooms. Rather, explicit grammar teaching is given secondary importance and, like NA, sequenced according to communicative need. Impromptu grammar lessons are common in CLT classes when the teacher notices that several students need the same grammatical structure to communicate their ideas. As is the case with NA, the development of listening comprehension is a strong focus of CLT.

VOICES FROM THE *COMMUNICATIVE CLASSROOM*

What Teachers Do:

- Conduct class primarily in the target language.
- Engage students in conversation.
- Teach communication strategies.
- Supply interesting and comprehensible input such as stories and jokes.
- Use culturally appropriate small-group and role-play activities.
- Engage students in scaffolded conversations.
- Negotiate meaning.
- Correct errors that interfere with communication.

What Students Do:

- Participate in small-group and conversational activities.
- Listen to and read input.
- Study grammar related to communicative needs.

Proficiency-Oriented Instruction

Complementary SLA Theory	*Proficiency-Oriented Instruction*
Conversation Theories	■ Encourages well-formed target language responses.
Output Hypothesis	■ Uses pair- and group-work extensively.
First Language Theories	■ Uses explicit grammatical consciousness-raising and error correction.
Cognitive Learning Theories	■ Emphasizes cultural appropriateness.

Proficiency-Oriented Instruction is an approach associated with Alice Omaggio Hadley and the American Council of Teachers of Foreign Languages (ACTFL) developed in the 1980s in an attempt to maintain the communicative focus of CLT while at the same time fostering greater grammatical accuracy. While CLT is primarily based on the Input Hypothesis and conversation theories, Proficiency-Oriented Instruction is more consistent with first language and cognitive learning theories as well as the Output Hypothesis. Proficiency-Oriented Instruction favors communicative teaching with more explicit grammar explanations and error correction. This perspective is based on the work of a number of scholars who argue that the type of error correction typically done by CLT teachers is too subtle to have the desired effect. These scholars favor **grammatical**

consciousness-raising, which calls for teachers to make learners aware of a grammatical structure before they listen to it or are asked to use it in conversation. In that way, learners are believed to be more likely to notice the grammatical point and therefore use it correctly when they speak. Proficiency-Oriented Instruction also favors explicit correction of learner errors. These practices are similar to the noticing described by the Output Hypothesis. The debate as to whether teachers should focus on what students are trying to communicate (meaning) or how they communicate (form) remains an important controversy in language teaching.

VOICES FROM THE *PROFICIENCY-ORIENTED* CLASSROOM

What Teachers Do:

- Conduct class primarily in the target language.
- Use gestures, pictures, props, and dramatic flair.
- Engage students in conversation.
- Supply interesting and comprehensible input such as stories and jokes.
- Alert students to grammatical structures that they are about to encounter (consciousness-raising).
- Teach grammar.
- Use small-group and role-play activities tied to specific grammatical concepts.
- Correct errors.

What Students Do:

- Participate in small-group and conversational activities.
- Listen to grammatical explanations and complete meaningful grammatical exercises.

What Is the Best Language Teaching Method?

Most language educators feel that it is no longer appropriate to talk about language teaching methods with a capital *M* since studies have not shown any language teaching method to be superior *overall* to others. This is not a surprising conclusion since there is such a wide variety of teaching situations, types of students, and learner needs, not to mention teacher motivation and skill in using the methods! It is clearly unlikely that one language teaching approach would be better in all situations or with all types of students. (Chapter 1 discussed how much language learners differ and how these differences may affect language learning.) It is also possible that some aspects of language learning are more compatible with one language teaching method while other methods are more appropriate for other language skills or stage of learning. For example, while the Contrastive Analysis Hypothesis and the Audiolingual Method are generally out of favor today, many teachers find them effective for pronunciation improvement in older and more advanced learners. (The language teaching methods described so far in this chapter are more oriented to beginning language learners.)

Teacher implementation is another important methodology issue. Most language teachers find it impossible to adhere to a single teaching approach due to the variety of student needs that they encounter. Even teachers who claim to follow a particular language teaching method tend to modify it to better fit their students. Of course, as is the case with second language acquisition theories, many teachers are eclectic and use some combination of language teaching methods and approaches. In addition, teachers in all content areas have become increasingly interested in **Differentiated Instruction,** or the variation of instruction based on the student characteristics within each class. Since many ESL classes include students at a variety of language and content levels and foreign language classes often include several proficiency levels as well as **heritage** and nonheritage learners, language teachers must often use multiple instructional approaches.

Content-Based, Sheltered Instruction, Learner-Centered, and Task-Based Approaches to Language Teaching

Content-Based Approaches

Complementary SLA Theory	*Content-Based Instruction (CBI)*
Conversation Theories	■ Goes beyond a focus on conversational language to emphasize the development of second language literacy.
The Input Hypothesis	■ Uses academic tasks to foster second language learning.
The Output Hypothesis	■ Pairs language learning goals with content learning goals.
	■ Involves substantial use of negotiation of meaning tasks.
	■ Corrects errors within conversational contexts.
	■ Emphasizes cultural appropriateness.

Sheltered Instruction Observation Protocol (SIOP) Model

Complementary SLA Theory	Sheltered Instruction Observation Protocol (SIOP)
The Input Hypothesis	■ Goes beyond a focus on conversational language to emphasize the development of second language literacy.
Conversation Theories	■ Uses academic tasks to foster second language learning and use.
The Output Hypothesis	■ Pairs language goals with content learning goals and communicates those objectives to students.
Sociocultural Theories	■ Emphasizes building background knowledge and linking new concepts to student's previous personal, cultural, and academic experiences.
	■ Integration of language skills.
	■ Makes language and content comprehensible by utilizing supplementary materials and providing substantial amounts of teacher scaffolding.

The teaching methods described so far in this chapter were specifically designed to teach second languages and use a language-based syllabus. In contrast, two recent teaching approaches, **Content-Based Instruction (CBI)** and **Sheltered Instruction (SI)** are designed to teach both content and language. CBI and SI are based on the premise that people learn new languages in the course of learning other things. For example, tourists may take cooking classes in Italy in order to learn new recipes *and* improve their Italian proficiency, or English learners may develop language proficiency in their content classes.

In addition to the dual focus on content and language, content-based approaches are defined by their use of authentic materials: the same materials used by native speakers to learn the same content rather than materials specifically designed for language learners. It is important to note that CBI and SI differ substantially from the far too common situation where language learners are left to their own devices in the same classes as native-speaking peers. Though these learners would clearly experience content learning, and authentic materials would be used, this situation lacks several essential components of CBI and SI. Both CBI and SI require (1) that the content instruction be tailored to the needs of the language learners, (2) that teachers have both content and language learning goals for their students, and (3) that teachers have the necessary preparation to work with language learners. (Content-based teaching is discussed more fully in Chapter 8.)

CBI and SI do not simply throw language learners into content instruction with authentic materials; they organize the content instruction to make it appropriate for language learners. Instructors typically modify their speech so that they are more comprehensible to nonnative speakers; for example, the instructional pace may be slower, visual aids are used, and very importantly, the cultural backgrounds of the learners are taken into consideration. By organizing instruction for language learners, content-based language instruction recognizes that the ultimate academic success of English learners is based on learning the content associated with their grade level as well as developing English language skills. Furthermore, CBI gives ELs experience using academic varieties of English, while conventional language teaching methods place greater stress on conversational language.

Sheltered Instruction goes one step further than simple content-based approaches because it does not mix language learners and native speakers in the same class. When content is taught to mixed groups of native speakers and language learners, it is natural for instruction to be geared to the language level of the proficient speakers. Even when instructors recognize and try to accommodate the two learning groups, the language learners remain at a disadvantage because they must struggle to learn content through a new language, while their classmates only have to deal with the subject matter. The idea of "sheltering" language learners is very appealing. Teachers support the learners as they simultaneously develop content knowledge and facility in the second language.

One specific approach to Sheltered Instruction called the **Sheltered Instruction Observation Protocol (SIOP) Model** (Echevarría, Vogt, and Short, 2008) is widely used with ELs but may also be a useful approach with foreign language learners. Indeed, the SIOP developers maintain that it represents good teaching for all learners in all content areas not just language learners. More so than the other language teaching methodologies discussed in this chapter, the SIOP Model offers detailed guidance for developing integrated content and language instruction. It encompasses eight components.

1. *Lesson Preparation.* All lessons should have both content and language objectives appropriate to the age and educational backgrounds of the students, and the objectives should be communicated ("clearly defined, displayed and reviewed") to students in words they can easily understand. This list of verbs reproduced from Echevarría, Vogt, and Short (2008, p. 31) gives examples of language and content (subject matter) objectives and how they differ.

Verbs for Content Objectives	Verbs for Language Objectives
Identify	Listen for
Solve	Retell
Investigate	Define
Distinguish	Find the main idea
Hypothesize	Compare
Create	Summarize
Select	Rehearse
Draw conclusions about	Persuade
	Write

FIGURE 3.1   Verbs for Writing Content and Language Objectives.

Lesson preparation also involves the frequent use of supplementary materials (graphic organizers, **manipulatives**, multimedia, visual aids, demonstrations, leveled study guides, outlines, etc.), the adaptation of content to multiple levels of student proficiency, and the inclusion of meaningful activities that integrate content learning with language practice.

2. *Building Background.* As will be discussed in Chapters 4, 6, 7, and 8, background knowledge is essential to understanding the language that learners encounter. Consistent with the Input Hypothesis, the SIOP Model emphasizes the importance of making language input comprehensible for learners. Teachers should build background by linking new concepts to students' previous personal and/or cultural experiences wherever possible, making connections between past learning and new concepts, and by introducing, highlighting, and reinforcing key vocabulary.

3. *Comprehensible Input.* Since the idea of making input comprehensible is central to SIOP, any of the suggestions throughout this book for helping learners understand written and oral language would be appropriate. The SIOP developers specifically note that teachers should use language that is appropriate for the students' proficiency levels, give clear explanations of the academic tasks, and use a variety of techniques and **meaning support** (Chapter 4) to make the content clear.

4. *Strategies.* The SIOP Model draws on insights from sociocultural theories of SLA here. It emphasizes the importance of strategy use in both language and content learning. Teacher scaffolding is also essential, and teachers should use a variety of questions and tasks that foster higher-order thinking skills. The integration of content with language reminds language teachers that they (we) must also pay attention to students' cognitive and academic development. The goal is for students to become more **autonomous,** and teachers should decrease support as students' language proficiency and academic knowledge develops.

5. *Interaction.* SIOP classes are meant to be highly interactive with plentiful opportunities for structured language use. There should be many and varied opportunities for language interactions using both small-group and whole-class activities. Teachers are also advised to encourage students to elaborate on their answers, give students adequate **wait-time** before they must answer and the opportunity to clarify important concepts in their first language.

6. *Practice/Application.* The integration of language skills and of language and content are central to the delivery of SIOP instruction. Teachers should provide activities that allow students to apply both content and language knowledge. Manipulatives and other hands-on materials help students practice new content.

7. *Lesson Delivery.* Lessons should be thoroughly consistent with both the language and content objectives. Pacing should correspond to students' ability

levels, and students should be actively engaged in learning throughout the lesson.

8. *Review and Assessment.* Lessons should systematically review key vocabulary and content concepts, and teachers should monitor students' progress and provide regular constructive feedback on their responses.

VOICES FROM THE *SIOP* CLASSROOM

What Teachers Do:

- Conduct class primarily in the target language, ensuring that the content and language is comprehensible to students.
- Engage students in the learning of content concepts and in academic conversations.
- Set integrated content and language objectives and communicate the objectives to students.
- Teach and encourage the application of learning strategies.
- Provide a large variety of approaches to meet the needs of all learners.
- Scaffold student attempts to communicate.
- Monitor student progress and give students feedback.
- Model good language usage.
- Use authentic assessment.

What Students Do:

- Participate in a large variety of hands-on content learning activities that promote language skills.
- Engage in self-assessment.
- Apply learning strategies.
- Ask for clarification of content and language concepts in the L1 or the L2.
- Collaborate with and assist other students.

From Teacher-Centered to Learner-Centered Approaches

So far this chapter has emphasized the activities and materials teachers use in the classroom. Many language educators feel, however, that these classic teaching methods—with the possible exception of the SIOP Model—focus too much on what teachers do and do not pay enough attention to the role of students in language learning or to their specific language learning needs. By focusing on methods, teachers do not pay sufficient attention to supporting **learner autonomy** or to differentiating instruction according to learner needs and differences. Some language educators advocate an approach called **language for specific purposes,** which maintains that language teaching methods and materials should be tailored to the specific needs of a group of students. Very few learners, they argue, need "general English," so the syllabus of any language course should be designed so that learners will be able to practice using the language for the topics and situations they need. Some language educators go so far as to suggest that teachers should negotiate the language syllabus with their students.

Another important concern with traditional language teaching methodologies such as CLT and NA is that they tend to teach listening, speaking, reading, and writing separately. While content-based approaches have a natural integration of language skills, traditional language teaching methodologies typically use activities that focus on only one aspect of language at a time. A teacher using a content-based approach, for example, may show students how to work a particular type of math problem, have students work in groups to solve some example problems, and then have each group describe their procedures to the other students. In this way, the students will have listened to the appropriate math vocabulary and sentence types when the teacher explained the math problems. Then they will have practiced speaking using similar language when they worked in groups and again when they explained their group's effort to the class. Later, when they read their math book, they will encounter language similar to the language they have already listened to and practiced orally. Thus, the content of the math problems allows listening, speaking, and reading practice to be integrated and gives students the opportunity to use similar concepts and language structures several times. Traditional language teaching methods do not have these natural connections between language skills to draw on.

Task-Based Language Instruction

Task-Based Language Instruction is a new approach to language teaching that incorporates several of the advantages of Content-Based Instruction. **Tasks** make communication in language classes more realistic, give students access to authentic target language sources, and better integrate listening, speaking, reading, and writing in culturally appropriate ways. According to Bygate, Skehan, and Swain (2001), tasks are activities where students must use the target language in a meaningful way to achieve a specific objective. Too often, activities in language classes seem unrealistic to students (write a letter to your "friend" in Buenos Aires) or seem solely designed to get students to use certain grammatical forms (tell your aunt that you never go to the store on Thursdays). Tasks can range from retelling a story, to writing a class newsletter, to preparing a research paper. The more realistic and appropriate the task for the particular group of students, the better. (See Chapter 8 for a fuller discussion of language tasks and how to use them.)

FINDING YOUR WAY

REFLECTIONS

Now that you are more familiar with various language teaching methods, which ones do you think you experienced as a language learner?

_____

_____

_____

_____

_____

Which ones do you think are most appropriate for your teaching context?

_____

_____

_____

_____

_____

Do some of the methods seem better suited to a particular stage of language learning?

_____

_____

_____

_____

_____

Do you think that the idea of language teaching methods with a capital _M_ is obsolete?

_____

_____

_____

_____

_____

PLANNING FOR YOUR CLASSES

Which language teaching method(s) would you like to use? Do you foresee any difficulties using those approaches in your teaching situation?

_____

_____

_____

_____

_____

What content could you incorporate into language-centered classes in your teaching situation?

_____

_____

_____

_____

PROJECTS

- Observe several language classes at different levels. What language teaching methods do you notice? Do there seem to be different methods at different levels?
- Select an SLA theory to discuss with a partner or group of students in your methods class. Discuss how the various language teaching methodologies described in this chapter are compatible or incompatible with the theory.

IN YOUR JOURNAL

- If you have thought of yourself as a content teacher, how do you feel about combining language objectives with your content objectives?
- Which teaching methods would you feel most and least comfortable using?
- How do you feel about the idea of negotiating your syllabus with your students?

TEACHING CHECKLIST

Yes _No_

☐   ☐   I think about my instructional goals and my students' needs when selecting teaching methods.

☐ ☐ I vary my teaching methods according to my instructional goals for a specific lesson.

☐ ☐ I use task-based activities that incorporate several language skills whenever possible.

☐ ☐ I read about language teaching methodologies. Some good publications about new language teaching approaches include: *TESOL Journal, NABE* (National Association for Bilingual Education), *ACIE* (American Council on Immersion Education) *Newsletter, ELT Journal, Modern Language Journal, Foreign Language Annals, Canadian Modern Language Review, Language Teaching, TESL-EJ, System, Asian EFL Journal, Hispania, French Review, Language Educator, Language Learning and Technology, Internet TESL Journal, CALICO* (Computer-assisted Language Instruction Consortium) *Journal, NECTFL Review, Al-Arabiyya Journal, Journal of the Chinese Language Teachers Association, Die Unterrichtspraxis/Teaching German, Slavic and East European Journal.*

☐ ☐ I think about my students' individual characteristics and their proficiency levels.

☐ ☐ I vary my teaching methods according to my students' needs.

☐ ☐ I talk to other teachers about language teaching methodologies.

REFERENCES AND SUGGESTIONS FOR FURTHER READING

Asher, J. J. (1986). *Learning another language through actions: The complete teachers' guidebook.* Los Gatos, CA: Sky Oaks.

Blaz, D. (2006). *Differentiated instruction: A guide for foreign language teachers.* Larchmont, NY: Eye on Education.

Breen, M. P., Hird, B., Milton, M., Thwaite, A., & Oliver, R. (2001). Making sense of language teaching: Teachers' principles and classroom practices. *Applied Linguistics, 22,* 470–501.

Brooks, N. (1975). The meaning of audiolingual. *Modern Language Journal, 59,* 234–240.

Brunfit, C., & Johnson, K. (Eds.). (1979). *The communicative approach to language teaching.* Oxford, UK: Oxford University Press.

Bygate, M., Skehan, P., & Swain, M. (2001). *Researching pedagogic tasks: Second language learning, teaching, and testing.* New York, NY: Longman.

Canale, M. & Swain, M. (1980). Theoretical bases of communicative approaches to second language teaching and testing. *Applied Linguistics 1,* 1–47.

Celce-Murcia, M. (2001). *Teaching English as a second or foreign language* (3d ed.). Boston, MA: Heinle & Heinle.

Chastain, K. (1988). *Developing second-language skills: Theory to practice* (3d ed.). San Diego, CA: Harcourt Brace Jovanovich.

Davidheiser, J. C. (2001). The ABC's of total physical response storytelling: A new and effective method of second-language teaching. In C. Cherry (Ed.), *The Odyssey continues: Dimension 2001* (45–63). Valdosta, GA: Southern Conference on Language Teaching.

Doughty C., & Williams, J. (1998). *Focus on form in classroom second language acquisition.* New York, NY: Cambridge University Press.

Echevarría, J., Vogt, M. E., & Short, K. (2008). *Making content comprehensible for English learners: The SIOP Model* (3rd ed.). Boston, MA: Pearson Education.

Herrera, S., & Murry, K. (2010). *Mastering ESL and bilingual methods: Differentiated instruction for culturally and linguistically diverse students* (2nd ed.). Boston, MA: Pearson Education.

Kelley, L. G. (1976). *25 centuries of language teaching*. Rowley, MA: Newbury House.

Krashen, S., & Terrell, T. (1983). *The natural approach*. New York, NY: Pergamon.

Norris, J., & Ortega, L. (2000). Effectiveness of L2 instruction: A research synthesis and quantitative meta-analysis. *Language Learning, 50*, 417–528.

Omaggio Hadley, A. (2001). *Teaching language in context* (3d ed.). Boston, MA: Heinle & Heinle.

Ray, B., & Seely, C. (2008). *Fluency through TPR storytelling: Achieving real language acquisition in school* (5th ed.). Berkeley, CA: Command Performance Language Institute.

Savignon, S. J. (1991). Communicative language teaching: State of the art. *TESOL Quarterly, 25*, 261–277.

Savignon, S. J. (Ed.). (2002). *Interpreting communicative language teaching: Contexts and concerns in teacher education*. New Haven, CT: Yale University Press.

Seely, C., & Romijn, E. K. (1998). *TPR is more than commands* (2d ed.). Berkeley, CA: Command Performance Language Institute.

Sharwood Smith, M. (1988). Consciousness raising and the second language learner. In W. Rutherford & M. Sharwood Smith (Eds.), *Grammar and second language teaching*. New York, NY: Harper and Row.

Shrum, J., & Glisan, E. (2009). *Teacher's handbook: Contextualized language instruction* (4th ed.). Boston, MA: Heinle.

Skehan, P. (2003). Task-based instruction, *Language Teaching 36*, 1–14.

PART TWO

How Do You Teach
a Language?

4

What Should I Know About Teaching Listening?

- Why is listening comprehension important in language learning?
- Why might students be able to understand some types of oral language and not others?
- What kinds of second language listening experiences do your students have access to outside of the classroom?
- How do content and language knowledge work together in listening comprehension?

LISTENING AND SECOND LANGUAGE ACQUISITION

Several second language acquisition theories and language teaching methodologies are specifically interested in the development of listening comprehension. The Input Hypothesis and its associated teaching methodologies the Natural Approach and Total Physical Response see listening comprehension as key to acquiring a second language. From this perspective, providing appropriate listening input and ensuring that the input is comprehensible is one of the teacher's major responsibilities. The SIOP Model makes the comprehensibility of both academic and language input central to both language and content learning. The cognitive learning theories favor using consciousness-raising activities to increase learners' awareness of grammatical structures when they listen. The conversation theories associated with Communicative Language Teaching also stress the importance of second language listening since it is not possible to participate in a conversation and take advantage of conversational feedback without understanding what your partner is saying. Sociocultural theories see language learners as using the tools they have available to them to actively construct meaning from the language they encounter.

When we think about learning a new language, we usually imagine ourselves participating in unplanned conversations just as we do in our first language. We think of running into an acquaintance and making small talk, or getting exactly what we want in a store after asking a number of questions, or communicating our hopes and dreams to a friend. In order to participate in spontaneous conversations, we have to be able to understand what our conversational partners say and formulate responses that are both appropriate and consistent with the ideas we are trying to communicate. This chapter and the following one discuss the development of second language listening and speaking abilities. I start with what instructors can do to help students develop and improve their listening comprehension skills.

Listening Comprehension: Some Important Concepts

Background Knowledge	■ A student's preexisting knowledge of a particular topic.
Previewing	■ Helping students anticipate the content they are about to listen to or read.
Advance Organizer	■ David Ausubel's term. An advance organizer is used to help integrate new information into the student's preexisting knowledge. Before teaching new material, the teacher provides an oral or written statement or outline of the new information, which links the content to learners' background knowledge.
Meaning Support	■ The practice of providing pictures, sound effects, and the like to make listening and reading materials more comprehensible to students.
Recall	■ An activity asking students to write down or orally record all of the ideas remembered from an oral or written text to determine what was understood. Recalls can be performed in the students' L1 so that they will not have difficulty expressing their ideas.
Recall Question	■ A question that calls for the recall of a piece of information from an oral or written text. Recall questions can often be answered by simply repeating words or phrases from the text.
Inference Question	■ A question that cannot be answered by simply repeating the words in an oral or written text. The student must have *understood* the material in order to answer the question correctly.
Intonation	■ Refers to the rising and falling of the tone of voice when speaking.

The Importance of Listening Comprehension

From a practical perspective, listening is an essential language skill. Even if a person were somehow able to speak understandably, this ability would be largely useless without the ability to understand other speakers. In addition, many language learners are expected to learn academic content by listening. Input researchers like

Stephen Krashen believe that listening is the most important language ability. Listening, along with reading, is a **receptive** language skill that requires a person to take meaning from the oral language produced by another speaker. Previous generations of language teachers were told that listening and reading were "passive" skills as compared with the "active" skills of speaking and writing. Today, however, language scholars recognize that listening and reading are by no means passive processes and that both listeners and readers must actively construct the meaning of any language they encounter. Of course, whenever we listen, the words themselves are not the only source of meaning. Gestures, facial expressions, tone of voice, our knowledge of the topic, and the setting and context of the conversation all contribute to our understanding of what other people are saying. From a sociocultural perspective the conversational participants **co-construct** the meaning of their conversation.

Obstacles to Teaching Listening Comprehension

In light of the importance of listening in language learning and use, it is somewhat surprising that listening comprehension does not receive greater emphasis in many language classes. On the other hand, there are several important obstacles to teaching listening effectively.

Classroom Listening and Real-World Listening. It is difficult to simulate authentic speech in the classroom. Classroom language is often artificial; the teacher may provide stories, anecdotes, and explanations in the new language, but realistic conversations are difficult to arrange. It is also difficult to provide language at the right level of difficulty. Some teachers feel that it is important to speak only in the target language and may speak too quickly, use language that is too complicated, or simply anticipate too high a level of listening ability from their students. Other teachers may speak at an exaggeratedly slow rate that hardly resembles the speech that learners would hear in the target language community. Even *second* language learners can have difficulty finding good listening experiences due to subtle barriers that keep them from participating in conversations with native speakers. For example, students in many American school cafeterias separate into English and non-English–speaking "zones," giving the non-English–speaking students fewer opportunities to develop their listening abilities than one might expect because of the social distance.

Listening experiences in the language classroom often differ greatly from the authentic speech students would encounter in the target language community. Many language learners have been distressed to find that understanding natural speech is much more difficult than understanding the clearly enunciated sentences in commercially produced materials. Natural speech does not proceed clearly and without interruption from the beginning of a sentence to the end. Rather, speakers often start sentences in one way, then pause and start over a different way. There are often long digressions as well (I was talking to Cindy . . . have you seen her hair? Can you believe it? Anyway, we were at the mall, and Cindy starts talking about that party . . .). Speakers frequently interrupt each other or try to change the topic to one they want to talk about. In natural speech, speakers often drop word endings or entire words and slur word boundaries. Thus, learners of English have a difficult time recognizing "I'm gonna . . ." as "I'm going to."

All languages have such inconsistencies between careful formal speech and informal, everyday speech, and language teachers are often confused about which forms to present to students. If students only hear careful speech, they are likely to have great difficulty when they talk to L2 speakers or listen to movies or videos. On the other hand, students may find informal speech difficult to understand if it does not clearly correspond to the written forms they have been studying. Second language learners are constantly confronted with contrasts between their textbook materials and the speech they hear in the community and may wonder when they are going to learn "real" English. Even when ESL teachers are careful to provide authentic listening experiences, they usually supply authentic adult speech when their students are encountering authentic child or teenager speech every day in school.

Ironically, commercially produced listening materials can be more difficult to understand than authentic language. Natural listening experiences almost always include a **context.** People rarely have to understand speech without knowing in advance who is speaking, why the conversation is taking place, and what kind of information is likely to be communicated. Thus, language students are at a distinct disadvantage when their teacher abruptly announces, "I am going to play an audio-file for you" and they have to listen without any background information. In addition, linguists have found that natural language contains many communicative redundancies and generally offers each piece of information in several ways. Therefore, listeners have other chances to understand information if they missed something the first time it was offered. These redundancies also give listeners valuable time to process incoming information. Consider the following example.

VOICES FROM THE CLASSROOM

An American student is telling a classmate about a movie she saw. Underline the redundancies in her speech.

Emily: Yesterday I went to the movies with some people from my dorm. Have you seen that new horror movie yet? It was really good! Anyway, Sofia and Blake came and so did Lindsay, even though she hardly ever leaves the dorm, especially for something frivolous like a movie.

In the classroom, a language student is likely to hear straightforward sentences with few or no redundancies, such as, "Rachel is going to do her science homework this afternoon." Unlike natural conversation, if a student misses any part of the utterance, either due to an unknown word or phrase or a momentary attention lapse, there is no chance to recover. To add to students' frustrations, classroom listening activities often tend to focus on minor or irrelevant details rather than the general message. Consider the following classroom exchange.

VOICES FROM THE CLASSROOM

To complement a unit on food, Mr. Johnson has just played a video clip containing an American television commercial about breakfast cereal. He then gauges his students' comprehension with a few questions. Do you think his comprehension questions are effective? Are some more effective than others? Explain your answers.

Mr. Johnson: What was the commercial about?

Esteban: Food. Breakfast . . . cereal.

Mr. Johnson: Excellent, Esteban! How long did the commercial last?

Elsa: I don't know. Only a little while.

Mr. Johnson: It wasn't a long commercial . . . only 25 seconds. According to the commercial, why is this cereal so nutritious?

Elena: Natural. It contains natural ingredients.

Mr. Johnson: Great. How much does it cost?

Roberto: Four dollars. No. Three dollars. Three dollars.

Mr. Johnson: Right! How many different actors and actresses were eating this cereal in the commercial?

Juana: I don't remember. Three?

Mr. Johnson: No, four. Would any of you buy this cereal?

Silvia: I would. I would.

Mr. Johnson: Really? Why?

Mr. Johnson's students were probably frustrated by the question "How many different actors and actresses were eating this cereal?" because it focused on an apparently irrelevant detail. On the other hand, the question "Why is this cereal so nutritious?" was appropriate and probably more engaging because it focused on important information and encouraged students to draw conclusions based on what they had heard. And the follow-up question about why Silvia would buy the cereal was probably the best question in eliciting overall understanding of the commercial rather than just recall of details.

Knowledge of the communicative context is very helpful in understanding interactions in natural settings. Since beginning language learners often have a limited knowledge of the communicative context and must fill in the information that L1 speakers intuitively know, language learners typically find it difficult to understand what they hear, especially if there is significant background noise or other distractions. Language researchers also know that speech needs to be louder and clearer for beginning language learners. Thus, a classroom full of fidgeting students is not an ideal environment for learning to listen.

Finally, in most natural listening experiences, the listener gets to see and interact with the speaker. In face-to-face conversations, we can watch the speaker's mouth, posture, and gestures to help us understand what is being said. When we become confused, we can ask for clarification. Thus for many reasons, classroom listening can be more difficult than understanding language in the "real world."

Unrealistic Expectations

Listening comprehension can be further complicated by students' unrealistic expectations that they should be able to understand every word that their teacher says.

A few years ago, I interviewed students in three first- and second-year college language classes while their teachers were out of the room. Their responses about listening were surprising and troubling. Almost all of the students were extremely anxious about understanding their teachers. Since they thought that they were supposed to understand every word their teacher said, these students would feverishly try to apply what are known as **bottom-up processing** strategies. That is, they tried to understand the meaning of every explanation or anecdote by translating word by word into English. Their teachers, on the other hand, believed that their students' listening comprehension abilities would improve while listening to amusing anecdotes, assuming that the students would apply their **background knowledge** and focus on understanding each anecdote as a whole (**top-down processing**). Understandably, the students found classroom listening extremely frustrating and anxiety provoking, and their anxiety further interfered with their ability to understand what their teachers were saying. The teachers were equally frustrated; the interesting and thoughtful listening lessons they thought they had planned were not enjoyable for their students and did not have the desired results. This disconnect does not mean that top-down processing will always be successful, or that bottom-up processing inevitably leads to failure. Rather, the experiences of these students tell us that teachers cannot expect that their students will automatically know what is expected of them in listening activities and that it is important to explain the purpose of listening activities and suggest appropriate strategies.

While older learners may feel it is necessary to understand every word, younger learners may be used to ignoring many listening opportunities because they feel that many conversations do not concern them. When children are living in a new culture, they may find listening opportunities especially overwhelming because of their general lack of cultural knowledge. In fact, as the cognitive learning theories note, background knowledge of any kind is a great aid to listening comprehension. Children can be at a particular disadvantage in listening because they also lack much of the knowledge of the world that older learners possess. For example, an older learner might observe a conversation among adults at a pharmacy and easily infer that the adults are discussing how to administer a prescription medication while a child would likely be puzzled by the interaction.

The Listening Process

In addition to the inherent difficulties of classroom listening, it is essential to recognize that learners do not jump directly from no listening ability in the second language to being able to comprehend spontaneous speech. Taylor (1981) describes the following stages in the development of listening comprehension abilities in language learners. Interestingly, it appears that listening comprehension abilities begin to develop before students ever start to actually understand sentences or even words in the new language.

Recognition of the Target Language.   In the beginning stages of listening, learners come to recognize the overall sound of the target language. This first stage of listening comprehension has been reached when learners can distinguish their target language from other languages. At this point, learners do not actually understand any of the listening material.

Activities associated with this stage include listening to songs and rhymes and extended conversations. Teachers might play popular music, movies, or other audio programs in the background whenever possible. At this stage of listening comprehension, students should be told that they are not expected to understand what they are listening to and to try to get used to the sounds and rhythms of the language. After a time, some teachers ask their students to pretend they are talking in the new language. The resulting gibberish can help students become accustomed to the sound of their new language.

Recognition of Isolated Words.   Until this stage, learners only hear a "blur" when listening to the target language. Now they begin to notice *some* isolated words. These words might be **cognates,** famous and common names, or vocabulary words they have previously encountered in class.

Teachers may help students begin to recognize familiar words by providing short passages containing many easily recognizable words and phrases. Recordings of familiar commercials and nursery rhymes, short narrations about famous people, places, or events, or simple **recombinations** of material practiced in class are all excellent materials for this purpose. Students should be told to listen for familiar words and to try not to translate. Students who can already read in their first language and who are familiar with the target language writing system can benefit from following along with a script of the text they are listening to and signaling when they hear words they know. Repetition and predictability of listening materials can be especially helpful with children. A daily classroom routine using a variety of favorite familiar songs, rhymes, proverbs, stories, and conversational questions is especially appropriate for young learners but can also be used effectively with older learners.

Recognition of Phrase Boundaries.   At this point, language learners *begin* to recognize individual words, phrases, and sentence boundaries. Spoken language begins to sound more distinct to them and less like a blur of sounds. But students *do not yet* understand much of what is being said.

The activities described for "Recognition of Isolated Words," especially the use of recombination materials with written scripts, are also appropriate for this stage of listening comprehension. Students would also benefit from multimedia materials where they can click on phrases in a written text and hear how they are pronounced and/or see translations.

Total Physical Response activities also work well at this stage because they typically require students to physically demonstrate their understanding of brief commands and narrative statements (e.g., Olga goes to the board and writes her name).

Listening for the Gist.   During this stage, language learners begin to have some feel for the global meaning of a listening passage. While they are still unable to understand many details, they *may* be able to identify the topic or understand the main point.

Preparation for listening and the use of **meaning support** are essential at this stage, as is relistening. Meaning support refers to the practice of providing pictures, sound effects, and so forth to make listening (and reading materials) more understandable to students. Because of their familiar content and easily identified pictures, listening to children's books can help learners bridge the gap from "listening for the gist" to "true listening."

True Listening.   Language learners finally begin to follow the meaning of a passage and are better able to process the listening material in **chunks** rather than word by word. Even so, they will continue to encounter many words and phrases they do not understand. Although this is the stage that teachers and students normally associate with "real" listening comprehension, learners will have more difficulty remembering the content of what they listen to than they would when listening in their L1. At this stage of listening development, a momentary lapse of attention can cause a breakdown of the comprehension process. In addition, students' ability to understand will differ based on the topic being discussed and the amount of background knowledge they have about that topic and their familiarity with the specific vocabulary and structures they are encountering. First language learners have already developed a great deal of listening ability before they have to use the language to learn academic content. Giving a context for listening materials, allowing students to listen to them several times, pairing the listening material with reading material, and following up with appropriate questions are very helpful in supporting students' newly developing listening abilities.

Implications of the Process View of Listening

The existence of various steps or stages in the development of listening comprehension abilities has a number of important implications. It is crucial for teachers to provide activities that are consistent with the stages of listening development.

Language teachers often expect beginning students to listen and respond orally, but beginners should be allowed to listen to the language without responding just to get the feel of its sounds, cadences, and **intonation** patterns. This practice is consistent with the Natural Approach and Total Physical Response philosophy of allowing a silent period. Listening to songs, nursery rhymes, commercials, and stories would be very useful at this level of listening comprehension. These kinds of impressionistic listening activities are more commonly used with children, and listening activities for older learners are typically meaning-focused from the outset—leaving students little opportunity to experience and accustom themselves to the overall sound and "music" of the language.

The old ALM textbook series had exercises that asked students to listen to sentences and indicate whether they had heard structures such as a declarative sentence or a question. This type of exercise helps students recognize typical intonation patterns in the target language. As students begin to build up vocabulary and grammar, these identification exercises can be expanded to include grammar consciousness-raising. When students learn how to form negative sentences, for example, they can be asked to listen to sentences and indicate whether they are positive or negative. From a more conversational perspective, students can be asked to identify the emotion of the speaker—whether the speaker is happy or sad, for example. When new verb tenses are introduced, students can be asked to indicate whether an action is taking place now or in the past. It is important to remember, however, that although students can identify questions in a listening exercise, they may not be able to recognize the same types of questions when they hear them in authentic conversations.

Instructors also often tie listening materials to the grammatical structures and vocabulary that students are learning to use in speaking. This practice is called **targeted input** and can be a useful way of getting students to notice particular vocabulary and structures as recommended by the cognitive learning, pushed output, and sociocultural theories. After students learn how to introduce themselves and exchange greetings in the new language, for example, they can be asked to respond to questions after listening to a passage containing simulated meetings between two or more people. Students should be at least at the "listening for the gist" stage to deal successfully with this type of targeted input. (A beginning student would have to skip several stages of listening comprehension to be able to do targeted listening.) It is also likely that students will be able to understand listening materials based on already studied grammar and vocabulary but still feel overwhelmed when faced with less familiar material, not to mention genuine conversations.

As students develop more listening and overall language abilities, they can begin to listen for familiar words and try to distinguish sentence boundaries in longer listening materials. Students will still be unable to follow the words as they do in their first language, however, and will likely have only a general understanding of what a passage is about. Comments like "it was a news story about the earthquake" or "they were talking about school" would indicate that students are dealing appropriately with the listening material for their early level of listening comprehension ability. Of course, students will be better able to follow listening materials when the topics are familiar and interesting.

It is also very important that listening and reading materials be at an appropriate level. According to the input hypothesis, acquisition will not occur if input is not comprehensible. On the other hand, if the input is too simple, acquisition will not occur because the learners are not pushed beyond their current level of competence. As noted in Chapter 2, Stephen Krashen uses the phrase **i + 1** to describe input that is neither too complex nor too simple. If "i" is the learner's current level of listening ability, i + 1 input is language that is just a bit beyond the learner's existing ability.

Krashen has also suggested an approach to teaching listening specifically directed at intermediate and advanced listeners. **Narrow listening** involves listening several times to the same short texts. This approach has the advantages of using natural language with its inherent redundancies and repeated listenings, which makes input more comprehensible. This approach is similar to the experience of children who repeatedly hear the same sentences used by their families and teachers ("OK, it's time to put your things away!") or who demand that the same book be read to them every evening. Similarly, students could listen to a number of texts about the same topic (which would also help develop content knowledge).

The following chart lists some teaching approaches that correspond to each stage of listening comprehension development.

Stages of the Listening Process and Appropriate Teaching Approaches

Stage	Approaches
Recognition of the Target Language	■ Listening to songs, rhymes, commercials, movies, podcasts, or extended conversations to get used to the sounds of the language. ■ Having students pretend they are speaking the language.
Recognition of Isolated Words	■ Listening to short passages that contain familiar phrases. ■ Listening for familiar phrases or words while listening to commercials, familiar nursery rhymes, or descriptions of famous people, places, or events. ■ Listening to recombinations of material presented in class.
Beginning Recognition of Phrase Boundaries	■ Listening to recombination materials with scripts. ■ Using digital materials that allow students to click on objects or phrases and hear pronunciations, transcriptions, and/or translations. ■ Participating in Total Physical Response activities. ■ Utilizing narrow listening.

Listening for the Gist

- Previewing listening materials.
- Establishing realistic listening goals with students.
- Having students select pictures that correspond to oral descriptions.
- Utilizing narrow listening.

True Listening

- Previewing listening materials including important concepts and vocabulary.
- Assisting students in developing personal listening strategies.
- Utilizing narrow listening.
- Having students summarize conversations they have heard.
- Asking students their opinions of what they have heard.
- Having students relate what they have heard to their own lives and experiences.
- Incorporating listening experiences on a variety of academic and nonacademic topics.

Some Guidelines for Developing Listening Activities

Teachers should always strive to make listening activities as comprehensible as possible. The following guidelines highlight important ways you can foster your students' listening abilities by developing realistic expectations, encouraging effective listening strategies, and providing meaning support. Technology, as well as any special talents you might have in drawing, drama, puppetry, and so forth, can help make the development of listening skills meaningful, interesting, and fun.

1. *Have realistic expectations about your students' listening abilities.* As discussed, beginning, intermediate, and even advanced learners will not be able to understand listening materials in their entirety. If they get the general idea of the material they are listening to, they are demonstrating appropriate progress in listening comprehension. Having realistic expectations also involves choosing materials and activities that are appropriate for your students' level(s) of listening comprehension development (for example, allowing a silent period in which students listen but are not required to respond).

2. *Help your students develop realistic expectations.* As is the case with all other aspects of language learning, it is important that students understand what they are supposed to be doing. If they think they are supposed to understand every word, but they are really supposed to be listening for the general

meaning of a passage, they are likely to become very frustrated. Give clear directions about your expectations for listening tasks. Sometimes you may want students to listen for the sound and rhythm of the language, sometimes for individual forms, sometimes for the gist, and when students are advanced enough in their listening abilities, to listen for information.

3. *Be aware of the role of affect in listening comprehension.* When choosing listening materials, keep in mind that students often feel nervous when they have to listen to long passages or particularly rapid speech. They may also feel especially anxious if they are asked to recall insignificant details or listen to material on unfamiliar topics.

4. *Provide a context and meaning support.* Materials based on interesting topics or familiar childhood stories, paired with advance organizers, are particularly effective because students already have background knowledge they can use when listening. Visual support (such as posters, photographs, clippings from newspapers and magazines) also helps provide a context and activate students' background knowledge.

5. *Provide natural listening opportunities as often as possible.* Language teachers today have greater access to authentic materials than in any time in history. Audio and video downloads from websites (search for "language listening activities" and "ESL listening activities"), cable and satellite television, YouTube videos, and DVDs all provide authentic listening experiences for students. Meaning support and clear expectations are particularly important when using authentic materials since they can be intimidating for language learners.

6. *Keep the age, interests, and listening needs of your students in mind.* When choosing listening materials remember that younger learners will have different interests and listening needs, as well as shorter attention spans. It is especially important that learners have practice listening to discussions and other types of conversations that they will likely encounter in their content classes. ESL teachers should also be a resource to help students interpret things they hear in other classes. Foreign language teachers can help students understand material they encounter on the Internet.

7. *Be aware of problematic cultural references.* Even when students know the words and structures in a listening passage, their listening comprehension can be short-circuited by references to people, places, or events they are unfamiliar with.

8. *Use "foreigner talk."* Similar to "motherese" and "fatherese," **foreigner talk** refers to the somewhat slower and simplified speech many people use when they address foreigners. Teacher speech is an ideal source of listening material because teachers can watch their students' facial expressions and modify their speech (repeat, use simpler vocabulary, act out an idea, translate a single unknown word or phrase, etc.) when students do not appear to understand.

9. *Allow for relistening.* Students may feel less anxious if they know they will be able to hear the material several times. You may want to give students a specific goal each time they listen so that they have a reason for listening again (**directed listening**).

10. *Teach listening strategies.* Students should be exposed to various types of listening strategies and encouraged to use them. Listening strategies increase comprehension and bolster students' confidence in their listening skills.

11. *Take advantage of technology to help students develop their listening abilities.* Many of today's technologies are ideal for the development of listening comprehension because they provide meaning in several ways. For example, captioned television often provides the choice of subtitles in the target language or the students' L1. You might want students to first watch a program with native language subtitles, next with target language subtitles, and finally without subtitles. Multimedia programs have similar flexibilities; DVDs often allow a wide choice of languages for the soundtrack.

12. *Give students an opportunity to talk about listening experiences they have had outside of class.* Students can benefit from hearing about challenges their peers have faced and the strategies they used to address those challenges. Students who are anxious about listening comprehension may take comfort from the words of others who have similar concerns.

Activity Ideas

In language teaching there are no "one-size-fits-all" activities. The general activity templates in Chapters 4–8 can be modified to fit the knowledge level, target language, and listening needs and interests of different groups of students. Although the following activities are linked to specific stages of listening comprehension development, they can be reintroduced periodically to provide additional practice and reinforce listening skills.

STAGE 1: RECOGNITION OF THE TARGET LANGUAGE

Activity 1	*"Name That Tune"*
Implementation	Tell your students that every language has its own sounds and intonation patterns. Then tell your students you will play a few seconds of songs in several languages. Ask your students to identify the language based on the way it sounds, and assure them that they are not expected to understand what they hear. Ask them what sounds or rhythms they associate with the language they are learning.
Activity 2	*"Star Search"*
Implementation	Pick a popular song in the second language and play it a few times for the class. (Videos would be particularly vivid.) Then ask the class as a group to pretend they are singing the song in the target language, making up the words as they go along! Assure them that they are not expected to understand

what they are saying or pronounce the words perfectly. You may want to ask for a few volunteers to "perform" for the class, and then ask the class to vote on who would be the best singer or rock star in the target language.

Activity 3	***"What's on Sale?"***
Implementation	Play some commercials for familiar stores or products in class or have students watch them at home. Have students listen for how the store or product was pronounced in the commercial. Ask them to identify whether the store or product was said in their L1 or the L2. Students could also keep a list of the commercials they have heard on their own or report to the class every time they have heard a new one.

STAGE 2: RECOGNITION OF ISOLATED WORDS

Activity 1	***"Is This 'Hello' or Is This 'Goodbye'?"***
Implementation	Read out some basic greetings and farewells and ask your students if you are starting a conversation with them or ending one.

Activity 2	***"Knock Three Times"***
Implementation	During a unit about health, play students a video of a soap commercial. Have students knock three times on their desks every time they hear certain target words they have learned, such as soap, wash, clean, and hands. Remind students that they do not need to understand every word of the commercial in order to do this activity.

Activity 3	***"I Heard That!"***
Implementation	Play students a listening passage containing several words and phrases they know. Have students check off the words or phrases as they hear them. For example, if you are playing a mouthwash commercial, the list might look like this:

_____ mouth   _____ breath
_____ gum disease   _____ mouthwash
_____ fights germs   _____ great taste
_____ fights bad breath   _____ works all day
_____ cavities

STAGE 3: RECOGNITION OF PHRASE BOUNDARIES

Activity 1	**"Mark It Up"**

Implementation   Give students a script of material they are familiar with, and then read it to them with slightly exaggerated pauses between phrases (including pauses at natural points within sentences). Have students mark the pauses on the script.

Activity 2   **"Instant Recall"**

Implementation   Read aloud a familiar story using vocabulary students know. Pause periodically and ask students to say aloud the last sentence or phrase you read.

Activity 3   **"What's Missing?"**

Implementation   Take a script of a story your students are familiar with and white-out a few phrases. Then read the story and have students fill in the blanks with the missing phrases.

Activity 4   **"Total Physical Response"**

Implementation   Give individual students, groups of students, or the whole class brief commands or implied commands contained in brief phrases. For example: "Write your name on the board"; "Now Tammy writes her name on the board." You can gradually increase the complexity of the activity by giving commands that contain multiple phrases: "Tarik picks up his pencil, puts it on Marga's desk, and goes to the window."

Activity 5   **"May I Ask You a Few Questions?"**

Implementation   Take a hand-raising poll on any subject. For example, if the class is studying clothing, ask people to raise their hands if they are wearing a dress, blue pants, etc. Provide targeted listening input by tailoring poll questions to any grammatical topic being studied.

Activity 6   **"Are They Open?"**

Implementation   Identify stores that your students are familiar with that have recorded messages in the target language. Have students call the phone numbers to listen for store hours, locations, etc. Remind students to listen to the messages several times. It would also be a good idea for them to listen to the same message over a period of several days.

STAGE 4: LISTENING FOR THE GIST

Activity 1   **"Who Won?"**

Implementation   In connection with a vocabulary unit about feelings and emotions, tell students they are going to watch a video that shows interviews with the winning and losing players after a tennis match. Remind them that they are not expected to understand every word. Ask students to brainstorm aloud about the kinds of things the two players might say, and then play the video. After playing the video, ask your students a few inference questions, such as "Who won?" "How does the winner feel?" "How does the loser feel?" Discuss the visual and auditory clues that led them to their answers.

Activity 2   **"To Sum It All Up . . ."**

Implementation   Tell students they are going to watch a video of a shopping trip. As an advance organizer, play the video for them once without sound and ask them what they think is happening during the video. Then hand out a sheet with a series of summary statements about the video. After playing the video, have students place a check mark beside the description that best sums up the video.

_____ Kyle went to the mall and bought two new shirts, a red one and a blue one. They were very expensive.

_____ Kyle went to the store and bought two blue shirts. Each shirt cost only $25.00.

_____ Kyle went to the store and bought two new shirts, a red one and a blue one. He didn't pay very much because the shirts were on sale.

Activity 3   **"Who Am I?"**

Implementation   Tell students they are going to hear a description of a famous singer/athlete/politician or possibly even a classmate. Before reading the description, point out the kinds of things they can expect to hear in the description, and then read the description 3 times.

1. The first time, tell students to listen for general meaning, without focusing on particular words.
2. The second time, tell them to listen for words and phrases that describe what the person looks like.
3. The third time, have students listen for words and phrases that indicate where the person is and what he or she does.

Finally, ask students to identify the mystery person, and then discuss with them the descriptive clues they picked up during each stage of the listening process.

Activity 4

Implementation

"How's the Weather?"

Show photographs of and read aloud several brief descriptions of different types of weather. Feel free to include some words students do not know. Tell students to focus on the global meaning of the descriptions rather than on specific words. Students should pick the photograph that corresponds to its description. To provide students an extra challenge, include some descriptions that do not correspond to any of the photos.

Activity 5

Implementation

"May I Ask You a Few Questions?"

This is the same activity as suggested for Stage 3 listening, but the questions can contain more complex sentence structures. Ask students for their opinions about any topic. For example, if the school has an upcoming basketball game, ask how many people think the home team is going to win, how many think the visitors are going to win, how many are not sure, and how many do not care. Students indicate their response by raising their hands. Expand this listening activity into a speaking activity by asking follow-up questions to the poll.

Activity 6

Implementation

"Surf the Web"

Identify a list of websites with good listening possibilities for students. Have students pick websites that are interesting to them, and then have them report to the class about the website they listened to.

Activity 7

Implementation

"Guess Who I Ran Into?!"

Help students identify a speaker of their target language to interview. Have them prepare a few brief interview questions and audio- or videotape their person's responses. Play the tapes for the class. (NOTE: By helping students meet target language speakers, this activity can also help lessen social distance.)

STAGE 5: TRUE LISTENING

Activity 1

Implementation

"Rumor Mill"

Start a rumor by whispering in the ear of a student a bit of gossip about a famous actor or sports figure. The student must immediately pass the rumor on to the person sitting next to him or her, without stopping to think of the individual words he or she heard. After the rumor has been passed along by several people, ask the last person who heard the rumor to tell you what the piece of gossip is. Have the class discuss the differences between the original rumor and the rumor in its final form.

Activity 2

Implementation

"Advice Show"

Have students take turns pretending to be a talk show host and the people who call the show asking for advice. The talk show host should listen to the caller's problems and offer appropriate advice.

Activity 3

Implementation

"Mystery School"

Give Student #1 a picture of the outside of a school, or of the floor plan of a school. Student #1 sits back-to-back with Student #2, who draws the school or the floor plan based on the oral description given by the first student. Have the two students compare pictures after the drawing is done and talk about the similarities and differences between the original picture and the drawing. (NOTE: This activity can help students become familiar with school facilities and services.)

Activity 4

Implementation

"Breakout"

Give Student #1 a copy of a fairly simple maze. Give Student #2 a copy of the same maze. With the two students sitting back-to-back, Student #1 will give directions for getting out of the middle of the maze, and the second student has to draw his or her escape path on the maze as the directions are given. The second student can also ask for Student #1 to repeat or clarify the instructions. This game may also be played between teams; the first team to break out successfully wins!.

Activity 5

Implementation

"Soap Opera"

Tell students they are going to view a soap opera–like video episode. Ask them what kinds of things they would expect to hear in a soap opera. Play the episode without sound and ask them what they think is happening during the episode. Write their thoughts on the board. Then play the episode again with sound. To follow up, ask students to sum up the plot in their own words. Discuss with them how their initial predictions differed from the summaries they gave after watching the episode. Playing the episode a third time would give students another chance to revise and discuss their summaries. Students could also provide their opinions about the episode and give any advice they might have for the characters.

Activity 6

Implementation

"Stop—Think"

Tell students they are going to view a dramatic video or listen to an audio dialogue. Preview the subject matter, and then play the dialogue, having students focus on listening for the gist. Periodically pause the episode and ask for a volunteer to sum up in his or her own words the last few things he or she heard. The rest of the class may collaborate in summarizing what they have heard.

Activity 7

Implementation

"You're the Director"

Play a dramatic video or audio episode, but pause before reaching the end. Ask the class as a whole to summarize what they have heard so far. Write their summaries on the board. Then ask the class how the episode should end. Write their opinions on the board before playing the rest of the episode. To follow up, ask students to compare their preferred endings with the actual one. Which do they like better, and why?

Assessing Listening Comprehension

Testing listening comprehension can be difficult because listening is a **receptive** process. There is simply no direct way to see what a student has understood. Listening input is also transitory; unlike reading, the learner cannot go back and reread the material. Misunderstandings or simple attention lapses early in a text can lead to new misunderstandings later on. Thus, when testing listening comprehension, it is especially important to provide a context and opportunities for relistening. The choice of listening items or material is also essential. Be sure that the text has enough redundancy that students have a chance to catch up if they miss part of what was said. You can avoid the necessity of students having to catch every word—which, in turn, encourages students to translate—by using **inference questions** rather than **recall** questions.

It is also difficult to test listening comprehension independently of other language skills. If you have students retell a story they have listened to either orally or in writing, it is difficult to know if any errors in recall are due to faulty comprehension or difficulties expressing the ideas. Similarly, if you use a multiple choice format with target language alternatives, it is hard to know if errors come from listening or reading. Some language educators advocate the use of multiple choice alternatives or recall of ideas in the student's native language, but this approach is impractical in mixed ESL classes where the teacher is not likely to be able to read all the L1s; it probably also encourages translation. Some listening tests rely on pictures in a multiple choice format, but pictures can be unclear or ambiguous, especially when photocopied or projected. Even when the visual quality is excellent, cultural misunderstandings are still possible. Language tests are usually developed by members of the target language group, and images that seem emblematic to members of one group might be confusing to another group. For example, a picture of an American middle-class house might be interpreted as some type of large building by a child who has spent most of his life in a small village. (You should also remember that listening comprehension is highly related to content knowledge and that difficulties often result from unfamiliarity with the specific topic.) Some teachers have students, especially younger learners, draw pictures to demonstrate their understanding of listening materials as an alternative to printed pictures.

Observation is probably the purest way to assess learners' listening abilities. Be alert for signs that students have or have not understood language that is addressed to them. Do they follow directions easily or do they look around to see what other students are doing? Do they answer the question you asked or offer some related but different piece of information? Do they smile and act shy when you or the other students say something to them in the target language? Do they have a buddy from their L1 group whom they often consult before responding? Do they seem to avoid situations where they would have to listen? You can follow up your observations with targeted questions or comments with individual students to check on the accuracy of your observations. Try to have as many private, "casual," target language conversations with your students as possible.

One simple technique to monitor comprehension in a large class is to have students use signs to indicate whether they understood what was said. One of my student teachers had her students fold a piece of notebook paper in half and paste a popsicle stick in the middle. The students then drew a smiley face ☺ on one side and a sad face ☹ on the other. Students were supposed to show the smiley face whenever they understood what was being said in the target language and the "frowny" face whenever they did not understand. Besides giving students a productive way to indicate their confusion, this technique had the advantage of giving my student teacher immediate feedback on student comprehension so that she had the opportunity to rephrase and repeat what she had said and offer more meaning support if needed. She soon knew which students usually understood quickly and which students generally had difficulty.

The "May I Ask You a Few Questions?" activity previously described offers a similar approach to the smiley-face signs. When you poll students about their opinions and experiences you get a quick response about whether they have understood. If you ask students to raise their hands if they are wearing a particular item of clothing, for example, you can quickly scan the class to make sure that the right people are raising their hands.

Dictation can also be a useful method of testing listening comprehension. Dictation tends to have a bad reputation among language learners and teachers because it has been used more as a spelling test than a test of listening comprehension. But Sandra Savignon has suggested that dictation can be graded based on the student's comprehension of specific ideas. For example, a student might write "Children laugh at song" when the sentence "The children were laughing at the funny song" was dictated. According to Savignon's system, this response would be correct *on the basis of listening comprehension* because "Children laugh at song" captures the general meaning of the sentence. Of course, this response also demonstrates that the student missed several details and has not mastered the grammatical structures in the sentence.

FINDING YOUR WAY

REFLECTIONS

How do the types of language that students are exposed to affect their listening development?

_____

_____

_____

_____

_____

PLANNING FOR YOUR CLASSES

What special talents do you have that you could use to make listening experiences more comprehensible and enjoyable for your students? Pantomime, puppetry, computer animations, sound effects, and drawings are all wonderful sources of meaning support and may also reduce students' listening anxiety.

_____

_____

_____

_____

_____

What authentic listening sources, such as L2 speakers, podcasts, cable TV, or children's programs, are available in your community? How could you take advantage of them in your teaching?

_____

_____

_____

_____

_____

PROJECTS

- Work with a partner and try to communicate an idea or anecdote using only the target language, supplemented with charades and impromptu props and drawings.
- Listen to audiorecorded examples of natural speech and prepared target language materials. Listen for differences in the amount of context, redundancies, interruptions, stopping and starting, extralinguistic clues (sound effects, voice expression, etc.). Compare the degree of comprehensibility of the prepared audio files with the recordings of natural speech.
- Create a context for a listening passage from a publisher-prepared audio file.
- Write advance organizers for common fairy tales such as _Cinderella, Little Red Riding Hood,_ and _The Three Bears._
- Write a set of preview questions and inference questions for the same stories.
- Prepare a short audio or video file (1 to 3 minutes) in your target language. You may record a newscast, someone giving a brief lecture, yourself reading a picture book or poem, people acting out a story, or any type material you think your students would enjoy. Use meaning support to make your passage comprehensible to _beginning_ students. Meaning support can be separate from the file, such as a list of vocabulary words or a photograph, or it can be incorporated into the file in the form of advance organizers, sound effects, and so on. Share your audio or video file with the rest of your class and keep a record of the different methods of meaning support that your classmates used.

IN YOUR JOURNAL

- Is listening a source of anxiety for you either in your L1 or in a second language?
- How was listening taught when you studied a second language?
- What do you want to remember about your own experiences in learning to listen in your second language?

TEACHING CHECKLIST

This checklist will help you quickly evaluate the way you teach listening.

Yes   *No*

☐   ☐   I devote an adequate amount of class time to listening.

☐   ☐   I use listening activities that are consistent with my students' stages of listening comprehension development.

☐   ☐   I assess my students' background knowledge and listening needs to be sure that my listening comprehension activities are appropriate.

☐   ☐   I provide meaning support for listening comprehension materials. I always let students know the context of what they are listening to, and the materials themselves include textual redundancies.

☐   ☐   I expect students to focus on understanding the broad meaning of listening materials rather than on isolated details and grammatical forms.

☐   ☐   I use consciousness-raising in listening activities to support students' developing grammatical awareness.

☐   ☐   I provide opportunities for relistening.

☐   ☐   I help my students develop reasonable expectations for listening.

☐   ☐   I encourage my students to use listening strategies.

☐   ☐   I include listening experiences in a variety of academic and everyday topics.

☐   ☐   I include listening comprehension in my assessment and testing procedures.

REFERENCES AND SUGGESTIONS FOR FURTHER READING

Anderson-Mejias, P. L. (1986). English for academic listening: Teaching the skills associated with listening to extended discourse. *Foreign Language Annals, 19,* 391–398.

Bacon, S. (1989). Listening for real in the foreign language classroom. *Foreign Language Annals, 22,* 543–551.

Berne, J. (2004). Listening comprehension strategies: A review of the literature. *Foreign Language Annals, 37,* 521–531.

Brindley, G. (1998). Assessing listening abilities. *Annual Review of Applied Linguistics, 18,* 171–191.

Buck, G. (2001). *Assessing listening.* Cambridge, UK: Cambridge University Press.

Elkhafaifi, H. (2005). Listening comprehension and anxiety in the Arabic language classroom. *Modern Language Journal, 89,* 206–220.

Ferris, D., & Tagg, T. (1996). Academic listening/speaking tasks for ESL students: Problems, suggestions, and implications. *TESOL Quarterly, 30,* 297–320.

Field, J. (2008). Bricks or mortar: Which parts of the input does a second language learner rely on? *TESOL Quarterly, 42,* 411–432.

Flowerdew, J., & Miller, L. (2005). *Second language listening: Theory and practice.* New York, NY: Cambridge University Press.

García, P. A. (1981). Comprehension training in a high school setting. In H. Winitz (Ed.), *The comprehension approach to foreign language instruction* (pp. 277–300). Rowley, MA: Newbury House.

Glisan, E. (1988). A plan for teaching listening comprehension: Adaptation of an instructional reading model. *Foreign Language Annals, 21*, 9–19.

Goh, C., & Taib, Y. (2006). Metacognitive instruction in listening for young learners. *ELT Journal, 60*, 222–232.

Graham, S. (2006). Listening comprehension: The learner's perspective. *System, 34*, 165–182.

Harley, B. (2000). Listening strategies in ESL: Do age and L1 make a difference? *TESOL Quarterly, 34*, 769–777.

Hoven, D. (1999). A model for listening and viewing comprehension in multimedia environments. *Language Learning and Technology, 3*, 88–103.

Joiner, E. (1991). Teaching listening: Ends and means. In J. Alatis (Ed.), *Linguistics and language pedagogy: The state of the art* (pp. 179–193). Washington, DC: Georgetown University Press.

Krashen, S. D. (1996). The case for narrow listening. *System, 24*, 97–100.

Long, D. (1989). Second language listening comprehension: A schema-theoretic perspective. *Modern Language Journal, 73*, 32–40.

Lund, R. J. (1990). A taxonomy for teaching second language listening. *Foreign Language Annals, 23*, 105–115.

Morley, J. (1991). Trends and developments in listening comprehension: Theory and practice. In J. Alatis (Ed.), *Georgetown University Round Table on Languages and Linguistics: Linguistics, language teaching, and language acquisition: The interdependence of theory, practice, and research* (pp. 317–337). Washington, DC: Georgetown University Press.

O'Malley, J. M., Chamot, A., & Küpper, L. (1995). Listening comprehension strategies in second language acquisition. In H. D. Brown & S. Gonzo (Eds.), *Readings on second language acquisition* (pp. 138–160). Upper Saddle River, NJ: Prentice Hall Regents.

Oxford, R. (1993). Research update on teaching L2 listening. *System, 21*, 205–211.

Savignon, S. (1983). Dictation as a measure of communicative competence in French as a second language. *Language Learning, 32*, 33–51.

Taylor, H. M. (1981). Learning to listen in English. *TESOL Quarterly, 15*, 41–50.

Vandergrift, L. (2003). Orchestrating strategy use: Toward a model of the skilled second language listener. *Language Learning, 53*, 463–496.

Vandergrift, L. (2006). Second language listening: Listening ability or language proficiency. *Modern Language Journal, 90*, 6–18.

Vandergrift, L. (2011). Second language listening: Presage, product, process, and pedagogy. In E. Hinkel (Ed.), *Handbook of research in second language teaching and learning acquisition* (Vol. 2, pp. 455–471). New York, NY: Taylor & Francis.

Vidal, K. (2003). Academic listening: A source of vocabulary acquisition? *Applied Linguistics, 24*, 56–89.

Vogely, A. (1998). Listening comprehension anxiety: Students' reported sources and solutions. *Foreign Language Annals, 31*, 67–80.

Wong-Fillmore, L. (1985) When does teacher talk work as input? In S. Gass & C. Madden (Eds.), *Input in second language acquisition* (pp. 17–50). Rowley, MA: Newbury House.

5 What Should I Know About Teaching Speaking?

- How much does grammatical practice contribute to the ability to speak spontaneously in a second language?
- What are some of the differences between speaking in a language class and speaking outside of class?
- How does second language competence become internalized?
- How is cultural competence related to speaking ability?

SPEAKING AND SECOND LANGUAGE ACQUISITION

Speaking is the hallmark of second language learning. Although some learners may have personal goals for language learning that do not include speaking, most language educators accept speaking as an essential goal of language learning and teaching. All of the second language acquisition theories discussed in Chapter 2 attempt to explain how learners come to understand and speak their target language but offer very different explanations for this process. The Input Hypothesis states that speaking ability is the result of listening and reading. The conversation theories hold a complementary view; they maintain that learners develop their oral ability by participating in scaffolded conversations. The cognitive learning theories, in contrast, hold that speaking comes from meaningful practice so that new explicit linguistic knowledge becomes automatic. The Output Hypothesis and sociocultural theories emphasize the need to produce and reflect on well-formed language.

Although speaking is the professed goal of most second language instruction, it is sometimes neglected in language classrooms. Teachers often find it easier to present language drills and grammatical presentations than to ask students to participate in lifelike conversations. Consequently, language classes are often filled with oral activities such as dialogue practice, grammar presentations, and vocabulary lessons. Some teachers feel that activities like oral drills and dialogue practice are precommunicative activities necessary to prepare students for true communication, while other teachers, unfortunately, mistake these activities for true communication. Even when teachers are careful to ensure that **structured communication activities** have a communicative **context,** these kinds of activities do not constitute "real communication." **Authentic communication** requires students to *spontaneously* produce and understand culturally appropriate language. Sandra Savignon contends that communicative competence—or the ability to participate in a *spontaneous* interchange with a native speaker—should be the goal of second language learning. Scholars like Carl Blyth would modify Savignon's definition to include spontaneous speech with a variety of target language speaking partners—not just native speakers.

Speaking: Some Important Concepts

Communicative Competence	■ Refers to a language learner's ability to communicate in the target language. Learners are considered communicatively competent if they can participate in a spontaneous interchange with a target language speaker.
Zone of Proximal Development	■ Refers to the distance between the speech language learners can accomplish on their own and what they can achieve with the assistance of others. It implies that as the learner's interlanguage develops, it will be ready to integrate the next appropriate language structure(s).
Errors	■ Consistent incorrect forms produced in speaking or writing. Errors are contrasted with mistakes which are simple slips of the tongue. Errors are consistent inaccuracies and represent gaps in the learner's interlanguage.
Interlanguage	■ The way that learners produce the target language. Learners' interlanguages are systematic and reflect their **implicit linguistic knowledge**.

The Importance of True Communication in the Language Classroom

During the heyday of the Audiolingual Method, variations of the following joke circulated among language teachers:

> FRIEND: Well, how did your trip to Germany go? You're such a good German student, you must have had a great time talking to Germans!
>
> GERMAN STUDENT: Well, actually it was kind of tough. [*Pause.*] I knew my lines, but the Germans didn't know theirs!

The German student in this joke is commenting on the dialogues that students learned in ALM classes which gave the false impression that target language questions had specific answers and that native speakers were standing around ready to offer those answers. If a question asked where the library was, the response was always the same, straight ahead, or on the left, or whatever. In the real world, of course, the library could be anywhere, and the person being asked about the library might not know where it is or might not want to be bothered to give directions. Consider these two conversations, the first representing a typical textbook dialogue and the second more similar to a natural or real-life encounter.

VOICES FROM THE CLASSROOM

Conversation 1:

> ***Visitor:*** Excuse me. Can you tell me where the mall is?
>
> ***Person in the Street:*** Certainly. It's on the corner of Chestnut and Vine. Just go three blocks and turn left. It's right next to the big church. You can't miss it!
>
> ***Visitor:*** Thank you!
>
> ***Person in the Street:*** You're welcome!

Conversation 2:

> ***Visitor:*** Excuse me. Can you tell me where the mall is?
>
> ***Person in the Street:*** I don't know. Which mall? Why don't you ask them?
>
> ***Visitor to Group of People:*** Excuse me. Can you tell me where the mall is?
>
> ***Group Person #1:*** Do you mean Lakeline Mall? I think it's north on Mopac.
>
> ***Visitor:*** I think Lakeline Mall. The one with Home Depot. What is Mopac?
>
> ***Group Person #2:*** Mopac is Loop 1, but Home Depot is in Gateway on 360.
>
> ***Visitor:*** How you get there?
>
> ***Group Person #1:*** You turn left at the next light and go about five, maybe ten miles, I'm really not sure, until you get to 183. Just cross 183, and I think it's on your right.
>
> ***Visitor:*** Thank you.
>
> ***Group Person #1:*** No problem.

In the first conversation, the visitor's question elicited the exact response the visitor was seeking in a comprehensible form. All the visitor had to do was thank the helpful person in the street, follow the clear directions, and arrive happily at the mall. Unfortunately, real-life conversations are seldom so easy. In Conversation 2, the visitor asked the same well-formed question, but the person in the street needed clarification, "Which mall?" Ultimately, the person in the street could not supply the requested directions and directed the visitor to a group of people. The group of people was more helpful, but even so, several exchanges were necessary before the visitor received the needed information. The second interaction shows how negotiation is necessary to a successful conversational outcome. The visitor did not originally know the name of the mall, and therefore the first set of directions was incorrect. In addition, the directions used a reference, "Mopac," that the visitor was not familiar with. Again, clarification was necessary. In this more normal conversation, the visitor needed to formulate several questions and to offer information that was not anticipated in advance. The visitor probably also needed to use extralinguistic information like gestures and facial expressions to facilitate communication. Savignon argues that communicative competence asks learners to use any means of communication possible, not just target language words. Speakers are much more likely to achieve their communicative goals if they supplement their words with appropriate gestures, facial expressions, tone of voice, and so on. These actions are examples of communication strategies (discussed in Chapter 1).

These two conversations illustrate the difference between structured communication activities and authentic communication. Since no one can predict the direction a conversation might take, or the exact structures and vocabulary students will need, true communication is unpredictable. Classroom activities such as role-play activities, problem-solving tasks, and interviews can be used to simulate the natural interactions that students might anticipate in the target language environment. The term **structured communication** refers to a less authentic form of communication where either the grammatical structure or the content of the response, or both, is dictated in advance by the teacher or the textbook.

Whenever language teachers discuss real communication activities, the question of errors usually arises. Many language teachers fear that asking students to speak spontaneously will cause them to make errors that will be difficult to correct later on; they fear that the errors will become **fossilized**. Some teachers, especially those who prefer the Audiolingual Method or believe in the Contrastive Analysis Hypothesis, feel that it is necessary for students to master the target language grammar before they are allowed to participate in real communication activities. Importantly, this view has not been supported by research. A number of studies have found that students can develop structured and spontaneous language simultaneously. These studies are consistent with the conversation theories that maintain that spontaneous conversations can actually help students master structured language. The Output Hypothesis and sociocultural theory see errors as a way for learners to test their developing knowledge of the second language.

Obstacles to Teaching Speaking

Since language teachers and learners usually agree that speaking is one of the most important goals of language learning, it is puzzling that language classes are not more communicative. As is the case with classroom listening, there are a number of obstacles to making the classroom an environment for natural speech.

Authentic Speaking and "Display" Speaking

It is difficult to simulate authentic conversations in the classroom. Real conversations are voluntary, and conversational participants have real goals for their interactions. Participants choose the people they want to talk to and the topics they want to talk about or the information they seek. Most classroom conversations are not voluntary, since the teacher usually selects the conversation participants and the topic. Many scholars have noted the artificiality of classroom conversations in general, not just those in language classrooms. Teachers usually initiate classroom conversations by asking a question related to the day's course topic. Students are supposed to answer the question by relating some piece of information that was contained in the day's reading assignment. This sequence of teacher question and student response is artificial because the teacher's question is not genuine. The teacher already knows the answer to the question and is only asking it to find out if the students know the answer or, even more artificially, to find out if the students did the assigned reading. Artificial questions of this kind are called **display questions** because they require students to display their knowledge of a piece of information that the teacher already knows. Consider these two interactions.

VOICES FROM THE CLASSROOM

Interaction 1:

Teacher: When did Columbus discover America?
Student: 1492.
Teacher: Good.

Interaction 2:

Mrs. Garza: What do people usually eat for breakfast in your country?

Ahmed: We eat hummus and falafel.

Mrs. Garza: Really? I always thought hummus and falafel were lunch or dinner foods. That's when we eat them here. I'm going to tell my husband. He loves to have hummus for lunch. He'll be surprised to find out that people really eat it for breakfast. What kinds of things do you have for lunch and dinner?

In the first interaction, the teacher is asking a question to which she clearly already knows the answer. When she responds with "good," she is indicating that the student offered the correct piece of information and that the conversation is over. She does not even follow up the student's response with a question that could lead to more discussion. She could have asked the student, for example, what he thought conditions were like on Columbus's boats in 1492. In contrast, the second conversation includes a true exchange of information. Mrs. Garza is curious about what is eaten for breakfast in the student's country and is clearly surprised at Ahmed's answer. The teacher's response that she is going to tell her husband shows that she values the information, and her question about lunch and dinner foods encourages the conversation to continue.

Although the hummus example above does not involve a display question, it still includes an important difference with real conversations. Authentic conversations are voluntary; the participants choose to talk to each other and choose what they want to talk about. For Interaction 2 to qualify as an authentic conversation, Ahmed must choose to communicate with Mrs. Garza about breakfast foods in his country and must care if she understands what he says. Ahmed, like most students, is more likely to want to communicate with Mrs. Garza if he believes that she is actually interested in what he is saying. It is, therefore, essential that language teachers show their students that they care about what they say. Too often, language teachers use questions to elicit particular grammatical forms rather than to establish a conversation. Consider the exchange between Señorita Wilson and Amber.

VOICES FROM THE CLASSROOM

Señorita Wilson: *Amber, ¿qué vas a hacer este fin de semana?* (What are you going to do this weekend?)

Amber: *Voy a la luna con mi hermana.* (I'm going to the moon with my sister.)

Señorita Wilson: *Bueno.* (Good.)

Amber appears to have figured out that Señorita Wilson does not really care about the content of her responses but only listens for a correct verb form. These types of questions are similar to display questions in that the student is really being asked to display grammatical knowledge rather than to communicate personal information. If Señorita Wilson had been paying attention, she could have taken advantage of a wonderful conversational opportunity to discuss how Amber planned to get to the moon, why she chose the moon, why she was going with her sister and not someone else, if other people in the class had ever thought about going to the moon, or why Amber found the question boring and chose to offer a silly answer. At the very least, Amber would have expected that Señorita Wilson would have noticed the content of her response and acknowledged it by laughing or rolling her eyes. By paying attention to and accepting the student's response, it is not difficult to turn a rote-like interaction into a more communicative one. Consider the following conversation.

VOICES FROM THE CLASSROOM

Señorita Wilson: *¿Qué vas a hacer este fin de semana?* (What are you going to do this weekend?)

Amber: *Voy a la luna con mi hermana.* (I'm going to the moon with my sister.)

Señorita Wilson: *¡Ay! ¿Vas a la luna? ¿No tienes tarea?* (Wow, you're going to the moon? Don't you have homework?)

Amber: *Pues sí, pero la luna es más importante.* (Well yes, but the moon is more important.)

Classroom conversation often uses an artificial variety of the target language that is rarely used by native speakers of that language. Languages have a variety of **registers** or levels of formality. We speak more casually to our friends than we do to our bosses or teachers. As noted in Chapter 4, second language materials often use a careful and formal variety of speech which does not correspond to the type of speech used by speakers in their daily lives. Sometimes language textbooks even insist on distinctions that have disappeared from normal conversational usage: the use of whom, for example. Even when second language materials are careful to use an appropriate register, they are likely to include vocabulary and expressions more suited to adults than children. Children need to know how to say "Yuck" and all its synonyms to talk with other children. If learners practice an inappropriate register, they can sound strange when they try to have conversations with peers and have more difficulty making friends.

Beliefs About Second Language Speaking

Teachers and students tend to have particularly strong beliefs about speaking in a second language. Many language learners and teachers believe that it is essential for students to practice only perfect, error-free sentences to be able to end up speaking the language well. They also believe that if errors are tolerated in learning, they will become very difficult to overcome later. Regardless of the actual truth of these beliefs, they are likely to influence teachers' selection of oral activities and learners' approaches to these activities. In fact, with the exception of the original versions of the Contrastive Analysis Hypothesis, most second language acquisition theories view errors positively. The conversation theories actually "require" errors so that learners can elicit the fine-tuned feedback that conversations provide. In the conversation between Takahiro and the adult (Chapter 2), the adult's offer of the phrase "upside down" came in response to Takahiro's incorrect use of "broken." It is also possible that Takahiro was using his "error" strategically to elicit the word he was looking for.

Teacher Anxiety

As discussed in Chapter 1, speaking is the aspect of second language learning most often associated with anxiety, and many language learners experience anxiety when they think about speaking the new language. Interestingly, however, language anxiety is not limited to students. Nonnative teachers may also be anxious about speaking and avoid conversational activities. In several studies, I have found that anxious preservice language teachers did not expect to use communicative teaching methods even though they believed that those were the best language teaching methods available.

Even native teachers may become anxious when no one volunteers to participate in a speaking activity. A large number of studies have found that teachers of all subjects have difficulty tolerating classroom silences. Teachers often answer their own questions after less than two seconds rather than waiting in silence for a student to volunteer. As students need extra time to understand a question and formulate a response in a second language, language teachers need to allow adequate time before moving on. (The SIOP Model, in particular, requires that students be given sufficient **wait-time.**) Judith Shrum suggests that if language teachers allowed more time between their original questions and talking again, language classrooms would become substantially more communicative. She found that classes where the teacher waited longer contained higher percentages of target language talk and lower percentages of native language talk. Ironically, Shrum found that language teachers gave students more time to answer questions in their L1 than in the second language. It seems reasonable to allow students to think for at least four or five seconds before stepping in and offering a response or posing a new question. (If the response requires the application of academic content, considerably more wait-time may be necessary.) Although five seconds may not sound like a long time, it can be an eternity to a teacher especially to a new teacher standing in front of a silent class, and it would probably be a good idea to start practicing waiting five seconds to prepare yourself to give your students adequate thought time.

Difficulties in Grading

Speaking is also sometimes neglected in the language classroom because it is difficult and time-consuming to grade. Many teachers do not know how to grade speaking, and even if they want to, it is difficult for teachers to organize a class so that each student can be graded individually. For that reason, written tests are often used as a substitute for oral tests because they can be administered and graded so much more conveniently. Unfortunately, students quickly learn that to do well they need to pass the written tests rather than to learn to speak spontaneously. In testing, this phenomenon is called a **washback effect.** Teachers usually state that the goal of the class is to learn how to speak the language, but grading is often based on an entirely different set of criteria: written tests. Students understandably decide to spend their time and effort on the activities that translate into good grades.

The Development of Speaking Ability

Simplification and Reduced Redundancy

Beginning second language learners—especially those in natural rather than class-room environments—tend to simplify the target language when they speak. Beginning English learners, for example, tend to use the word "no" to form negations. So sentences like "I no go" are common at this stage of learning. Some time later, the "no" is likely to be replaced with "not," and still later, the use of "don't" appears. Similar forms have been identified in learners' formations of English questions. The existence of simplified stages in learners' **interlanguage** implies that second language acquisition is developmental. That is, second language learners, like child L1 learners, go through a series of stages from simple to more complex and native-like in their language productions. The existence of developmental stages implies, in turn, that errors are not permanent and that the learner's interlanguage will become more native-like as acquisition progresses.

One particular type of simplification observed in language learner speech is called **reduced redundancy.** Redundancy refers to the amount of repeated information contained in an utterance. In the sentence "Yesterday, I went to the store," the fact that the action took place in the past is indicated by both the adverb "yesterday" and the use of a past tense verb. English speakers would have little difficulty understanding a sentence with reduced redundancy such as "Yesterday, I go to the store," but they would also perceive it to be nonnative-like. Language learners also tend to simplify their speech by reducing morphological complexity. Thus, sentences like "He go visit family" and "They have many friend" are typical examples of interlanguage in English. In the first sentence, the language learner did not put the third-person *s* on the verb "go." In the second case, the learner failed to pluralize "friend" because the adjective "many" implies more than one. Second language learners also commonly regularize verb forms as in the case of using "goed" instead of "went."

It is important to remember that simplification and reduced redundancy are not conscious choices on the part of the learner. Learners do not say to themselves, "Gee, if you use a time adverb like yesterday, you don't need to bother with past tense formation." Rather, there is a natural tendency to simplify as the human brain integrates the new language.

The Use of Formulaic Language

Both L1 and L2 learners tend to make great use of **formulaic expressions** in conversations. Formulaic expressions are set phrases that learners use strategically in conversation. Many learners learn phrases that they encounter in the L2 environment and begin to use those phrases before they understand exactly what they mean or how they are constructed. (Sociocultural theories call this practice imitation.) This phenomenon may be similar to American children not understanding the words to the Pledge of Allegiance when they are young (. . . and to the Republic for *witches stand . . .*). Formulaic and simplified expressions as well as nonverbal gestures make it possible for learners to participate in conversations and receive personalized feedback before they have developed a large amount of second language ability. While English learners may come into contact with many useful conversational phrases through the course of daily life, teachers may need to point out specific expressions that are appropriate for discussing particular academic topics.

Acquisition Sequence

Many researchers have been interested in determining whether learners learn the features of a particular second language in a specific order. If such a sequence exists, it would give teachers valuable guidance for syllabi and textbooks. It would also help teachers know how far along learners are in their language development. Although children learn the same first language in a similar order, there seems to be more variation in the sequence of second language learning.

In reviewing the studies of English learners of various first language backgrounds, Krashen concluded that learners tend to acquire English **morphemes** in the following sequence. Similar sequences have been found in the acquisition of other languages. (A morpheme is the smallest unit of language that indicates a difference in meaning. For example, *cats* is made up of two morphemes *cat* and *s*, since cat and cats convey different meanings.)

Krashen's Morpheme Acquisition Sequence

Group	Morphemes Included	Example
Group A	Ing	He sleeping.
	Plural	Boys, over there.
	Is, Are	Maria is happy.
Group B	Auxiliary	I am leaving.
	Article	The dog.
Group C	Irregular Past	Chu went home.
Group D	Regular Past	The dogs played.
	Third-Person Singular	Marcella runs.
	Possessive	Robert's ball.

Krashen's sequence is organized into groups of early-(Group A), mid-(Groups B and C), and late-acquired (Group D) morphemes rather than a sequence of individual morphemes. This grouping suggests that learners will acquire all the morphemes in an earlier group before they go on to acquire morphemes in the next group. In addition, learners may acquire the morphemes either one by one or a few at a time.

The existence of an L2 sequence implies that students may be more ready to learn some grammatical forms than others. From a sociocultural perspective, Lantolf speaks of a **zone of proximal development** with respect to language learning.

As the learner's interlanguage develops, her or his zone of proximal development becomes ready to integrate the next appropriate language structure(s). Thus, as learners acquire the morphemes in Group A they would become ready for Group B. Lantolf suggests that learners especially benefit from scaffolding and targeted input that correspond to their zone of proximal development. If an English learner is showing reasonable control of *ing,* plural, and *is* and *are* (Group A), for example, you might look for opportunities to scaffold the learner's utterances containing articles and auxiliaries (Group B). It would also be a good idea to use targeted input to raise the learner's awareness of these structures.

Implications of the Process View of Speaking

Although it is tempting to think that when you have "taught" a particular grammatical structure that students will "know" it, it is important to recognize that the grammatical accuracy of student speech is not static. Just because students have practiced particular grammatical structures and used them correctly in the past does not mean that they will always use those structures accurately. Students are more likely to produce accurate responses in structured communication activities than in spontaneous conversations. Spontaneous conversations make many cognitive demands on the speaker, and students will often make mistakes on "things they already know." In addition, when students learn a new grammatical feature, there is often a readjustment of their interlanguage that can result in new errors. For example, English learners, who consistently use an irregular verb such as "saw" correctly, might start to produce "seed" after they begin to use the regular (*ed*) past tense formation (**overgeneralization**).

In considering the accuracy of student speech, it is necessary to distinguish a true **error** from a simple slip of the tongue or **mistake.** Errors are *consistent* inaccuracies and represent gaps in the learner's interlanguage. Consistently leaving out definite articles is an example of an error. Mistakes are similar to the slips of the tongue that people make when speaking their L1. To distinguish true errors from simple mistakes, you should ask yourself, "Has that student made that same error before? Does she usually use that construction accurately?"

This chart suggests teaching approaches consistent with learners' developing oral ability. But the types of oral language listed in this chart do not correspond to a learning sequence similar to the one listed in Chapter 4 for listening comprehension. Language learners use simplified language, formulaic expressions, and reduced redundancy throughout their language learning.

Kinds of Oral Language and Suggested Teaching Approaches

Kind of Oral Language	Teaching Approaches
Simplified Language	▪ Allow students to answer questions and participate in conversations by whatever means possible. Do not require full sentence responses.

- Expand students' responses into more acceptable utterances. For example, if a student says, "I no go," the teacher should respond, "You're not going? Why not?" or "I'm not going either because I'm too tired."

Use of Formulaic Language

- Have students retell stories or dialogues from the perspectives of various characters and/or school personnel or celebrities.
- Use TPR Storytelling.
- Give students lists of common phrases and have them make the phrases into a dialogue.

Morpheme Acquisition Sequence

- Offer targeted input through listening or reading using morphemes corresponding to Krashen's English acquisition order.
- Be on the lookout for opportunities to scaffold and expand utterances including morphemes corresponding to Krashen's acquisition sequence.
- Encourage students to reflect on differences between how they speak and how more proficient speakers say the same thing.

Some Guidelines for Developing Speaking Activities

Teachers should try to make speaking activities as unthreatening and natural as possible. Although structured activities can be useful, do not confuse them with true, spontaneous conversation. Several strategies can encourage students to want to speak spontaneously in the language classroom.

1. *Encourage students to talk about themselves and to communicate their own ideas from the beginning.* If students get used to talking, spontaneous conversation becomes normal and expected. On the first day of class, teach students how to use an "I am" verb and give them a list of adjectives they can use to describe themselves. (If appropriate, have a separate list of adjectives for males and females.) Ask students to say one thing about themselves using the new language. Later, the third-person verb form can be introduced and students can be asked to recall what their classmates said about themselves. After simple negation is introduced, students can emphatically declare what they are not. This material can be used throughout the first year. Students can be asked to describe their friends and relatives, famous people, teachers, and

each other. You can also bring a stuffed animal to class and ask students to describe the toy. As students' language abilities progress, they can be asked to invent events in the toy animal's life.

2. *Get to know your students.* Conversations are more natural when people want to talk to each other and choose what they want to talk about. For classroom communication to be successful, students must want to tell you and each other about their lives, interests, and ideas. Be on the lookout for informal opportunities to talk with your students. Even if the conversations are in the students' first languages, they will give you an opportunity to establish a richer relationship with students and ideas about what they like to talk about and what they might be trying to say when they try to talk. In addition, students will be more motivated to communicate with you because they trust that you care about what they have to say.

3. *Be selective in error correction, especially during "real" communication activities (as contrasted with "structured" activities). Concentrate on errors that most clearly interfere with communication.* It is probably better to think in terms of trying to understand and clarify what a student is saying than in terms of "correcting errors." Although many parents claim that they correct all their children's first language errors, a parent is likely to ignore "I falled down," but to correct "That's a doggy" when the animal is really a cat. This apparent contradiction is easy to explain. "I falled down" is easily understood even though it contains a grammatical error. In contrast, mistaking a cat for a dog can have serious cognitive and physical consequences, and a parent is likely to want to correct this error in perception.

4. *Deal with errors gently.* When students concentrate on the ideas they want to communicate, they are likely to make mistakes even in the most basic structures. Many students report that fear of error correction is the chief reason they feel anxious in their language class. Moreover, when the message is important to students, they are even more likely to feel frustrated when they are corrected. Imagine excitely telling a friend about something that happened a couple of days ago and the friend stops you and asks, "Don't you mean last week?" Important errors can be pointed out to the entire class or illustrated in targeted listening or reading input when the activity has been completed.

5. *Personalize oral activities.* Your knowledge of your students' interests should be used extensively in oral activities. Instead of using fictitious names and places, use your students' names and familiar places. Many language teachers, however, prefer to use target language places and situations in oral activities in order to prepare students for cultural situations that they may encounter.

6. *Show genuine interest in what your students have to say. They will stop wanting to communicate if they think you are only interested in the verb forms.* I'm sure you've had the experience of talking to someone and noticing that they did not really seem interested in what you had to say. I was once observing a Spanish class where the teacher was asking individual students how they had spent their

weekends. One student struggled and struggled as he formed a past tense sentence about going to the movies and doing his homework. When he finally finished, he looked up expectantly at the teacher who offered a perfunctory *"bueno"* (good) and moved on to the next student. Classroom observers are not supposed to interrupt lessons, but it took all of my self-control to remain in my seat and not go over and thank that student for his hard work and determination (and ask him which movie he had seen and if he had liked it!).

7. *Use group work.* One way to reduce anxiety about speaking is to use pair and group work. Several studies have found that students feel more comfortable communicating with a partner or in a small group than in front of the whole class. These activities have the added advantage of giving students more speaking opportunities during every class session.

8. *Devise interesting oral activities.* The more interesting the activity, the more likely students will want to get involved and forget their self-consciousness. The department head at a school where I used to teach made even routine language drills into a game. After presenting a new verb, she would lead students in practice on the verb forms. She would offer a model sentence, and then the class would have to restate the sentence using the different subjects that she cued.

> **TEACHER:** I talk with the children.
> **TEACHER:** You.
> **CLASS:** You talk with the children.
> **TEACHER:** Michael.
> **CLASS:** Michael talks with the children.

To keep things interesting, my friend would give the class a point when they got the sentence right and herself a point whenever the class made a mistake or responded without sufficient enthusiasm. She would make a big deal about the points, making faces if the class was right, and gloating if they were wrong. The activity was really a very simple—and usually boring—pattern drill, but her students loved it. My friend was even able to use this strategy to call on individual students. Everyone noticed when a student made a mistake, but my friend would hug the student and pretend that the student only made the mistake so that the teacher would get a point. The fictional contest diverted attention from students and made their oral responses less attached to them personally.

9. *Use information gap activities.* To make classroom communication more authentic, language teachers often use activities called **information gaps.** Information gap activities are pair or small-group activities that are arranged so that each of the participants has only some of the information necessary to accomplish a particular task. For example, students could be asked to describe a new substitute teacher with each group member receiving different pieces of information about the person. (Activity 2 below for Beginning Speakers is an information gap activity.)

10. *Teach communication strategies.* Successful communication is not entirely a function of control over sounds, grammar, and vocabulary. Sometimes very competent second language speakers have difficulty achieving their communicative goals, while less competent speakers successfully make their point.

Successful communicators are adept at managing their conversations and using communication and compensation strategies. Simple strategies, such as asking conversational partners to repeat themselves or testing your understanding of what was just said ("OK, you're saying that I should ask John about homework and then talk to the teacher?"), can go a long way to help language learners make the most of the language they have.

11. *Foster realistic expectations about speaking.* Teachers and learners should recognize that speech that is less than native-like is still useful. In fact, sounding like a native can actually be a problem. When a learner's speech sounds too much like a native speaker's, members of that culture will expect a native-like cultural interaction as well. "Foreigners" are usually excused for cultural mistakes, but natives who make such blunders are considered rude or peculiar. Importantly, foreigners are also more likely to elicit scaffolding from their conversational partners.

12. *Encourage a nonthreatening environment.* Since some learners find the use of a second language anxiety provoking, and some learners may also be experiencing culture shock, teachers should make the language learning environment as supportive and nonthreatening as possible. It appears that a supportive class can actually reduce students' anxiety levels. (Remember that Pappamihiel found that her group of English learners was more comfortable speaking English in their ESL classes than in their mainstream content classes [Chapter 1].)

Activity Ideas

As with listening comprehension, the activities in this section are only suggestions that can be modified to fit the level and interests of your students and your educational setting. And you should always be on the lookout for spontaneous opportunities for conversations with your students; a school or news event might provide a topic for a true conversation. Since listening and speaking go together in conversations, many of the activities in Chapter 4 are also speaking activities, and the speaking activities listed here are also listening activities.

Beginning Speakers

Activity 1	***"As the Bunny Turns"***
Implementation	Bring a cute stuffed toy to class; ask the class to choose its name and tell you about its life. This is an ongoing activity that you can use throughout the year and even through several years. Each discussion of the toy should take previous discussions into account. (Keep notes! Each class will create a different life for the toy.) As a variation you could have students bring their own stuffed animals or toy figures to talk about.

Activity 2

Implementation

"Alien Invasion!"

Divide the class into pairs. Give one person in each pair a piece of paper with a drawing of a "spaceman" on it. The other member of the pair should have blank paper and something to draw with. The student with the drawing pretends to have seen a spaceman and describes it to their partner who attempts to draw the alien. When the drawing is complete, the drawer describes the space visitor to the teacher. If the drawings and descriptions are sufficiently similar, you should declare that there will be an official investigation of the sighting. (This activity structure has countless variations. You can use all kinds of pictures or even shapes or graphs. You can link this activity to vocabulary you are studying. For example, the spaceman could have a triangular head, hexagonal eyes, etc., to coincide with vocabulary being used in math class.)

Activity 3

Implementation

"Guess What!"

Bring an interesting object to class and ask students to guess what it is. Expand their utterances by commenting on their guesses: "Yes, I see why you think it is a rock, it's gray and rounded, but it's also pretty light (weight)." (The object is a dried mushroom.) This activity has many variations. You could put an object in a box and have students guess what it is, or you could ask them what they think you ate for lunch. Another simple variation is to play Twenty Questions and allow them to ask you or a designated student "yes" or "no" questions to guess the object. You could also give hints. Guessing is a particularly good way to get students to use language creatively. Although there is a "correct" answer, everyone understands in advance that most answers will be wrong and that the more guesses there are, the more likely the right answer will finally be revealed.

Activity 4

Implementation

"May I Ask You a Few Questions?"

Divide the class into groups of two or three. Give each group a set of personal questions to be answered orally by each member of the group. (These questions can be tied to the grammar and vocabulary you have been studying.) If you are using pairs, the students ask each other the questions and record the partner's answers. In groups of three, the first student interviews the second student and the third student records the answers. The second student next interviews the third student, with the first student recording the answers. Finally, the third student interviews the first student, and the second student records the responses. The student who recorded responses can either report the responses orally to the whole class or report them in writing. (Some students are less anxious when they are talking about other people rather than themselves.) The questions can vary from short and simple to thoughtful and involved. If you use simple questions based on textbook structures and vocabulary (e.g., "What time do you eat dinner?" "What do you usually eat for dinner?"), the activity is a structured communication task. If you use more open-ended questions (i.e., "How would you describe a good teacher?"), the task is closer to true communication.

Activity 5	***"May I Present . . . ?"***
Implementation	Have students bring or draw a picture of one of their friends or family members to class, and then have them describe the person to the class or to a smaller group of students. This activity can be used for a wide variety of "Show and Tell" subjects.
Activity 6	***"I'll Take One from Column A"***
Implementation	Give students the following handout:

	Column A		Column B
I like to play	games	*with*	my Dad.
	house	*with*	my friends.
	marbles	*with*	my neighbors.
	video games	*with*	my brother(s).
	basketball	*with*	the kids down the street.
	the piano	*with*	my teacher.
	hide and seek	*with*	the kids in my class.
	la víbora de la mar	*with*	my cousins.
	soccer	*with*	the kids in my neighborhood.
	lotería	*with*	my grandmother.
	??	*with*	??

(continued)

Have students take turns picking one expression from column A and one from column B to say things about themselves. The double question marks indicate that they can use any activity and partner they want.

Intermediate Speakers

Activity 1

Implementation

"Can You Figure It Out?"

Divide the class into groups and ask each group to come up with a list of answers to the question What can you do with a toothbrush besides brushing your teeth? Give the groups about five minutes to come up with their answers, and then bring everyone back together and have each group report its responses. You could give "awards" for the Most Creative, Most Unlikely, and Most Useful ideas. Alternatively, the class could vote for its favorite ideas. This activity is an example of a problem-solving task, and I'm sure you will come up with many entertaining variations.

Role-play activities are a staple of language classes. Here are a few suggestions.

Activity 2

Implementation

"Let's Pretend"

Pretend to be one of your students and choose one to be you. To encourage students who are not participating in the role-play to be attentive (and benefit from the listening comprehension opportunity), you could ask audience members to retell everything that they remember from the scene when it is over. You could also ask the audience to vote on which role-play participant was more likely to "win" the interaction. You could even stop the role-play from time to time and have the class decide what should happen next or have new students take over the parts.

Activity 3

Implementation

"Press Conference"

Designate one class member as a well-known personality (a television celebrity, the school principal, etc.).

The rest of the class acts as reporters and questions the person. The teacher acts as a press aide and calls on "reporters" if the questioning lags. Obviously, you want to choose a student who is comfortable in front of a group as the interview subject, but even shy students can participate in this activity as reporters since attention remains focused on the student portraying the celebrity.

Activity 4	**"Total Physical Response Storytelling"**
Implementation	Read the class a short story or children's story. Allow individuals or groups of students time to create their own version of the story. (This activity may be a speaking and/or writing activity as the students discuss or write their ideas for their story.) The groups then act out their stories for the rest of the class using action and props as well as speech.
Activity 5	**"Let's Make Some Plans"**
Implementation	Allow students to sign up for a few minutes of class time when they can talk to the class, as long as they do so primarily in the target language. I permitted my students to use the time to arrange study groups for tests in other classes or figure out one of their homework assignments. (They could not make social engagements that did not include the whole class or use the time to complain about other students or teachers.)
Activity 6	**"On the Campaign Trail"**
Implementation	Initiate a class election and have students prepare posters and campaign speeches supporting their positions. The election could be about where to go on a field trip, what to put on the bulletin board, or which film to watch on a special occasion. (You should only have an election if the election issue is actually under your control and all the possible outcomes are all right with you. They can't vote on a field trip to Disney World!) I'm not exceptionally proud of this, but my students would have an annual election about which was the worst—my singing, my drawing, or my handwriting. After their speeches about how much their ears hurt after I sang, singing would always win the award as my "least skillful skill."

Advanced Speakers

Activity	**"Class Soap Opera"**
Implementation	Give your students a list of citizens of a mythical town and a short personal history for each. The characters might be from the same culture as your students, or they might be members of the target culture. Each class member is assigned (or selects) an identity to be used regularly in the soap opera. To initiate an "episode," ask your class what has been happening lately in their mythical town.

When an interesting scenario is suggested, signal the class members whose characters are involved to act out the scene. As the plot develops, additional characters may be needed, and students should be alert to step into the scene when their character is involved. You might want to designate a specific day each week for the soap opera so that your students can come to class prepared with new plot twists. Younger students might enjoy using toys or puppets to act out the scenes.

All Levels

Activity   **"Virtual Field Trip"**

Implementation   Partner with another teacher or other teachers in your school. Have your class create something interesting in your classroom that the other classes can visit. It could be a village created for a social studies unit, a science terrarium, or outlandish room decorations. Send your class to visit your partner's classroom without you. When your students return, have them tell you what they saw. Ask reasonable and interested questions. This activity gives students an experience that you haven't had so you will be asking true conversational questions rather than display questions. Building the field trip "destination" will also offer many conversational opportunities for students in both classes.

Assessing Speaking

The assessment of speaking is a crucial but difficult part of language teaching. There are several professionally developed speaking tests available. For example, the ACTFL Oral Proficiency Guidelines rate students' speaking ability from novice through superior levels, and the **Test of English as a Foreign Language (TOEFL)** includes an Internet-administered test of spoken English (TSE). While these types of tests offer global information about a student's oral proficiency, classroom teachers generally want more specific information about the kinds of language tasks that their students can successfully accomplish. Moreover, in order to demonstrate to students that you are serious about the importance of speaking, they must see the connections between oral tests, the course curriculum, and their grades (washback effect). Fortunately, digital technologies offer many new options for the assessment of second language speaking.

Many teachers find the use of rubrics especially helpful in the evaluation of speaking. Rubrics let you highlight the aspects of speaking that are most important and appropriate for the specific speaking task. They can also be modified according to each student's degree of language proficiency or linguistic needs. Consider this example of a rubric for the assessment of an oral description.

Task: *Students are shown a picture of a happy child with a tattered doll. They are first asked to tell what they see in the picture, and second, to make up a story that led up to the picture they see. They are given up to two minutes to look at the picture and organize their thoughts before they are asked to start speaking.*

Amount of Information Successfully Communicated	Virtually no information was conveyed.	1 2 3 4 5	The picture was described fully.
	Alternatively, you could make a hash mark for every piece of understandable information communicated: / / / / / /		
Quality of Language Structure	One-word or L1 utterances.	1 2 3 4 5	A variety of sentence types used appropriately.
Flow	Many hesitations, false starts, and overly long pauses.	1 2 3 4 5	Language flows smoothly with appropriate pauses.
Pronunciation	Very nonnative-like. Incomprehensible to a native speaker.	1 2 3 4 5	Almost completely native-like; only a few mispronunciations which do not interfere with comprehensibility.
Word Choice	Use of L1 and false cognates. Repetition of unspecific labels (this, that, thing).	1 2 3 4 5	Precise and accurate.
Overall Impression	Especially poor for a student at this level.	1 2 3 4 5	Especially good for a student at this level.

This rubric is just an example of the types of charts you can develop for your own purposes. This one is probably longer than one you would use in your class, but it includes examples of different types of judgments that can be used in speaking assessments. The assessment rubric can be different each time you test speaking. It is a good idea to alert students in advance of the specific things you will be "listening for." For example, a speaking rubric associated with a social studies unit on the American Revolution could include vocabulary such as *revolt*, *taxation*, *colony*, *citizen*, and *monarchy*.

Self-assessments can also be very useful in the assessment of speaking, especially for older learners. Self-assessments are groups of statements that describe various ways a person might use the target language. Learners rate their ability to accomplish the specific task included in each statement. For example, the self-assessment item listed below concerns the individual's ability to order a pizza. The student responds on a scale from 1 to 5 indicating his or her ability to accomplish the task. You should notice that self-assessment statements are typically written in terms of the goal to be accomplished rather than whether specific grammatical structures were used correctly.

I can order pizza delivery by telephone in English.	*I am not usually able to order pizza.*	1 2 3 4 5	*I am always able to give the correct pizza order and directions to my house the first time I try.*

Self-assessments can help students see their language ability more realistically and encourage them to set specific and reasonable goals.

FINDING YOUR WAY

REFLECTIONS

How should teachers react to students' second language errors?

_____

_____

_____

_____

Why are students sometimes reluctant to speak in front of their peers?

_____

_____

_____

_____

PLANNING FOR YOUR CLASSES

How can you arrange authentic speaking opportunities for your students?

_____

_____

_____

_____

How can your students practice a variety of language registers?

_____

_____

_____

_____

PROJECTS

- Select a beginning, intermediate, and advanced textbook and evaluate the communicativeness of each book's oral activities. Are the activities closer to authentic or structured communication?
- Identify a learner who is currently trying to learn a second language. Report back to your class about how you assessed the person's speaking ability and what the learner can and cannot do in the language.
- Create a context for a structured communication activity you find in a textbook. A context is a plausible reason for someone to say what the exercise says they should say. Consider this conversation:

    JOHN: Hello, I'm John.
    MARY: Hi John, I'm Mary.
    JOHN: How are you?
    MARY: Fine thanks, and you?
    JOHN: Fine.
    MARY: Well, good bye.
    JOHN: Good bye.

    This dialogue was clearly designed to illustrate greetings and introductions to language learners, but it would be a rather unusual conversation in real life since people rarely introduce themselves and then leave. To make this dialogue more plausible, you could say that John and Mary are members of "Shy-Date," a matchmaking service for extremely shy people.
- Write a set of realistic self-assessment statements for the type of language learners you expect to be working with.

IN YOUR JOURNAL

- How do you feel if someone interrupts you when you are speaking?
- What communication strategies do you use when speaking in your first language? In your second language(s)?

TEACHING CHECKLIST

This checklist will help you remember what to do when you teach speaking.

Yes *No*

☐ ☐ I devote an adequate amount of class time to authentic communication.

☐ ☐ I get to know my students' academic backgrounds, interests, and communication needs so that I can plan appropriate conversational tasks.

☐ ☐ When I ask a question, I give my students adequate time to think about their responses.

☐ ☐ I show interest in what my students are trying to say.

☐ ☐ I scaffold my students' conversation attempts.

☐ ☐ I correct errors gently.

☐ ☐ I help my students develop reasonable expectations for speaking and help them understand that speaking is not translation.

☐ ☐ I encourage my students to use communication strategies.

REFERENCES AND SUGGESTIONS FOR FURTHER READING

Blyth, C. (1995). Redefining the boundaries of language use: The foreign language classroom as a multilingual speech community. In C. Kramsch (Ed.), *Redefining the boundaries of language study* (pp. 145–183). Boston: MA: Heinle.

Breiner-Sanders, K., Lowe, P., Miles, J. & Swender, E. (2000). ACTFL proficiency guidelines— Speaking (revised 1999). *Foreign Language Annals, 33,* 13–18.

Celce-Murcia, M. (1991). Grammar pedagogy in second and foreign language teaching. *TESOL Quarterly 25,* 459–480.

Celce-Murcia, M., Dornyei, Z., & Thurrell, S. (1997). Direct approaches in L2 instruction: A turning point in communicative language teaching. *TESOL Quarterly, 31,* 141–152.

Chun, D. (1991). The state of the art in teaching pronunciation. In J. Alatus (Ed.), *Linguistics and language pedagogy: The state of the art?* (pp. 179–193). Washington, DC: Georgetown University.

de Saint Léger, D., & Storch, N. (2009). Learners' perceptions and attitudes: Implications for willingness to communicate in an L2 classroom. *System, 37,* 269–285.

Dykstra-Pruim, P. (2003). Speaking, writing, and explicit-rule knowledge: Toward an understanding of how they interrelate. *Foreign Language Annals, 36,* 66–76.

Ellis, R. (2002). Does form-focused instruction affect the acquisition of implicit knowledge? A review of the research. *Studies in Second Language Acquisition, 24,* 223–236.

Ellis, R. (2006). Current issues in the teaching of grammar: An SLA perspective. *TESOL Quarterly, 40,* 83–107.

Ferris, D., & Tagg, T. (1996a). Academic oral communication needs of EAP learners: What subject-matter instructors actually require. *TESOL Quarterly, 30,* 31–58.

Ferris, D., & Tagg, T. (1996b). Academic listening/speaking tasks for ESL students: Problems, suggestions, and implications. *TESOL Quarterly, 30,* 297–320.

Goldschneider, J. M., & DeKeyser, R. M. (2001). Explaining the "natural order of L2 morpheme Acquisition" in English: A meta-analysis of multiple determinants. *Language Learning, 51,* 1–50.

Gregersen, T. S. (2003). To err is human: A reminder to teachers of language-anxious students. *Foreign Language Annals, 36*, 25–32.

Horwitz, E. K. (1985). Getting them all into the act: Using audience participation to increase the effectiveness of role-play activities. *Foreign Language Annals, 18*, 205–208.

Horwitz, E. K. (1986a). Adapting communication-centered activities to student conceptual level. *Canadian Modern Language Review/La Revue Canadienne des Langues Vivantes, 42*, 827–840.

Horwitz, E. K. (1986b). Will they say the secret word? You bet your life! *AATF National Bulletin, 11*, 4–5.

Horwitz, E. K. (1996). Even teachers get the blues: Recognizing and alleviating non-native teachers' feelings of foreign language anxiety. *Foreign Language Annals, 29*, 365–372.

Jenks, C. (2009). Exchanging missing information in tasks: Old and new interpretations. *Modern Language Journal, 93*, 185–194.

Johnson, K. (1995). *Understanding communication in second language classrooms.* Cambridge, UK: Cambridge University Press.

Lantolf, J. P., & Pavlenko, A. (1995). Sociocultural theory and second language acquisition. *Annual Review of Applied Linguistics, 15*, 108–124.

Lee, L. (2002). Enhancing learners' communication skills through synchronous electronic interaction and task-based instruction. *Foreign Language Annals, 35*, 16–24.

Loewen, S., Li, S., Fei, F., Thompson, A., Nakatsukasa, K., Ahn, S., & Chen, X. (2009). Second language learners' beliefs about grammar instruction and error correction. *Modern Language Journal, 93*, 91–104.

McCarthy, M., & O'Keeffe, A. (2004). Research in the teaching of speaking. *Annual Review of Applied Linguistics, 24*, 26–43.

Molholt, G. (1988). Computer-assisted instruction in pronunciation for Chinese speakers of American English. *TESOL Quarterly, 22*, 91–111.

Murphy, J. M. (1991). Oral communication in TESOL integrating speaking, listening, and pronunciation. *TESOL Quarterly, 25*, 51–75.

Nakahama Y., Tyler, A., & van Lier, L. (2001). Negotiation of meaning in conversational and information gap activities: A comparative discourse analysis. *TESOL Quarterly, 35*, 377–405.

Nassaji, H., & Fotos, S. (2004). Current developments in research on the teaching of grammar. *Annual Review of Applied Linguistics, 24*, 126–145.

Salaberry, R. (1997). The role of input and output practice in second language acquisition. *Canadian Modern Language Review, 53*, 422–451.

Savignon, S. J. (1972). *Communicative competence: An experiment in foreign language teaching.* Philadelphia, PA: Center for Curriculum Development.

Segalowitz, N., & Freed, B. (2004). Context, contact, and cognition in oral fluency acquisition: Learning Spanish in at home and study abroad contexts. *Studies in Second Language Acquisition, 26*, 173–199.

Shrum, J. (1985). Wait-time and the use of target or native languages. *Foreign Language Annals, 18*, 305–313.

Taylor, L., & Wigglesworth, G. (2009). Are two heads better than one? Pair work in L2 assessment contexts. *Language Testing, 26*, 325–339.

Toth, P. (2011). Social and cognitive factors in making teacher-led classroom discourse relevant for second language development. *Modern Language Journal, 95*, 1–25.

VanPatten, B. (1986). Second language acquisition research and the learning/teaching of Spanish: Some research findings and implications. *Hispania, 69*, 202–216.

Volle, L. (2005). Analyzing oral skills in voice e-mail and online interviews. *Language Learning and Technology, 9*, 146–163.

6 What Should I Know About Teaching Reading?

- Why is reading such an important part of language learning?
- How does written language differ from oral language?
- Are there different types of reading?

READING AND SECOND LANGUAGE ACQUISITION

Reading as well as listening is an important source of comprehensible input according to the Input Hypothesis. In addition, since language learners often have easier access to reading materials through print media and the Internet than to listening experiences, reading has the possibility of reducing social distance. Reading can also be a tool for learning more language; students can learn sound-symbol correspondences, vocabulary, and academic content through reading. And, of course, the ability to read and comprehend academic materials is essential for the educational success of many learners.

Many second language learners have limited opportunities for authentic listening experiences, but reading can give learners easier access to many types of language they would not otherwise encounter. Reading is also the route to academic success for many second language learners. Teachers can help learners develop effective reading strategies so that they can acquire more language through reading on their own. Thus, the development of students' reading abilities can contribute to their development as autonomous language learners.

Reading: Some Important Concepts

Intensive Reading	■ Students read a relatively short text for a thorough understanding of the content, grammar, and vocabulary.
Extensive Reading	■ Students read a longer text with the goal of achieving a general rather than a close understanding of the material.
Reading to Learn	■ Students use reading to learn content material.

Sound-Symbol Correspondences	■	Associations between the sounds of a language and its writing system.
Background Knowledge	■	A reader's preexisting knowledge of a particular topic.
Bottom-up Processing	■	Learners read by sounding out individual words and attempting to understand a text by individually processing every sound and word. Bottom-up processing is associated with a phonics approach to reading.
Top-down Processing	■	Learners apply their background knowledge and focus on understanding a written text as a whole. They use their understanding of the text and the predictability of the grammatical patterns in their target language to guess the meaning of unfamiliar words or phrases.

The Importance of Reading

Reading is fundamental to the development of full second language competence. Many people across the world develop some listening and speaking ability in a second language through contacts with target language speakers or through television or movies, but reading is necessary to use a language for academic or professional purposes.

Reading can provide a wide range of language input unavailable to learners in other ways. Through reading, learners have a window on the day-to-day lives of L1 speakers and their culture and can experience a much wider variety of conversational situations than they would through their own interactions with target language speakers. Reading is also an excellent means of vocabulary and grammar development.

The Reading Process

Like listening, reading involves the construction of meaning, and therefore much of the material discussed in Chapter 4 with respect to second language listening is also true for reading in a second language. In addition, many scholars believe that reading in a second language parallels reading in a first language. Thus, if you have ever studied the process of first language reading, you will find many similarities in this chapter. There is, however, an important difference between first and second language reading: when reading in a second language, a second language learner must deal with a much higher percentage of unknown words and language forms. Therefore, the simple decoding of words is typically much more problematic in a second language than in a first. When you read in your first language, your already developed language ability allows you to recognize the words that you are sounding out relatively easily; but in a second language, many of the words may still be unfamiliar even if sounded out correctly. Moreover, grammatical features, such as verb endings and word order, are less useful in helping to understand a second language reading text. For those reasons, many second language reading scholars feel that a minimum **threshold** level of language ability is necessary before true second language reading can occur. Until learners have developed an adequate amount of internalized second language ability, they will be more likely to translate than to draw meaning directly from the text.

Types of Second Language Reading

The distinguished language educator Wilga Rivers speaks of two approaches to teaching reading in the second language classroom: **intensive reading** and **extensive reading.** Intensive reading involves understanding relatively short texts in depth. Students are expected to understand the content of the passage as well as its grammar and vocabulary. Intensive reading has been a mainstay of Grammar Translation classrooms and is often used to reinforce grammatical instruction or preview grammatical structures to be introduced at a future time. Intensive reading is a good method for introducing vocabulary and nuances among words; it helps students develop a very secure knowledge of a small piece of language and understand how the target language is constructed. Even though intensive reading stresses a precise understanding of a text, it should not be confused with translation. Students are still expected to process the text in the target language without resorting to word-for-word or phrase-by-phrase translation.

Extensive reading is associated with the Input Hypothesis and second language acquisition and encourages students to achieve a *general* understanding of longer texts. This type of reading might be more properly called reading for the gist or reading for the main ideas, and it parallels what we think of as **reading for pleasure** in our first language. As contrasted with the poems, short essays, and **extracts** associated with intensive reading, extensive reading usually employs short stories, magazine articles, novels, or essays.

Rivers's distinction between intensive and extensive reading is consistent with distinct goals readers have. For example, with respect to extensive reading, a reader might **skim** a magazine article to get a general idea of its contents or **scan** it to find a specific piece of information. Similarly, readers might study an essay carefully to see how the author constructed his or her argument, a practice associated with intensive reading. Many times, however, reading in a second language involves aspects of both intensive and extensive reading. When reading a textbook for a course, the reader needs both general overall content and specific information. Since the success of many language learners depends on their ability to learn content material from written texts, it is useful to add **reading to learn** to the categories of intensive and extensive reading. Reading to learn contains elements of both intensive and extensive reading and recognizes that the development of reading comprehension is a secondary goal to many second language readers whose primary goal is to learn the content material required in their classes or work environment.

Learning to Read in a Second Language

For some time, American educators and the public at large have been debating whether **phonics-based** or **whole language approaches** should be used to teach native English speakers to read. In a phonics-based approach, the teacher emphasizes correspondences between sounds and symbols (letters) and encourages students to sound out words. The whole language approach emphasizes predictability in texts, has students develop **sight vocabulary words,** and encourages students to guess the meaning of unknown words from the context of the reading passage. The context of the reading passage as well as the student's own background knowledge are seen as crucial to reading comprehension from a whole language perspective. Researchers often refer to phonics-based reading as **bottom-up processing** because the reader begins with the individual sounds of a text and builds them into an understanding of the content of a text. In contrast, whole language approaches to reading use **top-down processing** (see Chapter 4) because readers begin with a general sense of the meaning of a reading passage and use their general knowledge of the world and the predictability of the grammatical patterns in their target language to guess the meaning of unfamiliar words or phrases.

Without taking a position on the best way to teach first language reading, it seems clear that second language readers need to use both bottom-up and top-down reading strategies. That is, second language learners need to develop a feel for the way sounds are represented in their target language so that they can decode individual words; but they also need to galvanize their knowledge of the world and the particular text in order to predict the meaning of the words and phrases they encounter.

Think back to the times you have read a text on an unfamiliar topic. Although you likely recognized most of the words, you might have experienced a sense of disorientation because you could not easily organize the words into a comprehensible message. When reading in your L1, you can count on your understanding of your culture to help make sense of what you read. But unfamiliarity with the new culture can make second language reading materials difficult to understand. I have read English-language newspapers in Hong Kong that were thoroughly incomprehensible to me because of my unfamiliarity with current events there. Second language readers may be able to decode the literal meaning of the words and phrases but still be unable to grasp the real sense of a passage. Indeed, a number of studies have found that students are more successful when reading about personally interesting and *familiar* topics.

Second language readers also often have to deal with the difficulty of learning a new alphabet. Many languages do not share a common alphabet, and even when the L1 and the target language use essentially the same alphabet (in the case of Spanish speakers learning English, for example), a new set of sound-symbol correspondences must be learned. As a result, second language readers will see a letter used in their L1 and have to learn to think of a different sound or sounds when they see that letter used in a written text.

New alphabets typically pose even greater challenges for second language learners. English-speaking learners of languages like Russian, Greek, Korean, Arabic, Hebrew, and Farsi must learn entirely new scripts, and learners of certain

Asian languages such as Chinese or Japanese must cope with the intricacies of **logographic** (character-based) writing systems. Some languages, such as Japanese, require the mastery of multiple alphabets. Speakers of Asian languages studying English often have to move from their own logographic writing systems to a **phonetic** or sound-based alphabet.

Finally, second language readers must struggle with their sheer lack of second language proficiency. When we first learn to read in our first language, our oral ability in that language is already well-developed, and words are familiar to us when we sound them out or infer them from context. Our oral ability typically exceeds our reading ability. Unfortunately, this is often not the case in second language reading, and a word that has been successfully sounded out can still be totally unrecognizable to the learner. In fact, many learners cite lack of vocabulary as their most important impediment to successful second language reading. Paradoxically, many second language scholars believe that reading is one of the best ways to build up second language vocabulary. Since beginning language learners have not yet developed enough language proficiency to approach a text in the same way they approach a text in their L1, teachers should be careful to select reading materials that match their students' level of second language ability. That is, until learners have internalized an adequate amount of language to read easily, their early efforts will likely include more translation, memorization, and sheer puzzle solving than is associated with mature reading.

Types of Reading Materials

Just as with listening materials, reading materials can be classified as authentic or constructed. In addition to typical classroom texts, such as stories and essays, language teachers use a wide variety of authentic materials that target language speakers encounter in their daily lives, such as advertisements, movie schedules, classified ads, and food packaging. These materials can be very exciting to students because they include current slang and other commonplace daily language. Any written material used in the target culture can be used in the language classroom. Such **realia** provide useful short reading passages for beginning students and help students learn about everyday life in the target culture. Many language teachers also use children's books and adolescent literature. In addition, the Internet gives language students and teachers easy access to an exciting variety of authentic reading materials.

Language teachers often wonder whether constructed or authentic materials are better for developing their students' reading abilities. **Constructed materials** have the advantage of using words and structures that are familiar to learners so that students have a feeling of recognition and a sense of accomplishment when they read, and these materials can be used to introduce and reinforce new grammar and vocabulary. Many language programs use a specific type of constructed material called **graded readers.** Graded readers are expressly written for second language learners and target specific vocabulary and grammatical structures for various levels of language proficiency. They are often simplified versions of well-known stories or books and may include only a limited number of common words and structures.

Constructed reading materials are seldom as inherently interesting to students as authentic materials, and they do less to prepare students for real-world reading. In addition, constructed materials do not typically contain the inherent meaning support found in authentic materials. Ironically, just as with constructed listening materials, constructed reading materials often have less built-in redundancy than authentic materials and can actually be more difficult for learners than well-chosen authentic materials. Both authentic and constructed materials can be used for intensive reading activities, but teachers generally prefer authentic materials for extensive reading.

The content of reading materials is also often an issue. Sometimes student interests can be very specific and tied to career goals. English learners often need to be able to read textbooks for their other classes, and English reading passages are often a major component of high school exit and college entrance examinations. Students who see language study as a step toward a career in business or medicine will want to read materials that will be useful to them in their future occupation. While it is probably impossible for a teacher to meet all these different reading needs within a single class, individual students can be encouraged to choose their own materials from a class library and/or to obtain a personalized set of electronic materials. As digital materials become increasingly available, it will be even easier to meet individualized reading needs.

Helping Students Develop Effective Reading Strategies

Just as it is difficult for people to read a story or article in their L1 without knowing what the material might be about, it is difficult for language learners when they do not know what kinds of information to expect in their assigned readings. Moreover, language students are often unprepared to understand the cultural or historical background of a required reading. The SIOP Model maintains that one of the teacher's most important jobs is to be aware of the background knowledge that students have and help them anticipate the content of an assigned reading. Indeed, a large number of both first and second language reading studies have found that the more background knowledge students have about a particular topic the more effectively they will be able to read. It is therefore critical for teachers to help students activate their background knowledge immediately before reading. Just as with listening, students should know about what they are about to read so that they can form reasonable hypotheses about the meaning of the passage as they read through it. Previewing and the use of advance organizers are essential in helping students read.

Activation of background knowledge can be achieved through teacher-led discussions and brainstorming activities, advance organizers, and preview questions. Since reading depends on both the decoding of words and the understanding of ideas, these activities help remind students of relevant information they already know. In addition, current language textbooks, as well as textbooks in content courses, typically contain pictures and other introductory materials which are intended to help students prepare for reading. By considering a written passage's title, section headings, and graphics, students can anticipate the type of information they will probably encounter and thus read more effectively. These are strategies students will also be able to apply to their content reading.

The permanent nature of the reading text affords the opportunity for two particularly effective prereading strategies: skimming and scanning. Skimming refers to looking through a passage quickly to identify the general content and format of the passage, while scanning refers to finding a specific piece of information. Teachers can encourage students to skim and scan by asking pertinent prereading questions. Students can be asked, for example, to look through a passage to identify the setting of the reading, the general topic, or the tone of the material (skimming), or to name the specific subtopics contained in a science chapter (scanning). If a passage depends on specific terms or vocabulary items, students can search the text to determine their meanings before they begin to read. In fact, it is often a good idea to have students look over several important vocabulary words before reading, especially if the terms would be difficult to infer from context. Rereading is an essential reading strategy especially in the case of intensive reading and reading to learn.

Unrealistic Expectations

Just as with listening comprehension, learners often have the unrealistic expectation that they should understand every word they read. Moreover, students often confuse reading with translation and employ a word-by-word approach to their reading. Consider the following classroom exchange.

VOICES FROM THE CLASSROOM

Mr. Vargas is holding his daily "study hall" where students in his ESL class have ten minutes to work on content homework and ask any questions they have.

Tony: I don't understand math.

Mr. Vargas: What don't you understand?

Tony: I understand this, problems, but then the questions are long.

Mr. Vargas: Show me a question.

Tony: See! It is long. I no can read it.

Mr. Vargas: Now, show me the problems you can do.

Tony: See, I add all these numbers together. I can do it.

Mr. Vargas: Good! Now see these numbers in the problem. What do you think you should do with them?

Tony: Add?

Mr. Vargas: Right! Good! Show me in the problem which words tell you to add.

Tony: She buy a lot things. Here it says, "How much cost."

Mr. Vargas: Good, when the problem says how much does a group of things cost, it's usually asking for adding.

Tony: But, look here, store and birthday.

Mr. Vargas: Math problems often have stories with them. That's why these kinds of problems are called story problems, but you don't need to understand the whole story to do the math. Look at the problem to see what math it is asking for. Let's look at the rest of the problems to see what kind of math you have to do.

ESL Teachers and Content Reading

ESL teachers are often responsible either officially or unofficially for helping their students understand the material taught in their content courses. This is especially true when it comes to reading. ESL teachers frequently are more accessible and better able to understand their students' spoken English, so students naturally turn to them for help. In some cases, ESL teachers speak their students' home language to an extent. Consider the following conversation between an ESL teacher in an elementary school and a fifth-grade teacher from the same school.

VOICES FROM THE CLASSROOM

An ESL teacher at an elementary school and a fifth-grade teacher talk about a new fifth-grade student who came to the school at midterm:

Ms. Applewhite (the fifth-grade teacher):   Hi Mark, I'm glad I ran into you. I wanted to talk with you about Kim, my new fifth-grader from Korea.

Mr. Crowder (the ESL teacher):   Sure, how can I help?

Ms. Applewhite: Well, I thought you could translate this history chapter for him so that he could do the history project with his group. And, well, the test over that material is in three weeks.

Mr. Crowder: Amanda, I really don't speak that much Korean, even though I spent some time there in the Army. Actually, I think it would be better if I, rather we, just helped Kim read it himself.

Ms. Applewhite: Do you think that's possible?

Mr. Crowder: Yes, I've been working with him for almost a month now, and we have a lot to work with. He has a good educational background in Korean—he can read and write at his grade level there—and he started studying English in third grade, so he knows the alphabet and can read some simple things. Why don't you and I get together after school and we'll plan a strategy. I've been working with him on using his background knowledge before he tries to read a textbook, and it would be helpful if you reinforced that strategy in your class.

As the teachers' conversation illustrates, ESL teachers do not simply teach English. They often serve as intermediaries between their students and their students' other teachers, especially in the area of reading. When Mr. Crowder suggests to Ms. Applewhite that it would be better to help Kim improve his own reading abilities than to translate his class materials into Korean (does she have any idea of how long it would take to translate even a single chapter in a content textbook?), he is trying to get her to see that there is a lot to build on with Kim and that translating materials is probably not a good instructional strategy. Mr. Crowder also subtly suggests that helping Kim improve in English is the responsibility of both teachers, not just his because he is the ESL teacher.

Some Guidelines for Teaching Reading

Since many scholars find parallels between second language listening and second language reading, you will notice many similarities in the guidelines here and the ones in Chapter 4 about listening comprehension. Importantly, the activation of background knowledge and the development of strategies are also essential components in successful second language reading. But unlike in listening, the permanent nature of reading texts can facilitate the learning and application of comprehension strategies; therefore, teachers might want to concentrate on strategy development connected to reading activities and then show students how to apply similar strategies when listening. Of course, as with listening materials, teachers should strive to make reading materials as comprehensible and appealing as possible. A wealth of interesting and familiar reading materials can be capitalized on. Childhood stories paired with advance organizers, or even magazine articles and websites devoted to pop culture figures, are particularly useful because students often have the appropriate background knowledge. Multimedia materials allow learners to process language in several modalities and may give them experience with the type of reading materials that will be increasingly available in the future.

As with listening comprehension, teachers can help their students better understand all types of reading materials by supplying appropriate meaning support. Meaning support for reading is generally supplied before students begin reading and again after they have read some of the text to facilitate rereading. Fortunately, most authentic print materials and many of those constructed for classroom use have substantial amounts of meaning support already included. Students should become accustomed to looking at titles, section headings, pictures, and the like to predict what the reading material might be about. These built-in sources of meaning support also help activate students' background knowledge.

1. *Have appropriate expectations for reading comprehension.* Students will have different levels of understanding depending on whether they are doing intensive or extensive reading, dealing with familiar or unfamiliar topics, or reading authentic or constructed materials. Opportunities for rereading will also increase students' comprehension levels.

2. *Help students develop realistic expectations for second language reading.* As it is for most language learning tasks, misunderstanding the task can lead students to adopt ineffective strategies. Specifically, if students think they are supposed to understand every word in a reading passage, they are likely to become frustrated or to confuse reading with translation. So it is important to be clear about your expectations for reading. Also, because different cultural groups may have different conceptions of what reading entails, a discussion of what students believe about reading might be helpful.

3. *Help students become aware of the background information they need to understand a particular reading.* Sometimes teachers do this explicitly, even in the students' L1, by pointing out specific historical events or cultural information that can aid comprehension. A discussion about the topic can remind students of information they already know. Think carefully about what your students already know and what they need to know when reading. If you are a nonnative teacher, you might want to think about cultural references that may have confused you at one time.

4. *Have students look over the title, headings, and any graphics associated with the reading and anticipate what it might be about. An advance organizer in the form of an outline or brief summary is also helpful.* By looking at the title, headings, graphics, and physical appearance of the text, students will get a good idea of the topic and the kind of text they are about to read. By encouraging students to make predictions about a text, you will help them develop an important reading strategy that is especially helpful for independent reading.

5. *Have students preview the text by giving them preliminary questions.* Students could be asked, for example, to skim through the reading to determine if they are dealing with fiction or nonfiction, how many characters there are, or the setting of the story. Have students review the text several times each time looking for new information.

6. *In the case of content textbooks, have students use end-of-chapter questions as preview questions.* Even L1 readers have difficulty dealing with the amount of information included in today's social studies and science textbooks. By employing the time-honored student strategy of using end-of-chapter questions to guide their reading, students can better maneuver through the abundance of information. This technique is probably an essential survival strategy for ELs who must deal with content assignments and tests at the same time they are learning to read English.

7. *Help students develop effective dictionary strategies and to distinguish important from unimportant words.* Encourage students to guess unknown words from context. After looking up unknown words, students should go back and

reread the whole paragraph before continuing. Many students find it helpful to keep a personal dictionary of words they anticipate needing in conversation or writing or with which they have difficulty.

8. *Ask inference rather than fact-recall questions.* Inference questions are as important, and possibly more important, in assessing reading comprehension than they are in listening comprehension. Since students can easily refer back to a text when reading, it is easy for them to find the answer to a recall question without actually having understood the text—or even the question!

9. *Provide authentic materials as often as possible.* Websites are a great source of authentic reading materials. Take advantage of current technologies and our increasingly interconnected world to help students gain access to a variety of personally relevant reading materials.

10. *Allow ample opportunities for rereading.* Students should be given the opportunity to reread materials several times. They should be given a purpose each time they read (directed reading).

11. *Take a multimedia approach to reading.* Today's digital technologies provide multiple ways for students to develop both reading and listening comprehension. E-books allow students to read texts on computers and other digital devices (including phones) and make notes and look up words. Some devices even let users translate text. Books on CDs and downloadable audiobooks allow students to improve listening by hearing spoken language. The combination of audiobooks and their text counterparts make an excellent resource for teaching reading and listening skills together.

Activity Ideas

Reading is essential for students' academic progress in content classes and on standardized tests; therefore, it is a good idea to coordinate classroom activities with your students' other reading demands. Fortunately, reading instruction lends itself very well to individualization.

Scanning Activities

The skimming and scanning activities suggested here could also be used for reading strategy training.

Scanning Activities

Activity 1	*"Treasure Hunt"*
Implementation	Divide the class into small groups, and give each group an instruction sheet for a math project. Place the needed materials (counters, Cuisenaire rods, M & M's, or whatever) in various places in your room. Have groups race to see which one can assemble the required materials first. Have groups check off each material from the list as they obtain it.

Activity 2	*"Cooking Sense"*
Implementation	Prepare several recipes for the class to look at. In each recipe include inappropriate ingredients (e.g., three pounds of dollar bills) and inappropriate cooking steps (e.g., put in the refrigerator and bake for 30 days). Have students scan the recipes and circle the improper ingredients and directions. (NOTE: This activity could be expanded into a writing activity by asking students to make the necessary changes to the recipe.)
Activity 3	*"Mad Libs"*
Implementation	Mad Libs is a party game that uses sentences with important words left out. Players are asked to supply the appropriate part of speech—noun, adjective, etc.—without knowing what the sentence will say. For example, a sentence could be, "Sandra always _____ with her mother on Saturdays." Students would supply a verb. Some of the sentences might be reasonable sentences, such as "Sandra always cooks with her mother on Saturdays," and some might be silly, such as "Sandra always parades with her mother on Saturdays." After the students have chosen their words, pass out copies of the Mad Libs script and have several students read their answers for each item. (You can use either published Mad Libs materials or create your own.) This game makes an excellent listening activity as well, and could be expanded into a grammar lesson about third-person *"s,"* for example.

Skimming Activities

Activity 1	*Is This "Hello" or "Goodbye"?*
Implementation	Have students read conversations between two or more people and determine if the people are greeting each other or saying goodbye. (NOTE: This activity has dozens of variations. Students could determine if the people are happy or angry, young or old, etc.)
Activity 2	*"Teacher of the Year"*
Implementation	Give students written descriptions of three fictional teachers who have been nominated for a "Teacher of the Year" award. For example, one

could be a geography teacher who spends a lot of time tutoring students but also gives two hours of homework every night. Tell them that they will have to vote for their favorite in two minutes. After two minutes, ask the class to raise their hands to vote for each of the award candidates. Declare a "winner." Now, give the class time to read the three descriptions and then ask if any of them would have changed their vote and why.

(NOTE: This activity can easily be expanded into an oral discussion of the three candidates and more generally the attributes of good teachers. Basing oral discussions on written materials gives students vocabulary and phrases they can incorporate into their comments.)

Activity 3

Implementation

"Celebrity Matching"

Give students paragraph descriptions of four celebrities who they would be familiar with. (You could also describe people who work at your school.) At the bottom of the page, list the names of six celebrities (the four described in the paragraphs and two distracters). Have students match the descriptions with the names. Students should work quickly to encourage skimming.

Intensive Reading

Activity 1

Implementation

"Knock, Knock!"

Select several common knock-knock jokes. Have students read through the first joke. After you are sure they have understood it, ask them if they thought it was funny, and if so, why. Have them locate the word or words that make the knock-knock joke a pun. Lead them in a discussion of the structure of a knock-knock joke (Knock, knock! Who's there? Response. Response who? Pun on response). Go on to the second and third joke. Have students analyze the structure of the new jokes. You might want students to make up their own knock-knock jokes as an application activity.

Activity 2	*"What Sparkle!"*
Implementation	Select a short authentic text such as a nursery rhyme, an accessible poem, or even a popular song. Include a gloss for important vocabulary words that would be difficult to infer from the text.

Sample Activity. "Twinkle Twinkle Little Star." First, lead a discussion designed to activate students' background knowledge. For example, you could ask about celestial objects or wishing customs in different countries. Ask students if they have ever wondered what stars are made of or what they would look like if they were up close. Play a recording of the song and have students read along with the text. Have students read the text again, and then ask inference questions to make sure that they understood what they read. After you are confident that students understand the song, it is time to discuss its structure. For example, you could ask students about the rhyming pattern, the words that create a sense of a personal relationship between the singer and the star, or the song's use of repetition. This activity could be expanded into a writing task by having students write a poem about stars or a paragraph describing their perceptions of stars.

Extensive Reading

Activity 1	*"Plain Vanilla"*
Implementation	Have students select books or magazines of their choice from the class or school library. This is not a time to be snobby! Extensive reading is about interesting reading, not the development of a sophisticated taste in reading materials. Direct students to materials that you think would be particularly interesting to them. Have them keep a log of the materials they have read.

(NOTE: Neither this activity nor the others in this section include discussions or comprehension checks of the content of the reading materials. Extensive reading is typically individualized, with students choosing their own materials, so a whole-class discussion is generally impossible. Extensive reading activities typically have students make a simple report on their reading such as making a reading log or drawing descriptive pictures.)

Activity 2

Implementation

"Class Book Idol"

Select three to five books (either fiction or nonfiction) or short stories for the whole class to read. The books can be read in any order and can be passed from student to student. Be sure that the books are easily comprehensible and have high interest value for your students. When the entire class has read all the books, hold an election to see which one should be named "Class Book Idol." During the election campaign, have students give reasons for and against each book. To incorporate speaking and writing, students could make campaign posters, campaign speeches, and even make video commercials for their favorite book.

Activity 3

Implementation

"Pass It On!"

Have students select a book or magazine from either a classroom library or the school library. (They should be free to choose a book below their grade level since their L2 reading ability is likely to be below their cognitive level.) When they are finished with the book, they should pass it on to another student in the class whom they think would enjoy it.

(NOTE: Classroom libraries are very useful in all language classrooms. The library should include a variety of fiction and nonfiction books and magazines that would be interesting to your age group. Be sure to include materials at a range of grade levels to accommodate many reading levels. Many students will enjoy extensive reading more if they can read materials that are not too difficult.)

Reading To Learn

Activity 1	*"My Friend's House"*
Implementation	Have students do research on each other's countries of origin for an oral presentation. Have them share their notes with a classmate from that country before they make their presentations to the whole class.
Activity 2	*"Academic Reading"*
Implementation	Ask students to bring to class a reading assignment from one of their content classes. Have students read the materials for a pretend quiz over the content. Meet with the students individually when they have finished their reading and ask them questions about the content. Follow the quizzes with a discussion about how students approached the reading, if they approached this kind of academic reading differently than they approached other readings in their language class, and if they had any particular difficulties.

Assessing Reading Comprehension

Since reading involves constructing meaning from text, many of the same approaches as well as the problems discussed in Chapter 4 with respect to the assessment of listening comprehension also apply to reading. On the other hand, unlike listening, written text is permanent and students can reread and go back over reading materials. Therefore, students do not usually misunderstand a written text simply because they were momentarily distracted.

When testing reading comprehension, it is important to use prereading activities to activate students' background knowledge and to give students enough time to reread a text. After all, if students are encouraged to use prereading strategies when they read in class or do outside reading, they should have the same opportunity when they are being tested. The choice of reading material is also important. Students may be able to read some types of writing but have difficulty with texts that include large amounts of content material. Literature poses particular problems since the true meaning of a literary passage often differs from the surface meaning and students may never have experienced this type of reading in their L1.

Like listening, it is also difficult to test reading comprehension independently of other language skills, so most language teachers rely on comprehension questions in the target language. If you choose this approach, it is important to ask true inference questions because students can often pick out the answers to simple recall questions without actually understanding the text. To avoid writing problems, some teachers have students answer inference questions in their L1. Self-assessment rubrics and straightforward conversations with students ("How much do you understand when you read the stories in our reading book?" "Tell me what happened in the squirrel story.") are also good choices for assessing students' general level of reading comprehension abilities, but they do not offer much information about how well a student has understood specific sentences in a text.

Cloze tests are often mentioned as a good way to test reading comprehension. Cloze tests are written passages in the target language that have had words deleted. Students read along and anticipate what should be put in each blank. Since students use only a single word to fill in each blank, problems resulting from writing difficulties are minimized. Even so, as can be seen in the cloze passage that follows, it is still difficult to entirely separate reading comprehension and content knowledge in this type of test.

VOICES FROM THE CLASSROOM

Cloze Passage **#1. This cloze passage is based on a paragraph from the beginning of this chapter. After the first sentence, every ninth word was replaced with an equal-sized blank. Cloze tests usually include the entire first sentence of a text to give students some context and an idea about the passage's writing style. Try to see how many blanks you can fill in without turning back to the beginning of the chapter.**

Like listening, reading involves the construction of meaning, and therefore much of the material discussed in Chapter 4 with respect to second language listening is also true for reading in a second language. In addition, many scholars believe that reading in _____ second language parallels reading in a first language. _____ , if you have ever studied the process of _____ language reading, you will find many similarities in _____ chapter. There is, however, an important difference between _____ and second language reading: when reading in a _____ language, a second language learner must deal with _____ much higher percentage of unknown words and language _____ .

According to John Oller, cloze tests tap into the student's **expectancy grammar.** As students read, they come to expect what will come next. These intuitions include guesses both about content and about sentence structure. For example, students may not know which noun to put in a blank, but if the cloze passage is at an appropriate reading level, they seldom try to put a verb in a blank requiring a noun or pronoun.

Cloze passage #1 is a standard cloze passage, which means that the words were deleted in a regular pattern—in this case, every ninth word. Several scholars suggest an alternative type of cloze test called **rational deletion cloze passage,** in which words are deleted intentionally in order to assess the student's knowledge of a specific grammatical structure or set of vocabulary words. Cloze passage #2 is the same cloze passage as #1, but this time all the prepositions have been deleted.

Although students still must read to complete a rational deletion cloze test, many scholars classify them as grammar or vocabulary tests rather than reading tests because students are required to use a particular part of speech. These scholars believe that rational deletion cloze passages do not tap into a student's expectancy grammar in the same way a reading task does. Other scholars believe that rational deletion cloze passages are preferable to traditional fill-in-the-blank grammar tests because the items are more authentic and include more context.

VOICES FROM THE CLASSROOM

Cloze Passage #2. **This passage is an example of a rational deletion cloze passage. All the prepositions after the first sentence have been deleted.**

Like listening, reading involves the construction of meaning, and therefore much of the material discussed in Chapter 4 with respect to second language listening is also true for reading in a second language. In addition, many scholars believe that reading _____ a second language parallels reading _____ a first language. Thus, if you have ever studied the process _____ first language reading, you will find many similarities _____ this chapter. There is, however, an important difference _____ first and second language reading: when reading _____ a second language, a second language learner must deal _____ a much higher percentage _____ unknown words and language forms.

These cloze passages were meant to be difficult because the readers of this book are language teachers rather than language learners. Since it is more difficult to read a passage with deleted words than it is to read a passage of intact text, cloze passages for students should be based on reading materials at or even below their current reading levels. It is also a good idea to use longer texts and to delete every eleventh, thirteenth, or even fifteenth word to maintain the flow of the text. By deleting every ninth word, I have created a truly challenging cloze passage.

FINDING YOUR WAY

REFLECTIONS

Do you agree with Krashen that both listening and reading function in the same way to facilitate second language acquisition?

_____

_____

_____

_____

_____

How does reading to learn differ from other types of reading?

_____

_____

_____

_____

How will electronic media influence what and how people read?

_____

_____

_____

_____

How much does vocabulary knowledge influence the ability to read?

_____

_____

_____

_____

PLANNING FOR YOUR CLASSES

What kinds of standardized reading tests do your students have to take? What will you need to do to better prepare your students for these tests?

_____

_____

_____

_____

What are some of the specific goals your students will have with respect to reading?

_____

_____

_____

_____

_____

PROJECTS

- Keep a record of reading materials you would like to use with your classes. Try to include a range of material types, such as authentic (websites, menus, content textbooks, etc.), literary (poems, short stories, children's books, etc.), and nonfiction. Try to obtain as many of these materials as possible to start a classroom library.
- Your methods instructor will show you some different types of reading materials. Look for differences in the amount of context, redundancies, and inherent meaning support (titles, pictures, headings, etc.) in the materials. Compare the degree of comprehensibility of the authentic materials with the constructed materials. What reading strategies would be helpful for each reading type?
- Write an advance organizer for a reading passage in a content textbook (science, social studies, math, etc.).

IN YOUR JOURNAL

- What kinds of reading do you find to be the most challenging? Why?
- What kinds of reading strategies do you employ?
- What can you do to retain or improve your current level of reading comprehension?

TEACHING CHECKLIST

This checklist will help you quickly evaluate the way you teach reading.

Yes	No	
☐	☐	I devote an adequate amount of class time to reading.
☐	☐	I assess my students' reading abilities and needs.
☐	☐	I provide a range of reading materials that correspond to my students' interests, L1 reading abilities, and L2 reading needs.
☐	☐	I assess my students' background knowledge to determine the information they will need for each reading text.
☐	☐	I use intensive, extensive, and reading to learn activities and have appropriate goals for each type of reading.
☐	☐	I provide opportunities for rereading.
☐	☐	I help my students develop reasonable expectations for reading.

☐   ☐   I help my students identify sources of available reading materials (libraries, websites, etc.).

☐   ☐   I include reading in my assessment and testing procedures.

REFERENCES AND SUGGESTIONS FOR FURTHER READING

Aebersold, J. A., & Field, M. L. (1997). *From reader to reading teacher: Issues and strategies for second language classrooms.* Cambridge; UK: Cambridge University Press.

Akamatsu, N. (2003). The effects of first language orthographic features on second language reading in text. *Language Learning, 53,* 207–231.

Anderson, J., & Gunderson, L. (2001). "You don't read a science book, you study it": An exploration of cultural concepts of reading. *Reading Online, 4.*

Ariza, E. N. (1999). Reaching Joseph: How a Spanish-speaking Anglo teacher helped a monolingual English-speaking Puerto Rican child learn Spanish. *Reading Improvement, 36,* 98–101.

Barton, M. L., & Jordan, D. L. (2001). *Teaching reading in science: A supplement to* Teaching Reading in the Content Areas Teacher's Manual (2nd ed.). Alexandria, VA: Association for Supervision and Curriculum Publishing.

Baumann, J., & Graves M. (2010). What is academic vocabulary? *Journal of Adolescent and Adult Literacy. 54,* 4–12.

Brantmeier, C. (2005). Anxiety about L2 reading or L2 reading tasks? A study with advanced language learners. *Reading Matrix, 5,* 67–85.

Carrell, P. L. (1991). Second language reading: Reading ability or language proficiency? *Applied Linguistics, 12,* 159–179.

Carrell, P. L. (2001). Influence of purpose for reading on second language reading: Reading procedural texts in ESL. *Reading in a Foreign Language, 13,* 567–591.

Carrell, P. L., & Wise, T. E. (1998). The relationship between prior knowledge and topic interest in second language reading. *Studies in Second Language Acquisition, 20,* 285–309.

Chihara, T., Sakurai, T., & Oller, J. W. (1989). Background and culture as factors in EFL reading comprehension. *Language Testing, 6,* 143–151.

Cho, K., & Krashen, S. D. (1994). Acquisition of vocabulary from the Sweet Valley Kids series: Adult ESL acquisition. *Journal of Reading, 37,* 662–667.

Cho, K., & Krashen, S. D. (2001). Sustained silent reading experiences among Korean teachers of English as a foreign language: The effect of a single exposure to interesting, comprehensible reading. *Reading Improvement, 38,* 170–174.

Cho, K., & Krashen, S. D. (2002). Reading in English as a foreign language: What a mother can do. *Reading Improvement, 39,* 158–163.

Cirino, P., Vaughn, S., Linan-Thompson, S., Cardenas-Hagan, E., Fletcher, J., & Fran, D. (2009). One-year follow-up outcomes of Spanish and English interventions for English language learners at risk. *American Educational Research Journal, 46,* 744–781.

Early, M., & Tang, G. M. (1991). Helping ESL students cope with content-based texts. *TESL Canada Journal, 8,* 34–45.

Elley, W. B. (1983). The impact of reading on second language learning. *Reading Research Quarterly, 19,* 53–67.

Field, M. L., & Aebersold, J. A. (1990). Cultural attitudes toward reading: Implications for teachers of ESL/bilingual readers. *Journal of Reading, 33,* 406–410.

Fitzgerald, J. (1995). English-as-a-Second-Language learners' cognitive reading processes: A review of research in the United States. *Review of Educational Research, 65,* 145–190.

Gonzalez-Bueno, M. (2003). Literacy activities for Spanish-English bilingual children. *Reading Teacher, 57,* 189–192.

Goodman, K. S., Wang, S., Iventosch, M., & Goodman, Y. M. (Eds.). (2011). *Reading in Asian languages: Making sense of texts in Chinese, Japanese and Korean*. Florence, KY: Routledge.

Grabe, W. (2009). *Reading in a second language: Moving from theory to practice*. Cambridge, UK: Cambridge University Press.

Koda, K. (2007). Reading and language learning: Crosslinguistic constraints on second language reading development. *Language Learning, 57*, 1–44.

Krashen, S. D. (1993). The case for free voluntary reading. *Canadian Modern Language Review, 50*, 72–82.

Lao, C. Y., & Krashen, S. D. (2000). The impact of popular literature study on literacy development in EFL: More evidence for the power of reading. *System, 28*, 261–270.

Laufer, B. (2009). Second language vocabulary acquisition from language input and from form-focused activities. *Language Teaching, 42*, 341–354.

Lee, J.-W., & Schallert, D. L. (1997). The relative contribution of L2 language proficiency and L1 reading ability to L2 reading performance: A test of the threshold hypothesis in an EFL context. *TESOL Quarterly, 31*, 713–739.

Lesaux, N., & Siegel, L. (2003). The development of reading in children who speak English as a second language. *Developmental Psychology, 39*, 1005–1019.

Lim, H. L., & Watson, D. J. (1993). Whole language content classes for second-language learners. *Reading Teacher, 46*, 384–393.

Lundberg, I. (2002). Second language learning and reading with the additional load of dyslexia. *Annals of Dyslexia, 52*, 165–187.

Nation, I. S. P. (2008). *Teaching vocabulary: Strategies and techniques*. Boston, MA: Heinle ELT.

Odisho, E. Y. (1994). *The alphabet and spelling connection: Insights from nonnative learners of English* (Report No. ED371604). Washington, DC: ERIC Clearinghouse on Languages and Linguistics.

Oller, J. (1974). Expectancy for successive elements: Key ingredient to language use. *Foreign Language Annals, 7*, 443–452.

Randall, M., & Meara, P. (1988). How Arabs read roman letters. *Reading in a Foreign Language, 4*, 133–145.

Rivers, W. M. (1981). *Teaching foreign language skills*. Chicago, IL: University of Chicago Press.

Saito, Y., Horwitz, E. K., & Garza, T. J. (1999). Foreign language reading anxiety. *Modern Language Journal, 83*, 202–218.

Schmitt, N., Jiang, X. & Grabe, W. (2011). The percentage of words known in a text and reading comprehension. *Modern Language Journal, 95*, 26–43.

Swaffar, J., Arens, K., & Byrnes, H. (1991). *Reading for meaning*. Englewood Cliffs, NJ: Prentice Hall.

Upton, T. A., & Lee-Thompson, L. (2001). The role of the first language in second language reading. *Studies in Second Language Acquisition, 23*, 469–495.

Verhoeven, L. (1990). Acquisition of reading in a second language. *Reading Research Quarterly, 25*, 90–114.

Wang, M., & Koda, K. (2005). Commonalities and differences in word identification skills among English second language learners. *Language Learning, 55*, 73–100.

Yamashita, J. (2002). Mutual compensation between L1 reading ability and L2 language proficiency in L2 reading comprehension. *Journal of Research in Reading, 25*, 81–95.

7 What Should I Know About Teaching Writing?

- What purposes do learners have for second language writing?
- How does purposeful writing differ from the simple recording of speech?

WRITING AND SECOND LANGUAGE ACQUISITION

Speaking and writing are usually referred to together as productive language skills because they require learners to actually create language. As contrasted with listening and speaking, very few second language acquisition theories specifically address the issue of how people learn to write in a second language, possibly because even in a first language writing ability is highly variable and generally associated with higher levels of education. The Input Hypothesis sees the development of writing as similar to speaking (it is acquired through comprehensible input) except that writers have the opportunity to apply their learned knowledge through the use of the monitor. Conversation theories tend to view writing as a conversation between writers and readers and suggest that the use of dialogue journals between teachers and students can approximate the scaffolding learners receive in oral conversations. From the perspective of cognitive learning theories, writing affords efficient practice, the possibility of recorded feedback which students can consult when needed, and a slower pace allowing more focused attention. Writing has a more prominent role in the Output Hypothesis and sociocultural theories of SLA. In these theories, learners benefit from the production of written text, with writing seen as a problem-solving activity that can contribute to further second language development.

Many language teachers use writing as a way to practice and encourage oral language development, but writing is an important ability in and of itself for many language learners. Writing is essential when the second language is needed for academic or professional purposes. English learners in the United States and many other countries must develop satisfactory L2 writing skills to be successful in school. High school exit examinations across the United States, as well as many standardized college entrance tests, are increasingly including compositions in their evaluations of academic competency.

Writing: Some Important Concepts

Writing Genres	■ Refers to the variety of types of writing students may have to accomplish.
Academic Writing	■ The type of writing students must do in content classes and other academic environments, including essays, compositions, outlines, and tests. Academic writing is purposeful and requires reflection and problem solving.
Free-Expression Writing	■ Refers to the type of writing where students select the topic and possibly the type of writing. Activities associated with free-expression writing include weekly free-writing assignments, diaries and journals, and dialogue journals.
Dialogue Journals	■ An extended written conversation usually between a teacher and a student similar to letter writing.
Monitor	■ Krashen's term for learned knowledge about the language. Similar to Bialystok's **explicit knowledge,** the monitor helps students write with more grammatical accuracy.
Prewriting Strategies	■ Practices like brainstorming and outlining which help students generate ideas and organization for writing.

The Writing Process

It is difficult to talk about a single second language writing process, since there are so many types of and purposes for writing. At the beginning levels of language instruction, writing is often used as a record of speech. Students are asked to write down the kind of information they communicate orally. Thus, after studying descriptive adjectives, students might be asked to write a paragraph describing one of their friends. Teachers can then examine the student's use of specific vocabulary, possessive pronouns, descriptive adjectives, and the like. This kind of writing involves very little problem solving, academic language, or organization. Students simply write down what they would say if someone asked them to describe one of their friends and, perhaps, proofread their effort. With the exception of the proofreading step, beginning second language writing resembles the kind of writing that children do at early stages of literacy development in their first language, and it is often used in language classes to foster the development of oral language.

When students are asked to write compositions, essays, and extended academic papers, writing becomes more purposeful. Many scholars view this type of writing as more similar to purposeful first language writing. That is, although students might start by recording what they would say, successful academic writing necessarily involves organizing and synthesizing thoughts; gathering, analyzing, and prioritizing information; and presenting thoughts in a cohesive, persuasive, and polished manner. Even if the assignment does not require any research, simple "off-the-top-of-the-head" comments will not satisfy the need for reflection and argumentation required in this type of writing.

Krashen maintains that the permanent nature of writing allows for the use of the monitor, or the learner's accumulation of knowledge *about* the target language. I like to think of the monitor as that language teacher in your head who reminds you to make your subjects and verbs agree. Since oral conversations move very quickly, the monitor has limited usefulness in speaking, but students can use their learned knowledge about the language to revise written texts. Krashen reminds us, however, that students must actually know the relevant grammatical rules and care about the accuracy of their writing for the monitor to be applied successfully. The Output Hypothesis and sociocultural theories of SLA see a larger role for writing. Writing allows learners to test hypotheses about how the language functions and to consolidate their internalized language proficiency.

Experienced first language writers are often frustrated by the different organizational patterns for writing in their second language. Many experienced L1 writers from Asian language backgrounds, for example, are frustrated by the directness of written American English. They may be used to starting a composition with a general introduction alluding to universal issues and filled with beautiful vocabulary—a practice that American teachers tend to find flowery, overly general, and irrelevant.

When writing educators talk about the "writing process," they are usually referring to a sequence of steps that can be used to help learners become better writers. They often speak of steps such as generating ideas (brainstorming), composing, writing a first draft, circulating the draft for comment, revising, producing a second draft, and so on. Since each writer approaches writing differently, there is no single writing process; but the term emphasizes the idea that no one, not even the most experienced writer, begins writing at the top of a piece of paper (or computer screen) and keeps writing without pausing until a flawless product emerges. Writing necessarily entails thinking and revision. Writers must continually focus on what they want to say and whether their words are actually communicating their ideas. In fact, like the sociocultural theories, many writing scholars see writing as problem solving. Often writers are not certain what they want to say until they are in the process of writing and use writing to figure out the thoughts and opinions they want to communicate.

Types of Second Language Writing

Writing in the second language classroom can be divided into **structured writing** and **communicative writing**. Structured writing corresponds to structured speaking, while communicative writing corresponds to authentic oral communication.

In structured writing activities, students use writing to practice specific grammar or vocabulary as well as any material they are learning orally: practices that are most consistent with the cognitive learning theories. Typically, structured writing includes such activities as copying dialogues, completing grammar worksheets, and keeping a vocabulary notebook.

In communicative writing, the focus is on meaning, and students are not limited to the vocabulary and structures they have already studied. For this reason, students may ask for needed structures and vocabulary, and a bilingual dictionary can be useful if students are able to read in their first language. Just as with oral communication activities, students will likely make more errors in communicative writing activities than in structured writing. Since beginning writers often rely on pat phrases (analogous to **formulaic** oral language), intermediate and advanced writers can sometimes make more errors than beginners when they attempt to communicate more sophisticated ideas. (One of the projects at the end of this chapter will ask you to examine some student writing samples to prepare you for the types of writing you will likely see from your students.) First language interference is also a common problem when learners attempt to write in a second language. The interference can become more pronounced when students translate from their first language rather than composing directly in the second language.

Free Expression

Second language teachers often employ a type of communicative writing called **free-expression writing**. Free expression has a more personal focus than simple communicative writing. Activities associated with free-expression writing include weekly free-writing assignments (see "Friday Specials" in the activities section), diaries and journals, and a type of interactive writing between the student and teacher called **dialogue journals**. Dialogue journals are frequently used with both first and second language writers and involve written correspondence between the teacher and student. Typically, students start by writing something about themselves, and then the teacher responds. My own students especially enjoyed talking about themselves or their families, and some would take the opportunity to point out some problem in their (my) class. E-mail, social networks, and even texting make dialogue journals more convenient than when teachers and students had to exchange pieces of paper.

Free-expression writing reinforces the idea that the goal of language learning is communication and not simply the manipulation of grammatical structures. Since students often use dialogue journals as an opportunity to discuss personally important events and feelings, it is important to focus primarily on what students are trying to say rather than on how they say it. Respond *in the second language* to the student's message as if responding to a note or e-mail message. The response should be sincere and personal. As it is with speaking, learners will not want to communicate with you if they do not believe that you care about what they say. Your responses also serve as a kind of personalized reading input for the student. After your communicative response, you could point out one or two important grammatical errors in a casual tone (and in the native language, if desired): "Remember that the plural of child is children." You could also employ a written recast and embed grammatical corrections in your "communicative" response similarly to the way you would scaffold an oral error.

Academic Writing

While language teachers tend to concentrate on the quality of the second language writing, content teachers are concerned with the logic and the specific ideas communicated as well as how well thoughts are communicated in the second language. Academic writing is purposeful and requires reflection and problem solving. The essays, compositions, outlines, tests, and other types of writing that students must do in content classes and other academic environments require both a more formal written style (see next section on registers) as well as content knowledge. It is, thus, difficult to know if writing difficulties are the result of difficulties expressing ideas in the second language or gaps in content understanding. There could also be issues with respect to cognitive development and the ability to make generalizations and apply knowledge in new situations.

Computer-Mediated Communication

It is impossible to discuss second language writing activities without mentioning the approaches made possible by digital media. Language teachers use class exchanges to involve students in free-written communication with each other. In addition to dialogue journaling with the teacher, students are able to "talk" to each other individually and in groups. This kind of activity is called **computer-mediated communication (CMC)** and can be used both synchronously (immediate exchange of messages) and asynchronously (some time lag in exchange of messages, like social media or e-mail). Consider the following synchronous CMC exchange in a Spanish class.

VOICES FROM THE CLASSROOM

A Spanish teacher (Señora Escamilla) has arranged a CMC session for her third-semester class. The session takes place in the language computer lab at her university. In preparation for the session, the class has read a chapter (in Spanish) on youth culture in a number of Spanish-speaking countries, and Señora Escamilla starts the "conversation" by posting the first message. (Please note that this CMC discussion is meant to take place in Spanish, but I am using English here to make it easier for readers of all language backgrounds to follow.)

Señora Escamilla: (To Everyone.) Well, actually I found those summaries interesting but a little bit overwhelming. If I hadn't grown up in Ecuador and didn't know better, I think I would be thinking that teenagers in Spanish-speaking countries have it very difficult.

Elizabeth: Me too! So many times and things, things to do. And always family! I was a little afraid.

Kathleen: Señora, it's not difficult. It's like my family!

Señora Escamilla: Elizabeth, what do you find scary?

Elizabeth: I don't know. Maybe not scary, but I would be afraid to make a mistake if I went there.

Señora Escamilla: Elizabeth, if you went where? The point of the chapter is that there are important differences in all the countries.

Joe: Kathleen, it's like my family too! Do you all eat dinner together every day?

Spanish Guy: (Some teachers allow or even encourage students to use pseudonyms for CMC discussions.) Elizabeth, every place is scary, until you're there.

Kathleen: Joe, every day and every Sunday!

El Jefe: (To Everyone.) What did everyone think about that school in Buenos Aires?

Elizabeth: Spanish Guy, you're a real philosopher ☺

Señora Escamilla: (To Everyone.) Do descriptions like this help you understand Spanish-speaking cultures better, or do you think they just create more stereotypes?

Unlike typical oral discussions, this CMC discussion is really a group of conversations. Señora Escamilla first addresses the whole class, but then addresses a comment only to Elizabeth, Kathleen and Joe start talking to each other, Spanish Guy starts talking to Elizabeth, and El Jefe and Señora Escamilla attempt to start new topics with the whole group. CMC allows students to start or find a conversation they like and ignore other conversations. People even sometimes change their screen names in the middle of a CMC session to start a new conversation or get out of one they want to avoid. I can imagine Elizabeth getting tired of all the comments being directed at her and attempting to change the topic. Could she be El Jefe? CMC also allows students to participate at their own pace. CMC discussions often can seem choppy, since a student can respond to a previous comment at any point in the conversation. This feature can be especially helpful for language learners who feel that by the time they have decided what to say and how to say it in a normal class discussion, their comment is no longer relevant.

Some teachers, like Señora Escamilla, use written materials as a basis for CMC discussions while others simply allow students to use the CMC session to talk to each other in the target language. Many teachers also use CMC to accomplish explicit learning goals. In this case, the chapter likely contained a great deal of important cultural information, but Señora Escamilla seems more interested in the students' emotional reactions than their understanding of the chapter's specific content.

A number of studies have shown that CMC, like other types of free-written expression, gives students more opportunities to communicate in the target language, less anxiety (learners who are reticent to talk in class often participate actively in written discussions), and the opportunity to reflect before they have to "speak." The use of a written text as a discussion focus also gives students a model for their "written" comments and may elicit a more formal variety of language than standard class discussions. Especially in teaching situations where large class sizes make it difficult to give students turns speaking, electronic conversation is an attractive alternative. CMC is also a good way to include both ELs and English speakers in content discussions, and a number of foreign language educators use electronic discussions to pair language learners and target language speakers. Language educators disagree about whether the type of language produced in CMC is really writing. Some scholars believe that electronic communication is more similar to recorded speech (oral language), though most conclude that it is its own variety of language, containing features of both oral and written language as well as unique computer-based elements (e.g., emoticons). With the integration of digital media into all aspects of life, CMC is similar to writing your students will do in their daily lives.

Digital Storytelling

Having children create and "publish" their own picture storybooks has been a mainstay activity in L1 language arts programs for a long time. Recently, many second language teachers have been using an exciting new technological approach called **digital storytelling (DS)**. There are a number of websites and software options available (search for "digital storytelling") in a number of languages with varying capabilities that allow students to create their own animated storybooks. Typically, the programs add written scripts to the animations based on the choices the learner makes. For example, the learner could choose a particular cartoon character and decide that the character is happy. After pressing the correct icon, the sentence "Once upon a time, there was a happy panda" appears. If the student decides that the character is old rather than happy, he or she could click on the "old" icon and the script would change. Students are also able to change the script as they wish, changing "once upon a time" to "a long time ago" or rewriting the script entirely. When students have finished their story, they can print it and/or post it.

Depending on the particular program and the content addressed in the story, DS has the potential for developing listening, speaking, reading, writing, cultural understanding as well as academic language. Each time the program generates a new caption, students must read it to check if that is what they want to say. They can also listen to different versions of the script, talk to other students about their book, and so on. DS is adaptable to learners of all ages and ability levels and allows students to "write" even before they have developed the ability to form letters in the new language.

Writing Genres

One large complication in the teaching of writing is the wide variety of types of writing that students may need to do. Depending on their individual circumstances, students may have to fill out registration forms, write a letter to a relative or a note to a classmate, prepare a college entrance essay, or outline content material. Similar to oral registers, each **writing genre** has conventions for format, organization, necessity of grammatical correctness, and level of formality. For example, some misspellings and grammatical errors are tolerated in e-mail, but similar errors in a college essay could easily result in a rejected application. Teachers, too, may have very different genres in mind when they think about teaching writing to their students. Some teachers think of writing as recorded speech while others imagine research papers or essay examinations or even poetry and other forms of creative writing. Writing genres associated with school tasks (essays, compositions, research reports, term papers) require formal academic language, while those associated with expressive writing (diaries, letters, plays) can use more conversational language. It is important to consider students' specific writing needs before deciding which writing genres to concentrate on. Whenever possible, it is helpful to consult with potential consumers of your students' writing (content teachers, employers, etc.) to determine the kinds of written tasks that will be expected of them. The fields of English for Specific Purposes and Writing for Specific Purposes study the kinds of writing required in particular work and professional settings.

Helping Students Develop Effective Writing Strategies

It is difficult to separate successful second language writing from a student's knowledge and ideas about the topic. When we think about how well students speak in a second language we tend to think about their accent, their grammatical accuracy, and their ease of expression; however, when we think about their writing we usually think about the quality of the ideas that they express. Thus, when students write in a second language, in addition to producing comprehensible second language sentences in a logical order, they must have something to say. Brainstorming can help students generate ideas to use in their writing and outlining can help them organize and sequence their thoughts. Brainstorming and outlining are generally considered **prewriting strategies**, but they could, of course, be used at any point in the writing process.

VOICES FROM THE CLASSROOM

Ms. Vu, a content-based ESL teacher at a middle school, is using a lesson on precolonial Native American tribes to teach her students how to outline. As she speaks, she writes her outline on an overhead transparency and the students copy it into their history notebooks. Later they will use it as a model for their own outlines. (You should also notice how good Ms. Vu is at expanding her student's comments.)

Ms. Vu: OK, I know that there were a lot of tribes in your history book, and I want to help you keep track of them. Let's start with the tribes in the southeastern United States. What were some of them?

Olivia: One was the Natchez.

Ms. Vu: Great! The Natchez were farmers. Was there another tribe of farmers in the Southeast?

Angel: The Muskogean live in Southeast. They also farmer.

Ms. Vu: Yes, that's right the Muskogean were also farmers. Both the Natchez and the Muskogean used tools to farm.

After all the tribes have been mentioned and listed, Ms. Vu continues:

Ms. Vu: OK, now that we've listed all the tribes that lived in the Southeast, what do we need to know about them?

Hue: Eat.

Ms. Vu: Right, we need to know what they ate. What else?

Sophia: What they believe.

Ms. Vu: Absolutely! We need to know about their beliefs and religions.

After the students have mentioned the important categories, Ms. Vu begins her outline:

Ms. Vu: OK, we are going to start with our topic. Our topic right now is Native Americans from the southeastern United States. So we are going to write that with a roman numeral *I* like this:

I. Native Americans from the southeastern United States

Next, I'm going to list all the groups that we mentioned. I'm going to use capital letters for that. So we have:

I. Native Americans from the southeastern United States

   A. Natchez

   B. Muskogean

Finally, after each tribe we can use regular Arabic numerals—regular numbers—for the things we know about each one, like this:

I. Native Americans from the southeastern United States

   A. Natchez

      1. What do they eat?

      2. How do they get their food?

      3. What are their beliefs?

      4. What do they produce?

   B. Muskogean

      1. What do they eat?

      2. How do they get their food?

      3. What are their beliefs?

      4. What do they produce?

Ms. Vu: Do you see how outlines work? They help you keep your information organized, and we sure have a lot of information about Native Americans to organize! Outlines also help you when you write. If we wanted to write about Native Americans and started without an outline, it would be hard to know what to talk about first, and we would probably leave out many important things.

When students think about important strategies for the actual production of written compositions, they usually think of using dictionaries. Although language teachers have varying opinions about how, and even if, students should use dictionaries when composing, with easy access to electronic bilingual dictionaries it is probably not realistic to think that students' out-of-class dictionary use can be controlled. Therefore, it is probably better to teach students to use dictionaries effectively than to hope they won't use them. Students should be made aware that when they look up a native language term in a bilingual dictionary they will find a number of possible alternatives and must make the difficult decision of which one to use. I will never forget the time one of my students used a bilingual dictionary to help him write a summary of a film I had shown. The film showed a young male customer flirting with the female salesperson. My student looked up "pick up" in a bilingual dictionary and produced the sentence "Michel tried to pick up Caroline." But instead of choosing a verb that meant "pick up" in the sense of dating, he chose a verb used for fallen objects. When he read his summary aloud, I burst out laughing as I imagined Michel trying to gather up all of poor Caroline after she had broken apart on the floor. After that incident, I always reminded my students to check the meaning of any word they had found in the native language section of their dictionary in the target language section to avoid using an illogical term.

In addition to dictionaries, teachers should be aware of new electronic tools which are becoming available to second language writers: **language corpora**. Corpora include large amounts of text which have been scanned into searchable databases. By searching one of these databases, a student can find which words in a language tend to go together, a phenomenon called **collocation**. In American English, for example, the noun "role" tends to go with the verb "play." So an American speaker would be more likely to say "My daughter *played* the *role* of the butterfly in her school play" even though the verb "acted" would seem to be a synonym for "played." By searching a corpus for "role," a student could find a number of sentences that use the term and see other vocabulary words that tend to be used with it.

Finally, revision is a crucial writing strategy. Students need to realize that whatever they write will be revised several times before it is finished. In many cases, revisions will bring about changes in the actual ideas being expressed. Since students often think in terms of producing a draft, proofreading it, and then turning the paper in, teachers need to build revising steps into writing assignments. For example, students could be required to show their compositions to two other students and include the other students' comments with their completed paper. Students could also turn in a preliminary version of the paper and have a conference with you before they turn in the final revised version.

Unrealistic Expectations

Learners often have very different ideas from their teachers about what it means to write in a second language. To some learners, writing in a second language means translating their first language thoughts word by word as best as they can into the new language. Others think they should write down whatever comes into their head and turn the paper in to their teacher. Students who can already write in their first language expect that writing in their second language will use the same organizational patterns as writing in their first language. In many cultures, writing is associated with artistic endeavor, and students are taught to emulate the writing styles of respected masters.

Consider the following classroom exchanges:

VOICES FROM THE CLASSROOM

Ms. Chang is teaching her high school English class in Taiwan how to write an American-style essay.

Ms. Chang: Americans usually start an essay with an introductory topic sentence or paragraph that announces what they are going to say.

Angela: But essays are supposed to show your knowledge and that you understand wise authors. Don't Americans know that?

Ms. Chang: American culture teaches them that each person should write personal thoughts.

Dr. Park is teaching a senior EFL writing class in a university in Korea. Some of the students want to go to graduate school in the United States, and Dr. Park has assigned them to write college entrance essays. He has underlined some of the words and is projecting an excerpt from one of the essays.

Excerpt: I want to study in your <u>esteemed</u> program because I hope to gain much <u>more practical knowledge</u> and learn to teach English more <u>efficiently</u>.

Dr. Park: I have underlined some terms in the essay that are more Korean in style than American. Americans like specifics, especially in graduate school application essays. One of my professors in the United States told me that phrases like "more practical knowledge" and "efficiently" are too general. To an American, this sentence means something like "I want to learn some things and teach better."

It would be better to say something like, "I want to study in your program because I hope to better understand how to teach students to communicate in English."

> *Ms. Ahn:* Why did you leave out "esteemed"? Now the sentence isn't polite.
>
> *Dr. Park:* My professor also told me that Americans think that words like *esteemed* sound like you are flattering them and that Americans feel uncomfortable if they think they are being flattered.

In these two examples both Ms. Chang and Dr. Park understand that there are cultural differences in writing styles that their students must overcome, but the two teachers used different approaches to teach their students about the differences. Ms. Chang described the kind of introduction that her students should write, while Dr. Park showed students an example of a writing style that would not be successful in English and suggested a better alternative. In both cases, the teachers recognized that their students would need to modify their expectations about how to write and what to include in order to produce a successful English essay.

Some Guidelines for Teaching Writing

Since there are so many types of written genres, it is important to select writing tasks that are connected to students' specific language needs, especially if they have academic or career purposes for writing. By coordinating reading and writing assignments, teachers give students models, language structures, and ideas that they can apply in their writing.

1. *Have realistic expectations for writing.* New teachers are often surprised and a little dismayed at their students' writing ability. Many language learners, even those with good oral proficiency, will write at the novice level since written language must be more precise and organized than oral language. (See Chapter 9 for a description of the ACTFL proficiency levels including *novice.*) It is also important to remember that students are able to use single words and phrases to participate in conversations, but that written text requires full sentences. In addition, novice writers often make mistakes in even basic structures, and you should expect that students will continue to make errors even in structures that you have "corrected" before.

2. *Include a variety of writing activity types.* Assign a variety of structured, communicative, expressive, and academic writing activities and help students understand the requirements of each type of writing. Structured writing helps students gain control of new grammatical structures, while expressive writing can help them learn to express their ideas with less hesitation. Communicative and academic writing should be used to help students express their ideas more accurately and precisely.

3. *The type of writing assignment should dictate the type of error correction and teacher response.* Explicit corrections are more appropriate for structured and academic writing than for communicative and expressive writing, but it is always important to respond to the students' ideas. Unfortunately, it is not always easy to figure out what a student is trying to say. In that case, mark the specific sentences and tell the student that you don't understand. I often found that sentences I could not understand were word-for-word translations from the learner's first language.

4. *Help your students develop realistic expectations about writing.* Since students have more time when they write than when they speak, they may be even more likely to try to translate from their L1. Try to discourage translation by telling students to think in the new language and reminding them that they will have opportunities to revise. They should understand that the ideas that they will be able to express in the new language will not be as sophisticated as the ideas they can express in their first language.

5. *Help students consider and organize their thoughts before writing.* Encourage students to brainstorm, outline, and plan their writing before they get started. Just as with reading, it is a good idea to include prewriting activities to remind students of information they already know that might be useful for a particular assignment.

6. *Point out specific conventions of the writing genre.* Do not assume that students will know what to include in their writing; give them clear guidelines about necessary components. If, for example, students need to write an argumentative essay in English, tell them it will need an introductory paragraph with a statement of their thesis, several arguments, and a concluding paragraph that takes their analysis a step beyond their original thesis. You also could show them several samples of argumentative essays so that they can see concrete examples of the type of writing you are assigning and remind them of specific vocabulary words and structures that may be useful in their writing.

7. *Try group writing.* We tend to associate group work with oral activities rather than written ones, but small-group writing activities can be effective as well. Group interaction and negotiation helps learners determine what they want to say and to phrase their ideas more comprehensibly.

8. *Use electronic communication.* Electronic writing can make writing more motivating and even fun for students. By communicating with a real person (you, their classmates, native-speaking peers), they have an authentic reason to write.

9. *Coordinate writing assignments with the materials students are reading and content material they are learning.* Due to differences in writing conventions or limited first language literacy, many students will have little idea of how a written text should be organized. Having students read authentic texts with a similar structure gives students a model for their work. In addition, having students write about content that they have learned gives them practice with the kind of writing they will need in academic classes.

10. *Give students guide questions.* Another way to help students organize their ideas into a particular writing format is to guide them through the writing with targeted questions. When they have answered your questions, they will have produced a draft of the assignment.

11. *Help students develop effective dictionary strategies.* Have a class discussion about how to use dictionaries and other writing resources.

12. *Encourage revision.* Encourage students to think of writing as a process and build revision into writing assignments.

13. *Be aware of the role of affect in writing.* Many people feel uncomfortable writing in their first language, and when writing in a second language they must deal with the additional problem of their limited language proficiency. Encourage students to stop and brainstorm or to break the writing task down into smaller steps, especially if they experience writer's block. Unfortunately, teachers sometimes add to their students' writing anxiety. Avoid telling students that a particular writing assignment or type of writing is hard, and try to correct errors gently.

Activity Ideas

Students have a particularly wide variety of writing needs. This section focuses primarily on beginning and intermediate writers and includes structured, communicative, and expressive writing activities. Chapter 8 includes more examples of academic writing.

Structured Writing Activities

Activity 1	**"Class Survey"**
Implementation	Prepare a survey questionnaire with questions about your students' interests, hobbies, favorite TV shows, favorite colors, etc., and have students fill it out. Groups of students could then summarize different parts of the survey and submit a written "report" to the class.
Activity 2	**"Recipe Swap"**
Implementation	After reading or using a recipe in class have students write their own recipes and share them with the class. The recipes could be gathered together as a class cookbook.
	(NOTE: If students have already seen written recipes, they will have a guide for writing their own. Writing recipes will give students practice using sequencing and transition terms.)

Activity 3	***"Put It in Writing!"***
Implementation	Give students a Mad Lib story format to fill in. Have students share and edit their Mad Libs in groups of three or four students. After students revise their Mad Libs, gather the papers to share with the class. You could read them to the class for listening comprehension practice or prepare booklets or Power-Points for students to read.

Communicative Writing

Activity 1	***"Dear Blabby"***
Implementation	Have students write letters about their "problems" to the well-known advice columnist "Dear Blabby." Put all the student letters into a bag, and then have each student draw someone else's letter and write advice for that person's problem.
Activity 2	***"Take My Advice"***
Implementation	Have students write a letter to new students who will be in your class next year. Ask them to tell the new students anything they need to know about the class and any advice they have for them.
	(NOTE: This activity has many variations. For example, students could write advice letters to younger siblings or new teachers in their school.)
Activity 3	***"First, He Puts on Plaid Pants and a Flowered Shirt"***
Implementation	Ask students to describe a day in the life of someone that the other class members would recognize. You could give them a page from a daily planner to use for the assignment. One of my students described our school principal starting with the title of this activity.
Activity 4	***"Let's Stay Connected"***
Implementation	Use social media or other appropriate electronic resources to create class groups. Students could discuss assigned topics or readings or just "talk" about whatever they choose.
Activity 5	***"Author! Author!"***
Implementation	Use digital storytelling.

Expressive Writing

Activity 1	*"Word Associations"*
Implementation	There are several variations to this activity, and they can be done over a period of several days.

1. Give students a word and ask them to write down the first target language word that comes into their minds. You can then ask several students for the word they wrote down. You can respond to their words with comments like: "How interesting!" "I thought of that one too." or "You had the same word as _____." "Did anyone else have that one?" Since there are no correct answers, this activity gives every student a chance to participate. After all, every response is correct for the student who gave it. I would repeat this process for five to ten words.

2. This type of word association is similar to the first one, but this time ask your students to write down the first five words that come into their minds. Ask various students to report one of their answers, perhaps the one that they think is most interesting or the one they like the best. You could also use a picture or an abstract design rather than a word for the word associations.

3. Give students a minute to write down as many word associations as they can think of. Call on some students to give their favorite word and ask others how many words they were able to list. Take a show of hands to see who was able to list the most words.

(NOTE: These activities are especially good for beginners since students do not have to actually do a lot of writing. Word associations give students practice putting together unusual combinations of words and gets them past the rote responses they may rely on as beginning learners.)

Activity 2	*"Stream of Consciousness Writing"*
Implementation	Ask students to get out pen and paper. Give students an amount of time starting with one minute and working up to five minutes to write in their target language.

(NOTE: This activity is designed to help students get past their tendency to think more about their grammar than about what they want to say.)

Activity 3

Implementation

"Friday Specials"

Friday Specials are short expressive writing assignments designed to emphasize the communication of
meaning. (Leemann and Waverly, 1977, coined the
term *Friday Special*.) The directions are as follows:
"Every Friday (or whatever day is convenient to the
teacher) you will write me three, four, or five sentences
in the target language." I think that this approach
would adapt very well to social media.

(NOTE: This assignment is a mini version of the
dialogue journal discussed at the beginning of this
chapter. It is important to write a personal target
language response to the students' comments. You can
also correct obvious errors. Sometimes beginning students copy sentences out of a book rather than writing
their own. In that case, respond to the sentences as if
they were meant to be communicative (e.g., "Oh, why
did Mr. Smith turn right to go to the library?").

Activity 4

Implementation

"Dear Diary"

Journal writing is a natural extension of Friday Specials and should be responded to in the same way. Ask
students to write at least one paragraph in a personal
journal or diary on a regular basis. I asked students to
write in their journals four or five times a week so that
the assignment wouldn't become burdensome.

(NOTE: Responding to any kind of journal writing—
Friday Specials, dialogue journals, or student
journals—is very time-consuming for the teacher.
You should plan the schedule of this kind of activity
carefully since students anticipate a quick response to
journal writing. When I had students keep journals in
my classes, I would limit the assignment to one class
at a time and collect one student's journal each night
rather than collecting the whole class at the same
time. It is not necessary to respond to every journal
entry. Just respond to the entries that interest you and
answer any questions the students address to you.)

Academic Writing

Activity 1

Implementation

"Getting Down to the Basics"

Have students prepare outlines of a textbook chapter
or a section of a textbook chapter that they are reading

for a content class. Divide students into groups of students who are outlining the same chapter. Each group of students should compare their outlines and then prepare a master outline for the group. Make copies of the master outline so that each group member gets one. If more than one group has outlined the same materials, have the groups compare their master outlines. Outlining content material gives students the opportunity to use more formal varieties of the language.

Activity 2	***"In Summary"***
Implementation	Have students write a summary of a short story that the whole class has read or part of a chapter from one of their content textbooks.

Assessing Writing

Due to the large variety of writing goals and genres, and the difficulty of separating the quality of the writing from the quality of the ideas, rubrics similar to the ones used for the assessment of speaking are probably the best option in evaluating a single piece of writing. Rubrics can be varied according to specific goals for each writing assignment. Rubrics can also include content objectives, as in this example.

Task: Students are asked to write an essay describing the lifecycle of a frog. They are told to include an introductory paragraph noting the frog's place in the animal kingdom and a concluding paragraph comparing the frog's lifecycle to another natural event.

Introduction (Content)	Classification is incorrect.	1　2　3　4　**5**	Classification is correct.
	Comments: *Good job!*		
Introduction (Writing)	Topic of essay is unclear.	1　2　3　**4**　5	Clear topic sentence includes good use of descriptive language.
	Comments: *I wasn't sure if you were writing about frogs or tadpoles. Tadpoles are just one stage in the frog's lifecycle. You should only use "tadpole" when you are talking about that stage of the lifecycle. Otherwise your introduction was very good.*		

Body of Essay (Content)	Some stages are left out, stages are not in the right order, or they are described incorrectly.	1 2 3 4 5	All stages of the lifecycle are included, described accurately, and in the correct order.

Comments: *You left out the female laying the egg. That is a very important stage in the lifecycle.*

Body of Essay (Writing)	It is very difficult to follow the sequence of the stages. Sequence and transition terms are either absent or not used correctly.	1 2 3 4 5	Stages are described clearly. Excellent use of sequence and transition terms.

Comments: *I was a bit confused when you talked about the legs falling off. Is that a separate stage or part of the "frog" stage? If you use terms **like "first" and "second," you wouldn't need to keep repeating "next,"** and it would be less confusing for the reader.*

Conclusion (Content)	Use of L1 and false cognates.	1 2 3 4 5	Precise and appropriate word choice.

Comments:

Conclusion (Writing)	Especially poor for a student at this level.	1 2 3 4 5	Especially good for a student at this level.

Comments:

Overall Quality of the Writing	Especially poor for a student at this level.	1 2 3 4 5	Especially good for a student at this level.

Comments: *I liked your essay very much. Your writing was very clear, and you really understand frogs!*

It would be better to use the present tense for this kind of essay. You used the past tense, and it made it sound like you were talking about one frog rather than frogs in general. Please rewrite this in the present tense and use "frogs" rather than "the frog" as your subject. When you rewrite this, please be sure to make the other corrections I have marked on your paper.

I can't wait to see your next draft. I think it is going to be great!

Portfolios are another excellent approach for evaluating student writing, with the added advantage of involving learners in the evaluation process. Some teachers have students include all their written work over a given period of time, while others ask students to choose representative works for their portfolio. At certain times throughout the year, students are asked to review their portfolios in preparation for a conference with their teacher. Some teachers give students a rubric, such as the following, to include with their portfolios.

Progress	I feel that I have made (substantial, some, little) progress in writing since my last portfolio conference.
	Reasons for your answer:
	I feel that I have made the most progress in these areas of writing.
	Why?
	I feel that I have made the least progress in these areas of writing.
	Why?
	Teacher comments:
My Favorite Writing Sample	This is my favorite piece of writing because . . .
	Teacher comments:
My Most Typical Writing Sample	I think that this piece of writing is most representative of my writing because . . .
	Teacher comments:
My Writing Goals for the Next Portfolio Conference	**Student comments:**
	Teacher comments:

FINDING YOUR WAY

REFLECTIONS

What role do you think writing should have in a second language curriculum?

_____

_____

_____

_____

_____

PLANNING FOR YOUR CLASSES

Is writing an important language skill for your students? What kinds of writing will they need to be able to do?

_____

_____

_____

_____

What kinds of writing will your students have to do on standardized tests?

_____

_____

_____

_____

PROJECTS

- Keep a record of writing activities that you want to try in your own classes.
- With a group of other teachers, compare the structure and style of various types of writing in your first language and your second language.
- Discuss the types of writing tasks your students will encounter in any required standardized tests.
- Your methods instructor will show you some examples of student compositions. How would you describe the kinds of written errors you see? Did the amount and kinds of errors surprise you?

IN YOUR JOURNAL

- How do you feel about teaching writing? Are you comfortable with your own writing abilities?
- Many adults wish that their teachers had corrected their errors more when they were young. Do you now wish that your language teachers had corrected your writing more?

TEACHING CHECKLIST

This checklist will help you quickly evaluate the way you teach writing.

Yes	No	
☐	☐	I devote an adequate amount of class time to writing.
☐	☐	I assess my students' writing needs.
☐	☐	I encourage my students to plan what they want to say before they begin to write.
☐	☐	I coordinate the way I correct and respond to students' writing to the type of writing assignment.
☐	☐	I use structured, communicative, expressive, and academic writing assignments according to my students' writing abilities and needs.
☐	☐	I provide opportunities for peer editing and revision.
☐	☐	I help my students understand that writing in a second language is not translation from their L1.
☐	☐	I respond to the *ideas* expressed by students in their writing assignments.
☐	☐	I encourage my students to reflect on differences between how they have expressed an idea in writing and how more proficient writers express their ideas.
☐	☐	I include writing in my assessment and testing procedures.

REFERENCES AND SUGGESTIONS FOR FURTHER READING

Birdsong, D., & Kassen, M. A. (1988). Teachers' and students' evaluations of foreign language errors: A meeting of minds? *Modern Language Journal, 72,* 1–12.

Breiner-Sanders, K. E., Swender, E., & Terry, R. M. (2002). Preliminary proficiency guidelines—Writing (revised 2001). *Foreign Language Annals, 35,* 9–15.

Cheng, Y. (2002). Factors associated with foreign language writing anxiety. *Foreign Language Annals, 35,* 647–656.

Chiang, S. (2003). The importance of cohesive conditions to perceptions of writing quality at the early stages of foreign language learning. *System, 31,* 471–484.

Cumming, A. (2009). Assessing academic writing in foreign and second languages. *Language Teaching, 42,* 95–107.

Dykstra-Pruim, P. (2003). Speaking, writing, and explicit-rule knowledge: Toward an understanding of how they interrelate. *Foreign Language Annals, 36,* 66–76.

Ferris, D., & Hedgcock, J. (2005). *Teaching ESL composition: Purpose, process, and practice* (2nd ed.). Mahwah, NJ: Lawrence Erlbaum.

Ferris, D., & Roberts, B. (2001). Error feedback in L2 writing classes: How explicit does it need to be? *Journal of Second Language Writing, 10,* 161–184.

Frankenberg-Garcia, A. (2010). Raising teachers' awareness of corpora. *Language Teaching,* 1–15. Available on CJO 2010 doi:10.1017/S0261444810000480.

Harklau, L. (2002). The role of writing in classroom second language acquisition. *Journal of Second Language Writing, 11,* 329–350.

Hudelson, S. (1988). Writing in a second language. *Annual Review of Applied Linguistics, 9,* 210–222.

Huie, K., & Yahya, N. (2003). Learning to write in the primary grades: Experiences of English language learners and mainstream students. *TESOL Journal, 12,* 25–31.

Hyland, K., & Hyland, F. (2006). Feedback on second language students' writing. *Language Teaching, 39,* 83–101.

Lee, I. (2007). Feedback in Hong Kong secondary writing classrooms: Assessment for learning or assessment of learning? *Assessing Writing, 12,* 180–198.

Lee, L. (2002). Enhancing learners' communication skills through synchronous electronic interaction and task-based instruction. *Foreign Language Annals, 35*(1), 16–24.

Leeman, E., & Waverly, L. (1977). Communication-based beginning college French: An experiment. In R. A. Schulz (Ed.), *Personalizing foreign language instruction.* Skokie, IL: National Textbook Company.

Li, X. (2007). Identities and beliefs in ESL writing: From product to process. *TESL Canada Journal, 25,* 41–64.

Luoma, S., & Tarnanen, M. (2003). Creating a self-rating instrument for second language writing: From idea to implementation. *Language Testing, 20,* 440–465.

Matsuda, P. K., & De Pew, K. E. (2002). Early second language writing: An introduction. *Journal of Second Language Writing, 11,* 261–268.

Paltridge, B. (2004). Academic writing. *Language Teaching, 37,* 87–105.

Reichelt, M., & Silva, T. (1995–96). Cross-cultural composition. *TESOL Journal, 5,* 16–19.

Santos, T. (1988). Professors' reactions to the academic writing of nonnative-speaking students. *TESOL Quarterly, 22,* 69–90.

Shin, D., & Nation, P. (2008). Beyond single words: The most frequent collocations in spoken English. *ELT Journal, 62,* 339–348.

Slater, T., & Mohan, B. (2010). Cooperation between science teachers and ESL teachers: A register perspective. *Theory Into Practice, 49,* 91–98.

Steinman, L. (2003). Cultural collisions in L2 academic writing. *TESL Canada Journal, 20,* 80–91.

Suh, J. (2002). Effectiveness of CALL writing instruction: The voices of Korean EFL learners. *Foreign Language Annals, 35*(6), 669–679.

Xi, X. (2010). Automated scoring and feedback systems: Where are we and where are we heading? *Language Testing, 27,* 291–300.

8 What Should I Know About Teaching Academic English in Content Classes?

■ How is teaching content different from teaching language?
■ How is teaching content similar to teaching language?

SECOND LANGUAGE ACQUISITION IN THE CONTENT CLASS

Many language educators have come to view content-based language classes as the ideal environment for language learning and teaching. Content-based language classes differ from ordinary language classes and ordinary content classes in that they involve both language and content objectives for students, and they gear instruction to the needs of language learners. Of the language teaching methods described in Chapter 3, only the SIOP Model specifically addresses the integration of content, language, and cognitive development. Unfortunately, many language learners and teachers do not have the luxury of true content-based language classes, and English learners are often put in regular content classes with native-speaking peers. However, when teachers pay attention to the needs of ELs, content classes can afford many experiences conducive to language learning. Specifically, since content courses focus on the teaching of a specific subject matter, they can provide large amounts of *contextualized* comprehensible input and the opportunity for authentic conversations and negotiation of meaning as well as tasks that foster problem solving and cognitive development. Perhaps the greatest advantage of content classes for language learners is that they require students to listen, speak, read, and write the academic variety of English (or other second language), thereby promoting the development of academic literacy.

For the most part, the SLA theories presented in Chapter 2 do not make a distinction between the acquisition of everyday oral language and either oral or written academic language but simply refer to the acquisition of a second language in general terms. They do anticipate, however, that learners will not develop particular language abilities if they do not receive comprehensible input, practice, and communicative experiences in that variety of the language. The Output Hypothesis goes further to specify that learners be pushed to produce increasingly refined language and feedback, while the sociocultural theories recognize that high-level language use is intertwined with the development of higher-order thinking skills. To be successful in school, ELs must progress in their cognitive development, become acculturated into the academic culture, and understand and use academic language.

When a second language is taught through the medium of a content area such as mathematics or science, students have many occasions where they can communicate personally important messages, negotiate their understanding of the subject matter orally and in writing, and listen to and read contextualized authentic input. In other words, content courses automatically include many of the experiences associated with successful second language learning. In addition, since teachers in these classes are familiar with the content being learned and with what students may want to communicate, they are able to scaffold learners' conversational attempts by supplying needed vocabulary or structures. The thematic units used in content courses give students the opportunity to process and express similar ideas and language structures through tasks that require listening, speaking, reading, and writing. Finally, since target language use is intrinsically connected to the academic subject matter in content classes, the classes automatically include substantial amounts of the academic variety of language as well as problem-solving activities that are essential for success in school and careers.

Teaching Academic English: Some Important Concepts

Language Domains	■ Different types of language required for the discussion of different topics. Many topics require specific vocabulary and sometimes even specific grammatical structures.
Academic Language	■ The variety of language used for academic purposes in school settings.
Basic Interpersonal Communication Skills (BICS)	■ One of two types of second language proficiency described by James Cummins. BICS refers to a type of everyday language that is commonly used for social interaction. Also referred to as social language or even "playground" language.
Cognitive Academic Language Proficiency (CALP)	■ The other type of second language proficiency described by James Cummins. CALP refers to the more abstract variety of language commonly

	used in academic classes. Abstract language is used to discuss objects or people that are not present in the "here and now," as well as less concrete concepts.
Academic Literacy	■ The development of reading and writing abilities in academic varieties of language. Also refers to the development of content and cultural knowledge necessary to school success and the ability to function in the school environment.

The Development of Academic Language

Sociolinguists speak of **language domains** and recognize that people are generally more adept linguistically in some domains than others. I sometimes think of language learners as having a vitamin-deficient diet. That is, they may have abundant exposure to some language domains or kinds of language but little or no access to other essential varieties. Although most language learners will not encounter a full range of language domains in the course of their daily lives, content classes hold the possibility of addressing a wider range of language than typical stand-alone language classes. Perhaps the most important advantage to content classes for language learning is that students have access to **academic language**. English learners typically hear and use English in everyday social situations and through media use, but have fewer opportunities to listen to, read, or use the more formal and abstract varieties of English used in class discussions, written compositions, and other academic tasks. In fact, ELs who appear to be very "fluent" in oral varieties of English can still have difficulty with school assignments that require abstract reasoning and formal writing. (EFL and other foreign language learners can have the opposite problem of being exposed to formal but not conversational language, resulting in difficulties establishing social relationships.) Since language use in content classes is intrinsically connected to learning the academic subject matter, they automatically give students opportunities to use the academic variety of language and expose learners to important language domains such as life and physical sciences, mathematics, history, literature, and social science.

The development of language in various domains has been recognized as essential to school success. James Cummins argues that language learners need to develop at least two types of second language skills: **basic interpersonal communication skills (BICS)** and **cognitive academic language proficiency (CALP)**. **BICS** refers to the everyday here-and-now language commonly used on playgrounds or even in nonacademic content courses such as art and physical education. It can also be called social language or conversational language. In contrast, CALP, which I have been referring to as "academic language," is the more abstract variety of language used in academic (content) classes.

VOICES FROM THE CLASSROOM

Here are two brief conversations that took place before a GED class. Which of the two conversations is more indicative of basic interpersonal communication skills? Which is more indicative of cognitive academic language proficiency?

Conversation #1

Hassan: Hi, how are you today? Did you finish the homework?

Michiko: Yes, did you finish it?

Hassan: Not all of it. I was sick last night.

Michiko: Are you OK?

Hassan: I'm better today.

Michiko: That's good.

Conversation #2

Li: Hi, what's going on? Did you finish reading the homework?

Fatima: Yes, did you?

Li: Yes, but I don't know why the book says that multiplication and division are the same thing.

Fatima: Because division is the same as multiplying by a reciprocal.

In a series of studies of immigrant children to Canada, Cummins has determined that language learners develop BICS and CALP separately and that BICS language is often developed *long* before CALP language in a second language setting. Although new English learners can develop a substantial amount of BICS in their first year of exposure to English, it can take from five to seven years for them to develop full CALP proficiency. It is thus very common to see students who understand English very well in the cafeteria but who are "lost" during a social studies lesson. Educational backgrounds can have a lot to do with CALP development. Migrant children, for example, may come to school with good BICS in English but little CALP because of repeated interruptions in their schooling. In contrast, international students may have a great deal of CALP language but very little BICS.

Relatively little research has focused directly on the development of CALP language compared to the development of general L2 proficiency. We do know that CALP development continues in first language learners at least into their early teen years and that L2 learners who already have CALP in their L1 tend to develop CALP fairly readily in their L2. The development of CALP language is related to schooling and home literacy. Children from literate homes tend to have CALP experiences before starting school and typically enter kindergarten with some amount of CALP language already in place. It is, therefore, understandable why Cummins maintains that the development of CALP language itself is essential for the academic success of learners. To be successful in school, and ultimately in the work world, students need both highly developed language and highly developed cognitive abilities in addition to the content knowledge acquired in school (mathematics, science, social studies, and the like). The activities and subject matter in content courses not only provide practice using CALP language they also foster cognitive development and ultimately, higher-order thinking skills.

In sum, according to Cummin's research, the development of CALP language is essential for content learning, normal cognitive development, and general success in school. Because content teachers regularly come in contact with students' ability to understand and use academic language, they are in an excellent position to determine if students are progressing satisfactorily in the development of CALP language. Many language educators use the terms CALP and academic language interchangeably. The term **academic literacy** goes a step further to specify that learners be able to use academic language both orally and in writing along with appropriate content knowledge and the ability to function in school settings.

Here are some questions to ask when considering whether a student is progressing adequately in the development of academic literacy:

Helping Learners Develop Academic Language in Content Classes

Assess your learners' degree of language and cognitive development.

- What kinds of educational experiences has the student had previously?
- What kinds of language experiences has the student had outside of school, such as at home or in church?
- Does the student's level of cognitive development seem to be appropriate for the age and grade level?
- Does the student's knowledge of the world (animals, geography, life skills, etc.) seem to be appropriate for the age and grade level?
- Does the student seem to speak English well but still have difficulty learning content?
- Does the student seem to learn more successfully when the content is presented orally rather than through reading?
- Is the student able to participate in class discussions on abstract topics but unable to express similar ideas adequately in writing?

Generation 1.5 and Transnational Students

The distinction between BICS and CALP is especially critical in understanding a group of learners who have come to be called **Generation 1.5**. Generation 1.5 learners are longtime immigrants to the United States who are not literate in their first language and who also have language problems in English. They are called Generation 1.5 because they have characteristics of both first- and second-generation immigrants. Like second-generation immigrants, they can seem thoroughly acculturated into

American society, but, like first-generation immigrants, they may not be literate in English. Like other students with good BICS but little CALP proficiency, Generation 1.5 students tend to do fine in oral activities in school; however, their English difficulties become more apparent in content classes, especially when they must do academic writing. In fact, teachers may not even realize that these students are still language learners until they see their written work. Unfortunately, Generation 1.5 students are typically exited from ESL or bilingual classes because of their good oral proficiency and therefore receive little if any help to improve their English proficiency. For this reason, often the only chance they have to improve their English proficiency is through the intervention of alert teachers in their content classes.

Some Generation 1.5 English learners may simultaneously be **heritage learners** of their family's native language. Heritage learners typically can understand and speak their family language much better than they can read or write it. Thus, it is unfortunately possible that some Generation 1.5 English learners will not have a good CALP foundation in either English or their heritage language.

In addition to Generation 1.5 students, many ELs and their families are **transnationals** who move back and forth between the United States and their countries of origin. These learners may have gaps in their literacy development in both their native language and in English due to interruptions in their schooling in both countries. They may also have especially complicated feelings about their true cultural identities.

Scaffolding, Contextualized Input, and Thematic Units

When children learn their first language, they are exposed to large amounts of contextualized language input. Language input is **contextualized** when it refers to objects and actions in the learner's immediate environment. Thus, L1 learners experience clear connections between what is being talked about and the "talk" itself. When a mother talks about a toy, she is usually referring to a specific object, not to "toys" in general. Second language learners seldom receive large amounts of **concrete** "here and now" input (although some scholars suggest that children are more successful as second language learners because they receive greater amounts of concrete and contextualized input than older learners do). Content classes, however, typically include much greater contextualization of input than traditional language-based courses. Specifically, the teacher usually announces the topic under consideration and directs students to specific materials such as a chapter in the textbook that the students may have looked at in advance. Warm-up activities are also used to activate related background knowledge. Nonacademic classes, particularly art and physical education, pair visual demonstrations with relevant language. For example, an art teacher displays the necessary materials and explains the processes required when assigning a new art project, offering comments like "I like the way you used a bright color here" or "You need to hold your brush near the bottom, like this." Both academic and nonacademic content classrooms afford teachers the opportunity to negotiate meaning with students and to expand their students' communicative attempts and for students to clarify and restate their ideas. Thus, the oral interactions in content language classes approximate authentic communication because everyone involved has a stake in understanding what the other participants are saying.

Finally, the contextualization of language in content classes facilitates scaffolding by helping teachers understand and respond helpfully to learners' oral comments. Teachers are better able to anticipate the kinds of things students will want to say and to help them articulate their ideas through feedback and scaffolding. (The SIOP Model in Chapter 3 also offers good advice for contextualization and learner support.) Consider this example.

VOICES FROM THE CLASSROOM

A fourth-grade social studies class is discussing Greek civilization.

Adriana: I don't understand. Athens and Sparta are states in United States?

Mrs. Callison: No, Athens and Sparta are called city-states because each one is like its own country. Sometimes the word *state* means country, and the Greek cities are called city-states because they are small like cities but they still were separate countries in many ways. (Mrs. Callison pulls down a map of Ancient Greece and asks students to point out the various city-states.)

Since everyone has read the same chapter about Greek civilization, Mrs. Callison could be pretty sure that most of the students' comments and questions would be related to what they had just read. Thus, when Adriana asks if the cities are states in the United States, she can answer that Athens and Sparta are called city-states because they have characteristics of both cities and countries. By using the map at this point, students can see that the city-states are not in the United States and how their size and geographic locations make the label city-state appropriate. If Mrs. Callison had heard Adriana's question outside of the context of this specific social studies unit, it probably would have raised confusing questions about the student's total lack of geographic and historical perspective. How could the ancient Greek cities be in the United States?! How could any student think that?! But since she knew that the Adriana had just read about city-states, the source of the confusion was clear and fairly easy to address.

Promoting Second Language Development in Content Classes

Although content courses have several advantages for second language learning, they may also pose considerable obstacles to ELs. Ordinary content courses, as contrasted with Content-Based Instruction, are designed for native speakers, and so it is challenging for teachers to offer appropriate levels of comprehensible input for both proficient speakers and language learners. Language learners often have difficulty getting the floor in content classes because they cannot formulate their responses or comments as quickly as their English-speaking peers. And, importantly, teachers in content-based language classes are careful to develop specific language objectives for their students, while content teachers often concentrate on their specific content area, expecting the ESL or bilingual teacher to take care of language development.

Establishing Language Learning Objectives

One important difference between content-based language classes and regular content classes is the explicit emphasis on both language and content learning. By examining information and concepts in their subject area, content-based language teachers develop language objectives for their students and coordinate those objectives with the content to be taught. Some examples of language objectives for a middle school science class follow. Notice that there are objectives for both general and academic language development. (Figure 3.1 includes objectives for content and language learning within the SIOP Model.)

VOICES FROM THE CLASSROOM

In conjunction with a unit on oceans, Mr. Khoury developed the following language objectives for the English learners in his eighth grade science course:

1. Students will be able to describe the stages of meiosis and mitosis.

   Targeted language:

   Academic   Vocabulary related to cell reproduction
   General: Ordinal numbers such as first, second, and third, and sequential adverbs such as before, after, next, and finally

2. Students will be able to describe the distribution of ocean plant and animal life.

   Targeted language:

   Academic: Vocabulary related to oceanic regions and categories of plant and animal life
   General: Comparison adjectives such as warm, warmer, warmest; cool, cooler, coolest; deep, deeper, deepest

There are generally two ways to organize language objectives: around grammar and around the kinds of things learners will need to communicate. Historically, second language curriculum developers and textbook writers have sequenced instruction grammatically using activities based on what can be communicated by particular grammatical structures. For example, language textbooks often include **structured communication exercises** about students' daily lives after teaching how to tell time. (When do you come home from school? I come home from school at four o'clock.) In recent years, however, language educators are more likely to use syllabi organized around communication tasks and the kinds of ideas that people need to communicate. Topics on this type of syllabus might include narration in the present and the past, hypothesizing about the future, making requests, supporting an opinion, and apologizing. Classroom activities are typically organized around specific communicative and academic tasks: narration in the past pairs well with the study of history, while narration in the present tense could be used in connection with mathematics by asking students how they go about solving particular kinds of problems. Communicative syllabi stress the context of communicative acts and the relationships among vocabulary and various grammatical structures.

To identify appropriate language objectives, think about the language that is naturally associated with your content objectives. (According to the SIOP Model and the Cognitive Academic Language Learning Approach [CALLA], discussed later in this chapter, many speakers of different varieties of English, such as African American or Appalachian English, would also benefit from an explicit focus on language development in content classes.) It is important to recognize that language objectives are not typically achieved as quickly as content objectives. Students will likely need to continue to focus on many language objectives for the duration of a course. In other words, while it is commonplace to think of content objectives sequentially (students will learn how to add two-digit numbers and then learn how to subtract them), language is not developed one unit at a time, and students will not "know" a particular language objective simply because it has already been addressed in class. It is also true that students may achieve a particular language objective orally but not be able to control the same language in writing, or vice versa. For all these reasons, it is helpful to think of **recycling** language objectives and concentrating on the same objective or objectives at different points during the year.

Providing Appropriate Listening and Reading Input

One important challenge for the content teacher stems from the fact that the same listening and reading input may be simultaneously too difficult for some students and not sufficiently challenging for others. When ELs are **mainstreamed** in regular content classes, teachers may use a speech style that is comfortable for some students but too complicated and colloquial for the language learners. Ideally, to accommodate a range of language abilities and content background knowledge, reading materials would be individualized based on students' comprehension levels and educational backgrounds. Listening input can be made comprehensible to more learners by using **foreigner talk**. Teachers should articulate clearly and use high-frequency vocabulary words ("kick the ball *hard*" rather than "kick the ball *firmly*") and simple sentence structures ("stand there" rather than "I would like you to stand over there"). **Narrow listening** is another useful way to make listening input more comprehensible and can be easily incorporated into thematic units.

Content courses also include an important but demanding type of listening experience: class discussions. Class discussions are particularly difficult for language learners to follow since people in different parts of the classroom speak and interrupt each other and topics change frequently. Second language learners often complain that they have difficulty even telling the various speakers' voices apart. Since it is likely that many language learners will have difficulty learning content through class discussions, teachers should summarize each discussion or elicit a summary from students. This approach has the advantage of reinforcing the content of the discussion for all students.

Academic Literacy

Except in the unfortunate case of "sink or swim" submersion content and language learning, learners in content classes in the United States already have some, and perhaps even excellent, oral proficiency in BICS English. The primary focus in content classes should, therefore, be the development of academic reading and writing (and, of course, learning the content).

Reading

Chapter 6 described several ways to approach reading instruction with second language learners. Since the purpose of reading in content classes is to understand and remember concepts contained in textbooks and other reading materials, **reading to learn** is the most important type of reading students in these classes must be able to do. Unfortunately, ELs who lack either important content knowledge or CALP proficiency or both may have particular difficulty with this kind of reading. They are especially likely to be confused when the English they encounter in written text does not correspond to the informal and even nonstandard language they hear and use elsewhere. If you have ever traveled to another country, you have probably noticed how different the speech was from the somewhat artificial conversations and stories you had studied. ELs have the opposite problem, especially when it comes to reading. They hear informal speech every day but must read formal speech. Thus, their classroom reading materials can be doubly "foreign" to them. That is, the texts are written in English, which of course is a foreign language, and they are also written in a variety of English that is different from the one they are learning to produce orally.

In addition to using formal CALP language, reading materials in content classes can also contain a high density of unfamiliar concepts and vocabulary words. For example, a social studies text may define an abstract concept such as "population" or "urban area" and then go on to use the newly defined terms in increasingly complex ways. If a student does not understand the concept of population when first introduced, the content which follows in the textbook is likely to be almost incomprehensible. For this reason, bilingual dictionaries may be necessary in reading to learn because of the large amount of new vocabulary words in content readings and the need for a precise understanding of the words.

There are several ways that content teachers can help readers develop their ability to read to learn. Here are some suggestions:

Helping Learners Read to Learn in Content Classes

Help students understand that the language used in class materials is different from the oral language they use in social situations.

- Point out specific common examples of the way BICS and CALP language express the same idea.
- Have students identify instances of BICS and CALP language in various texts.

Make certain that students have the background knowledge they need to read a particular text.

- Preview reading materials to determine the background knowledge that students need to know.
- Use advance organizers and other prereading strategies to activate background knowledge.
- When necessary, teach students the necessary background information before asking them to read.

Teach specific content reading strategies.

- Tell students how to skim text to get the general idea of the material and activate background knowledge before reading.
- Encourage students to scan text in order to identify specific information, especially when reviewing content reading materials.
- Teach students to take notes and keep a record of important information. Reviewing notes and then rereading the text is a very helpful reading strategy.

Help students develop good dictionary strategies.

- Help students identify important words and distinguish between important and less important words.
- Encourage students to finish reading a paragraph before they jump to the dictionary.

When ELs in content courses have reading difficulties, it can be difficult to determine the source of their difficulties. A student may simply be at an early stage of English development, but it is also possible that the student does not know how to read in his or her first language, has a reading disability, or does not have sufficient academic background. Students from immigrant or refugee families may have had little formal schooling due to frequent family moves or the political situations in their home countries. Although the idea of assessing a student's first language reading ability in a variety of world languages may seem daunting, there are some simple things that can be done.

David Schwarzer, an L2 reading specialist, gives the example of a student at a high school where he was working. Several of the teachers suspected that this student could not read in her native Vietnamese and that her lack of L1 reading ability was the cause of her reading difficulties in English. Unfortunately, no one on the school staff understood Vietnamese, and teachers were at a loss as to how to assess her L1 reading ability. Professor Schwarzer had an elegant solution. He asked the student to bring in a book written in Vietnamese. When she arrived the next day with a book, he asked her to read it aloud. Although Professor Schwarzer speaks no Vietnamese, he saw that her reading was confident and animated. The student seemed delighted to show off a story that she obviously enjoyed. Professor Schwarzer quickly concluded that she could indeed read in Vietnamese and that her teachers should look elsewhere to help her read in English.

Of course, even without Professor Schwarzer's elegant solution, there are many possibilities for determining if students can read in their L1. You should observe if students seem comfortable and familiar with books and if they seem to associate written symbols with words. Simple questions about any books the family owns or reading activities students engage in can be helpful. Students can be asked directly if they own any books and if they can read in their first language (**self-assessment**). Whenever possible, teachers should consult with families to understand their students' previous educational experiences.

Writing

Written expression is highly valued in content classes and is often used to test content knowledge. Teachers are often surprised when a student with excellent speaking ability writes poorly; but as it is for a first language, good speaking ability in the second language does not necessarily translate into good writing ability. As noted in the Output Hypothesis, good writing requires more precision in vocabulary and expression than oral language. And, again, speaking typically uses BICS language, while students must use CALP language for academic writing. Consequently, content teachers often have difficulty determining whether a student's writing difficulties are due to an inability to write in English, lack of CALP language, difficulties understanding the content material, difficulties organizing concepts, or a combination of these factors. Moreover, since students are often required to learn content material through reading, writing difficulties may also be a result of reading difficulties.

It is important to understand the nature of academic writing to help learners develop their writing skills. Most academic writing requires more than the simple recording of ideas; it requires synthesis, analysis, problem solving, and other cognitive and content skills. For example, students in content classes are often asked to compare and contrast two concepts. In order to accomplish this type of writing task, students have to first determine how the two concepts are similar and different. If they cannot provide the required similarities and contrasts, or, more basically, if they do not understand the concepts, they are going to have difficulty with the writing assignment even if they can produce written sentences with good grammar and sentence structure. This is exactly the type of difficulty that a content teacher might anticipate with a student who is not progressing in terms of cognitive development. Consider the difficulties that Jaime is having comparing addition and multiplication:

VOICES FROM THE CLASSROOM

Jaime is a sixth-grader who has been asked to write a paragraph describing how addition and multiplication are similar and how they are different. The other students are absorbed in their writing.

Jaime: Mrs. Lincoln, I don't know what to do. I keep starting, but I don't know what to say.

Mrs. Lincoln (the math teacher):   First, just list ways that addition and multiplication are the same and then make a list of ways they are different.

Jaime: I don't know how they are the same or different; they're just two things you do in math class. Do you mean they're the same because we get quizzes on both of them?

Mrs. Lincoln: Well, yes, they're both things we do in math class, but I was thinking more in terms of . . . if you add numbers or if you multiply numbers are you doing the same or different things to the numbers. Hum . . . When you add, what do you do to the numbers?

Jaime: You add them! You put them together.

Mrs. Lincoln: Exactly! When you add you put numbers together. How about when you multiply?

Jaime: Oh, I see. Multiplying is putting numbers together, too. Is that what you want me to do?

Mrs. Lincoln: Yes, and now think of any other ways that adding and multiplying are the same, and then think about ways that they are different.

Jaime: OK, I will think about it.

In this interaction, Jaime cannot start writing because he does not understand how multiplication and addition can be compared. It is also possible that he doesn't understand what it means to compare and contrast something. Mrs. Lincoln helps him see the type of comparisons and contrasts she is looking for in the assignment, but Jaime must still think of his own set of similarities and differences in order to complete the assignment.

As with reading, ELs are likely to have difficulties stemming from the differences between the oral BICS language they are in the process of developing and the more formal CALP language required by academic writing assignments. Good academic writing also demonstrates an important characteristic called **coherence**. Coherence refers both to the logical sequence of a text and to the way ideas are related to each other. Good writing is not a simple listing of ideas: the writer must show readers how the ideas are connected, and the ideas must follow each other logically. The sentences in a paragraph must connect to each other and advance the central idea of the paragraph, and all the paragraphs in a paper must relate to each other and to the overall unity of the written text. As it was for Jaime, writers need to decide on the relationships among the ideas that they want to communicate so that they can make their writing coherent.

It can be more difficult to demonstrate coherence in writing than in speaking because speakers are able to use nonverbal behaviors such as gestures and facial expressions to help them establish coherence. One important aspect of coherence in written texts is the use of transition words and phrases to show readers the connections the writer sees between and among the ideas. For example, articles are an importance source of coherence in English. In the sentences "Phil ran into a friend while he was at the store. As the two were talking, the friend realized he was late and quickly said good-bye," the switch from the indefinite to the definite article signals to the reader that the sentence is now talking about a specific friend. There are, of course, many ways to achieve coherence in writing such as repeating phrases from one sentence to the next or using synonyms and pronouns to avoid repeating the same phrase over and over.

Integrating Language Skills Using Thematic Units and Task-Based Activities

As mentioned in Chapter 3, **task-based activities** have become very popular recently in both stand-alone and content-based language classes. Teachers in language classes attempt to design tasks that are similar to the ones students will have to perform in their content classes. Tasks work especially well with thematic units, such as "Our Community" or "Elizabethan England," which are often used in content classes.

Most tasks require the use of several second language skills as well as learners' other cognitive abilities, and students generally work in groups. The listening and reading components give students targeted input that they can later incorporate in speaking and writing. Conversation theories maintain that reusing the same vocabulary, language structures, and ideas reinforces learners' second language development, and from the perspective of the cognitive learning theories of SLA, language becomes more automatic each time the learner uses it. Students might first do a lot of listening and speaking to decide how to approach the task and what they want to accomplish. A research phase might follow where students gather information by reading. Finally, the production phase might involve negotiation and writing as students decide on the form of their finished product and how to produce it. Tasks give students the opportunity to produce the "precise, coherent, and appropriate" language required by the Output Hypothesis and are central to sociocultural theories because they are culturally embedded and incorporate authentic problem solving.

For example you might ask students to produce a travel brochure for a state. In this case, the content would center on the history and geography of the state, and the language objectives might include the use of imperatives (Visit Texas!) and describing location (Texas is located in the southwestern United States. It is bordered by Arkansas, Louisiana, Oklahoma, New Mexico, and Mexico.). To complete the assignment, students first join a group based on their choice of state. Next, each group decides how to go about finding information and what format they are going to use for their brochure. (Are they going to do it by hand or computer? What size paper are they going to use? Will they draw pictures or search for pictures on the Internet that they can cut and paste?) Next, the students need to decide on a set of topics to be included in their brochure and divide up the research by topics. When the research is completed, students produce the brochure. This step will entail much negotiation about the length and spacing of various sections so that the finished brochure is attractive and includes all the required information. Each section should be written and then exchanged among the students for peer editing. When finished, the brochures can be displayed on a bulletin board or used as part of a presentation on the fifty states.

Some Guidelines for Teaching Language Through Content

Activities in content classes should focus on both language and content objectives for ELs. ESL teachers in stand-alone or pull-out classes should identify the kinds of tasks students will have to accomplish in their content classes and include similar assignments in their language curriculum.

1. *Assess students' existing knowledge in the content area.* It is essential that classroom tasks be at the appropriate level of content difficulty. If a student is having difficulty learning content or accomplishing tasks, it is important to know whether the difficulty is due to limited second language development or to insufficient content background.

2. *Assess students' CALP language development.* It is especially important to be sure that students are progressing in their CALP language development. Be sure to look for differences in ease of expression when students are talking

about concrete "here and now" social topics (BICS) and more abstract academic topics (CALP). Look for opportunities to have "CALP" conversations with individual students.

3. *Choose tasks that require a variety of language skills.* The use of various language modalities (listening, speaking, reading, and writing) enhances language learning. The input derived from listening and reading gives students patterns that can be used as building blocks in oral and written language production, and the repetition and negotiation of ideas through speaking and writing helps learners clarify their ideas and state them more comprehensibly.

4. *Include targeted oral and/or written input as part of the content task so that students have a model for the kind of language they will have to produce.* Complex final products such as summaries or reports are usually more demanding for students than the projects that they are doing or did in their ESL or bilingual classes. For that reason, it is very helpful to include an oral or written model of the kind of language students will need to accomplish the task. For example, Task 2 ("Prove It!") in the next section asks groups of students to prepare mathematical proofs and has the teacher both explain and write a sample proof as the first step in the task. Hearing and seeing the teacher do the proof first gives students an idea of the scope of the task, the steps involved, as well as specific phrases and vocabulary that can be used. They can also refer to the teacher's original proof for relevant language patterns.

5. *Remind students about language learning and communication strategies that will be helpful in accomplishing a specific task.* Since content assignments are organized around independent, individual, and group work, strategy use is especially important. These strategies will also be helpful to students if they find themselves in a "sink or swim" situation in other content classes where they must rely on themselves to figure out an assignment.

6. *Include problem-solving tasks that require hypothesis generation and abstract thinking.* Although CALP language is clearly associated with the learning of content material, content tasks do not automatically involve CALP language. Students could probably report the steps of a famous science experiment, for example, without necessarily using abstract language (Mendel bought the pea plants. He planted them. Etc.). In order to ensure that the CALP variety of language is used in the completion of a task, the task must involve hypothesis generation (If I melt the wax, I think that it will weigh less because some might evaporate.) and abstract thinking (Do you think it's a good idea to pay people based on how much they need to support their family rather than on the actual value of their work?).

7. *Apply the SIOP Model and CALLA* (see next section).

Activity Ideas

Since the activities suggested in this section are tied to the learning of content material, they are more task-based than the suggestions in previous chapters. They involve greater integration of language skills and use both BICS and CALP language. In many cases, the tasks require both group consensus building (BICS) and the accomplishment of an academic task (CALP).

Task 1 (Science)

Language: Descriptive words, locations, and plant vocabulary.

Content: Local plants, characteristics of plants.

Organization: Small groups.

"I Spy!"

Divide the class into groups and give each group a different list of plants with pictures that can easily be found on the school grounds. Send the groups out to find their plants and have them write down a description of where each plant was found. In a second phase of this activity, each group could lead other class members to the places where their plants can be found. The group describes the plant in question, and the rest of the class has to guess which plant is being described. When the plant is identified, the group teaches the class the name of the plant.

Task 2 (Math)

Language: Sequencing and math vocabulary.

Content: Mathematical proofs.

Organization: Whole class and small groups.

"Prove It!"

At an appropriate point in the math curriculum, lead the class through the steps of a mathematical proof based on mathematical concepts with which they are already familiar. You could either demonstrate the proof yourself or, if you have already done proofs with your class, call on students to try to figure out the steps in the proof. Be sure that each step of the proof is clearly stated. Repeat and expand on any student comments and show the steps in writing (blackboard, overhead projector, or PowerPoint). Leaving the proof visible, call on students to explain each step. Divide the class into groups and give each group a similar proof to the one you have just worked on as a class. Have each group work through the steps of their proof and record their solution in writing. Then have each group present its solution to the class, giving a rationale for each step. The groups should also be prepared to answer questions about their proof.

Task 3 (History)

Language: Apologizing, narrating in the past.

Content: American history (causes of the Civil War).

Organization: Whole class and small groups.

"I'm Sorry!"

After a unit on the causes of the American Civil War, use a whole-class discussion format to develop a list of the five most important causes of the war (cotton, slavery, agrarian vs. more industrial economy, etc.). Divide the class into five groups—or have them choose groups—so that each group is assigned one of the five causes. Have the groups prepare a written statement explaining how their "cause" helped to start the Civil War. Next, have each group present an apology to the class for contributing to the war. For example, someone from the group representing cotton might say, "They call me King Cotton! I am very sorry for helping cause the Civil War. When people started growing me in the South, I thought I was going to be helpful since people could make cloth and other useful products out of me. I didn't realize that I would become such a valuable crop that the South would base most of its economy on me. The cotton industry was so big that the South couldn't survive without it. I am very sorry for the problems I caused."

Task 4 (Music)

Language: Persuasion and music vocabulary.

Content: Music styles.

Organization: Whole class.

"What Should We Sing?"

Present your class with a list of the songs they have learned and have them decide which ones they should sing for the parents' program the following month. Give them some criteria by which they should select the program (length of songs, variety of musical styles, pacing of the program, etc.). Have students give reasons for their suggestions and end with a class vote on the songs. They might also decide on one new song that they could prepare for the program.

Task 5 (Social Studies)

Language: Description, narrating in the present.

Content: World geography.

Organization: Whole class and small groups.

"What's It Like to Be You?"

After a unit on families across the world, divide students into groups focusing on a particular area (e.g., rural United States, urban China, United States–Mexico border). Have each group talk about the daily life of a hypothetical family from their area and develop a written schedule of what they think a child their age would do on a typical day. Each group should then make a drawing or a doll representing the child from their area and introduce the child orally to the class. The introduction should include a description of how the child is dressed, the child's daily schedule, and reasons for the child's schedule. Alternatively, a group member could role-play the child and the class could ask the "child" questions about his/her daily life.

The Cognitive Academic Language Learning Approach (CALLA)

Content-Based Approaches

Complementary SLA Theory	*Cognitive Academic Language Learning Approach*
Socio-Cognitive Theory An SLA theory combining cognitive learning and sociocultural theories of SLA.	■ Draws language learning objectives from specific academic content. ■ Coordinates instructional objectives with appropriate national and state standards. ■ Stresses the development of second language literacy. ■ Employs explicit strategy instruction for both content and language learning.

Like the SIOP Model discussed in Chapter 3, Anna Uhl Chamot's **Cognitive Academic Language Learning Approach (CALLA)** is a widely used method for teaching language through content. It emphasizes the dual nature of learning in content-based language instruction—learners must develop both academic concepts and academic language—and accordingly, it is based on a hybrid cognitive learning and sociocultural theory of SLA. CALLA is designed to develop English skills through content learning and is made up of 3 components:

1. The instructional topics are chosen from major content subjects.
2. Instruction focuses on the development of academic language and literacy.
3. There is explicit instruction in both content and language learning strategies.

The strong emphasis on learning strategy instruction (training) makes CALLA different from other approaches to Content-Based Instruction. The SIOP Model also includes strategy instruction, but CALLA elevates it to one of the three major components of the model. In addition to strategy instruction, CALLA embraces several related teaching approaches including literacy across the curriculum, cooperative learning, process writing, inquiry approaches, and the Language Experience Approach (Van Allen & Allen, 1976). In CALLA, the content curriculum dictates the language curriculum through which students are to develop listening, speaking, reading, and writing ability in every content area. Chamot believes that content learning is inherently more motivating than stand-alone language learning, and in CALLA, language objectives are chosen because of their natural relationship to the content being taught. In addition, by using content to guide instructional objectives, teachers are also able to focus on higher-order thinking skills.

As noted in Chapter 3, the question of whether second language acquisition/learning is similar to or different from other types of learning is an important controversy among SLA scholars. This issue becomes more complicated in content-based language learning since students are learning content and language simultaneously. Without resolving the general question of whether language learning and content learning are the same or different processes, a hybrid learning model such as the one underpinning CALLA seems reasonable for language learning in content settings. The cognitive learning element of Chamot's approach is similar to the **controlled processing** and **automatic processing** components of the cognitive learning SLA theory described in Chapter 2. Chamot is concerned with how learning—either language or content—becomes automatic through the interaction of declarative knowledge and procedural memory. **Declarative knowledge** "consists of facts and information that we know" (Chamot, 2009 p. 18) and "includes words (forms and meanings), facts, and rules, including our memory for images and sequences of events" (p. 9). **Procedural memory**, in contrast, refers to "things we know to do" (p. 18), and "underlies our ability to understand and generate language" (p. 9). Thus, Chamot agrees with the cognitive learning theory of SLA in that language learning is very similar to other types of learning and that with sufficient practice language becomes automatic.

VOICES FROM THE *CALLA* CLASSROOM

What teachers do:

- Conduct class in the target language ensuring that both the content and language is comprehensible to students. Monitor student comprehension.
- Identify, teach, and promote the use of learning strategies for the specific content and language objectives. Teach test approach strategies.
- Coordinate instructional objectives with state and national **standards**.
- Promote higher-order thinking skills.
- Use a variety of activity types such as cooperative learning, process writing, and inquiry approaches.
- Use **alternative assessment** procedures.

What students do:

- Participate in content learning activities that are designed to develop language literacy.
- Apply language and content learning strategies.
- Participate in a variety of learning activities including experiential learning.
- Engage in self-assessment.

Assessing Language in Content Classes

In order to assess language in the content classroom, it is important to be clear about both language and content objectives. Although many content-based language teachers choose to give separate grades for the language and content components of an assignment, it is never possible to separate the two areas completely since poor language use might make it seem that the learner does not understand the content well. The use of group work in content classes can also make it difficult to detect individual difficulties in either language or content.

All in all, rubrics that combine language and content criteria are a good assessment choice in the content classroom. The following is a generic example that can be modified for specific assessment purposes.

Accomplishment of Targeted Language Function(s)	The communicative function was not achieved.	1 2 3 4 5	The function was fully achieved.

Note: *You would do a separate rating for each language function.*

Amount of *Accurate* and *Appropriate* Information Successfully Communicated	No *appropriate* information was conveyed or the information was inaccurate.	1 2 3 4 5	The issue was fully and accurately explored.

Note: *In a content task, it is inadequate to record only the amount of information conveyed. The information must also be accurate and appropriate to the topic. At higher levels, the precision of the language is important.*

Use of Appropriate Language Structures	Inappropriate structures are used.	1 2 3 4 5	Appropriate structures for the task type are used.

Note: *For example, if the task involves narration in the past, using the past tense would be appropriate and using the present tense would be inappropriate.*

Sequence	Content is presented in a random order.	1 2 3 4 5	Sequence is logical. Ideas are well-organized and build on each other.

Note: *Appropriate sequencing of content helps indicate that the content has been understood. If the content is presented in an illogical fashion, it could indicate that the student is only copying phrases from other people or from source materials.*

Understanding of Content	Student shows little true understanding of the content material. Comments are formulaic and student is unable to respond to follow-up questions or complete novel examples.	1 2 3 4 5	Student shows excellent understanding of the material. Student shows original thought, synthesis, and/or can answer original questions or complete novel examples.

Note: *To be successful in school, students need to analyze and synthesize content material. Simple recall is insufficient.*

Word Choice	Student uses general rather than specific vocabulary and/or unspecific labels.	1 2 3 4 5	Student uses domain-appropriate vocabulary.

Note: *Specific and accurate word choice is associated with the development of CALP language.*

Since task-based activities provide time for planning, opportunities for revision, and the possibility of negotiation of meaning, students may produce more polished speech during task-based activities than they do in spontaneous conversations or class discussions. It is important to remember that the quality of students' language will vary according to the demands of each specific task. Students will have more facility in some linguistic domains than others and with some forms of language production (essays, summaries, short-answer questions) than others. Thus, because of the potential for substantial variation in the kind and quality of language that students will produce from task to task, **portfolios** are especially useful in monitoring the progress of ELs in content classrooms.

Since students usually know whether they understand content material or not, self-assessments can also be particularly helpful in the evaluation of content learning. In addition to helping you understand your students' academic strengths and weaknesses, self-assessments can help students become more aware of their accomplishments and areas of difficulties. The following example asks students to reflect on their subject matter competence and at the same time initiates a dialogue with the teacher about the student's concerns. Ideally, self-assessments would be done orally as a conversation with the teacher so that there could be an immediate discussion of any problems. If a conversation is not possible, you could also use a dialogue journal approach.

Dividing Fractions	I don't know how to divide fractions.	**1 2 3 4 5**	I am usually able to get the right answer when I divide fractions the first time I try.

What would you like to tell me about dividing fractions?

Note: *I included a place for the student's comments about division of fractions in this example since a student might have something to say that is not reflected by the actual rating. For example, the student might say, "I usually get the right answer, but I really don't understand what I'm doing when I divide fractions."*

Finally, although these methods do not translate easily into grades, observation and direct conversation are probably the best ways to determine what students understand and what they can actually do with language and content. As your students are working on their assigned tasks, walk around the classroom, watching, questioning, and making suggestions about strategies and materials. These interactions should give you a good idea of which students are engaged and which ones are simply watching others work.

FINDING YOUR WAY

REFLECTIONS

Why do some language learners have difficulty developing academic language proficiency?

_____

_____

_____

_____

_____

Why do some language learners have difficulty developing basic interpersonal communication skills?

_____

_____

_____

_____

_____

How is the development of CALP language related to the development of higher-order thinking skills?

_____

_____

_____

_____

_____

What does CALLA add to our understanding of how to teach language through content?

_____

_____

_____

_____

_____

PLANNING FOR YOUR CLASSES

How can you coordinate with (other) content teachers in your setting to make sure the content and language tasks you design are consistent with what students will have to do in their other classes?

_____

_____

_____

_____

_____

How can you use tasks to differentiate instruction?

_____

_____

_____

_____

_____

PROJECTS

- Select a content textbook. What assumptions does the book make about learners' language ability? What help will your students need to be able to use the text to learn content material?
- Present a short content lesson to your methods class. Be sure to prepare the lesson with an audience of language learners in mind. What kinds of extra language support will they need? What opportunities for scaffolding and negotiation of meaning are there in your lesson? What opportunities for CALP language use are there in your lesson? After several students in your class have presented, compare the types of language that were available for the various contents that were taught.
- With a partner, select a content objective and a language objective. One person should prepare a lesson based on the SIOP Model and the other using CALLA. Compare and contrast the resulting lessons. What similarities and differences do you see?

IN YOUR JOURNAL

- How are L2 learners at a disadvantage when they have to learn content in classes with L1 speakers? Do L2 learners have any advantages in such a situation?
- Do you feel that you are stronger in BICS or CALP language? What CALP experiences have you had in your academic development?

TEACHING CHECKLIST

This checklist will help you evaluate the way you teach English in content classes.

Yes _No_

☐   ☐   I use small-group activities.

☐   ☐   I use oral and written activities that require both BICS and CALP language.

☐   ☐   I coordinate my language and content objectives.

☐   ☐   I provide meaning support including advance organizers and activation of relevant background knowledge when my students need to listen to or read content material in English.

☐   ☐   I listen carefully to my students to be certain that they understand the content material.

Yes   *No*

☐   ☐   I help my students develop and use appropriate language and content learning strategies.

☐   ☐   I provide contextualized oral and written input.

☐   ☐   I regularly use and highlight academic terms that are associated with my content field.

☐   ☐   I identify the language functions and vocabulary that are needed to discuss concepts in my content field.

☐   ☐   I use task-based and thematic activities.

☐   ☐   I foster higher-order thinking skills.

REFERENCES AND SUGGESTIONS FOR FURTHER READING

Anderson-Mejias, P. L. (1986). English for academic listening: Teaching the skills associated with listening to extended discourse. *Foreign Language Annals, 19*, 391–398.

Atkinson, D. (2002). Toward a sociocognitive approach to second language acquisition. *Modern Language Journal, 86*, 525–545.

Atkinson, D., Churchill, E., Nishino, T., and Okada, H. (2007). Alignment and interaction in a sociocognitive approach to second language acquisition. *Modern Language Journal, 9*, 169–188.

Callahan, R. (2005). Tracking and high school English learners: Limiting opportunity to learn. *American Educational Research Journal, 42*, 305–328.

Campano, G. (2007). *Immigrant students and literacy: Reading, writing, and remembering.* New York, NY: Teachers College Press.

*Chamot, A.U. (2009). *The CALLA handbook: Implementing the cognitive academic language learning approach* (2nd ed.). White Plains, NY: Pearson.

Crandall, J. (Ed.). (1987). *ESL through content-area instruction: Mathematics, science, social studies.* Englewood Cliffs, NJ: Prentice.

Crookes, G., & Gass, S. (Eds.). (1993). *Tasks and language learning: Integrating theory and practice.* Clevedon, UK: Multilingual Matters.

Cummins, J. (1991). Interdependence of first- and second-language proficiency in bilingual children. In E. Bialystok (Ed.), *Language processing in bilingual children* (pp. 70–89). New York, NY: Cambridge University Press.

Cummins, J. (1999). *BICS and CALP: Clarifying the distinction* (Report No. ED438551). Washington, DC: ERIC Clearinghouse on Languages and Linguistics.

Davison, C. (2006). Collaboration between ESL and content teachers: How do we know we are doing it right? *International Journal of Bilingual Education and Bilingualism, 9*, 454–475.

DeCapua, A., & Marshall, H. (2010). Serving ELLs with limited or interrupted education: Intervention that works. *TESOL Journal, 1*, 49–70.

Dubin, F., Eskey, D., & Grabe, W. (Eds.). (1986). *Teaching second language reading for academic purposes.* Reading, MA: Addison-Wesley.

Duff, P. (2001). Language, literacy, content, and (pop) culture: Challenges for ESL students in mainstream courses. *Canadian Modern Language Review/La Revue Canadienne des Langues Vivantes, 58*, 103–132.

Edwards, H., Wesche, M., Krashen, S., Clement, R., & Kruidenier, B. (1984). Second language acquisition through subject-matter learning: A study of sheltered psychology classes at the University of Ottawa. *Canadian Modern Language Review, 2*, 268–282.

Ferris, D., & Tagg, T. (1996). Academic listening/speaking tasks for ESL students: Problems, suggestions, and implications. *TESOL Quarterly, 30*, 297–320.

González, N., Moll, L., & Amanti, C. (2005). *Funds of knowledge: Theorizing practices in households, communities, and classrooms.* Mahwah, NJ: Lawrence Erlbaum.

Herrera, S., & Murry, K. (2011). *Mastering ESL and bilingual methods: Differentiated instruction for culturally and linguistically diverse (CLD) students* (2nd ed.). White Plains, NY: Pearson.

Janzen, J. (2008). Teaching English language learners in the content areas. *Review of Educational Research, 78,* 1010–1038.

Krueger, M., & Ryan, F. (Eds.). (1993). *Language and content: Discipline- and content-based approaches to language study.* Lexington, MA: D. C. Heath.

McKay, S. M. (1993). *Agendas for second language literacy.* Cambridge, UK: Cambridge University Press.

Pally, M. (Ed.). (2000). *Sustained content teaching in academic ESL/EFL.* Boston, MA: Houghton Mifflin.

Scarcella, R. C. (2003). *Accelerating academic English: A focus on the English learner.* Oakland, CA: Regents of the University of California.

Schleppegrell, M. J. (2004). *The language of schooling: A functional linguistics perspective.* Malwah, NJ: Lawrence Erlbaum.

Shih, M. (1986). Content-based approaches to teaching academic writing. *TESOL Quarterly, 20,* 617–648.

Short, D. (1991). *How to integrate language and content instruction: A training manual.* Washington, DC: Center for Applied Linguistics.

Stryker, S., & Leaver, B. (Eds.). (1997). *Content-based instruction in foreign language education: Models and methods.* Washington, DC: Georgetown University Press.

Thonus, T. (2003). Serving generation 1.5 learners in the university writing center. *TESOL Journal, 12,* 17–24.

Trueba, E. T. (2004). *The New Americans: Immigrants and transnationals at work (Immigration and the transnational experience).* Lanham, MD: Rowman and Littlefield.

Valdes, G. (1992). Bilingual minorities and language issues in writing. *Written Communication, 9,* 85–136.

Van Allen, R., & Allen, C. (1976). *Language experience activities.* Boston, MA: Houghton Mifflin.

Van Gelderen, A., Schoonen, R., Stoel, R., de Glopper, K., & Hulstijn, J. (2007). Development of adolescent reading comprehension in language 1 and language 2: A longitudinal analysis of constituent components. *Journal of Educational Psychology, 99,* 477–491.

Welsh, L., & Newman, K. (2010). Becoming a content-ESL teacher: A diaologic journey of a science teacher and a teacher educator. *Theory Into Practice. 49,* 137–144.

Zeungler, J., & Miller, R. (2006). Cognitive and sociocultural perspectives: Two parallel SLA worlds? *TESOL Quarterly, 40,* 35–58.

Zwiers, J. (2008). *Building academic language: Essential practices for content classrooms.* San Francisco, CA: Jossey-Bass.

*Note: CALLA was originally developed by Anna Uhl Chamot and the late J. Michael O'Malley: Chamot, A., & O'Malley, J. (1994). *The CALLA handbook: Implementing the cognitive academic language learning approach.* Reading, MA: Addison-Wesley.

PART THREE

How Do I Know
What to Teach?

9 How Do I Assess Language Learning?

- What does it mean to know a second language?
- How do international, national, and state-mandated standardized language tests influence language learning and teaching?
- What are the advantages and disadvantages of teacher-made tests?

LANGUAGE ASSESSMENT AND SECOND LANGUAGE ACQUISITION

People tend to associate the field of second language acquisition with language teaching. In fact, since it is impossible to determine how people learn languages without knowing if and what they have learned, language testing is also an important focus of second language acquisition research. The goal of language testing researchers is to develop practical tests for both research and classroom purposes that can *consistently* and *adequately* estimate a person's true second language ability. I use the word *estimate* because it is impossible to actually "see" an individual's language ability. It is only possible to observe some instances of their spoken and written language and make judgments about their actual ability based on those observations.

So far this book has considered how students learn second languages and what teachers can do to foster their learning, but testing is also an important part of a language teacher's job. Teachers must know about their students' incoming language abilities and the progress their students are making. In addition, language teachers are often responsible for using tests to make judgments about whether students should be placed in specific learning settings such as ESL, bilingual, or mainstream classes and how learners should be classified for state-mandated testing. Such tests have important consequences for students and ultimately can determine the educational resources and opportunities that are made available to them. For these reasons, language assessment is unquestionably an essential part of a language teacher's job.

Language tests are of necessity compromises. You could follow a student around for several months and record every time he or she listened to, spoke, read, or wrote in the second language. You could then review your recordings and notes and come up with a pretty good idea of the learner's true language ability. You would probably also be exhausted and still have dozens of other students to examine. A **language test** is a systematic and *practical* way of eliciting some samples of a language learner's oral and written performance as well as listening and reading ability to understand what the learner can and cannot do in the language.

ELs in the United States typically are required to take a variety of English tests, and various school districts use a number of **publisher-** and **locally-produced** tests in conjunction with their school district's ESL and bilingual education programs. These tests are used to place students in the appropriate level of English instruction, decide whether students' learning needs would be better met in an ESL or bilingual program, and determine students' **dominant language** (English or their home language) for **standardized testing** purposes, among other uses. University foreign language programs test students to determine the appropriate level for incoming high school students. In addition to standardized tests, many programs use **alternative assessment** procedures that emphasize authentic, holistic, and integrative language measures tailored to the specific educational context.

Although there have been a number of suggestions throughout this book for testing listening, speaking, reading, writing, and academic English, this chapter discusses the curriculum standards in the United States that have been developed for ESL and foreign languages as guides for language teaching and testing. It is impossible to develop a satisfactory language test without having a clear vision of what you want to test, and the standards are meant to give teachers an understanding of what students ultimately need to be able to do with the language. This chapter will also review some basic testing concepts to help you develop tests for your own students. The final section describes the TOEFL, the ACTFL OPI, the TOEIC, and the IELTS, four standardized language tests, which have had a great impact on language teaching and learning around the world.

Standards

One of the language teacher's greatest difficulties is to decide what to teach and consequently what to test. Languages are very large, and it is difficult for teachers to decide where to concentrate their efforts. Many people have personal concepts of what it means to know a second language, but it is difficult to use those individual definitions to develop a practical language test. My personal idea of full language competence is **authentic self-presentation** using the second language. I believe that people must be able to be themselves when using the second language and that their true selves must also be perceived consistently when they participate in the target culture. Unfortunately, my definition does not offer much practical guidance for language testing.

The TESOL organization and a consortium of American foreign language teaching organizations have developed general statements of goals or **standards** for teaching English as a second language and for world languages in order to help teachers establish appropriate learning goals for their students. Both sets of standards have already been highly influential in the development of language tests as well as language curricula and textbooks. You should also be aware of the **Common**

European Framework that was adopted by the Council of Europe in 2001 to guide curriculum development and language testing among member states.

The ESL Standards for Pre-K–12 Students

The ESL standards for students in prekindergarten through grade 12 were developed by the TESOL organization and include three essential goals for English learners. Each goal, in turn, has three standards or statements about the related language abilities students need in order to be successful academically and within American society. The ESL standards including Progress Indicators and Teaching Vignettes can be found in TESOL (1997).

VOICES FROM THE CLASSROOM

Goals for ESOL Learners

Goal 1: To use English to communicate in social settings.

Students will:

Standard 1: use English to participate in social interaction.

Standard 2: interact in, through, and with spoken and written English for personal expression and enjoyment.

Standard 3: use learning strategies to extend their communicative competence.

Goal 2: To use English to achieve academically in all content areas.

Students will:

Standard 1: use English to interact in the classroom.

Standard 2: use English to obtain, process, construct, and provide subject matter information in spoken and written form.

Standard 3: use appropriate learning strategies to construct and apply academic knowledge.

Goal 3: To use English in socially and culturally appropriate ways.

Students will:

Standard 1: use the appropriate language variety, register, and genre according to audience, purpose, and setting.

Standard 2: use nonverbal communication appropriate to audience, purpose, and setting.

Standard 3: use appropriate learning strategies to extend their sociolinguistic and sociocultural competence.

Source: TESOL, *The ESL Standards for Pre-K–12 Students*

Goal 1 concerns the development and use of social or BICS language. This goal recognizes that students must be able to interact socially in school and other settings in order to participate fully in American society and avoid "the negative social and economic consequences of low proficiency in English" (TESOL, 1997). In other words, it would be very difficult to overcome social distance without BICS English. Standards 2 and 3 reflect a concern for individual learner characteristics. Learners should feel confident when using English and develop effective learning strategies. Although the ESL standards document states that students should be able to interact socially in English, it does not imply that students must or should lose their ability to communicate in their first language.

Goal 2 addresses the importance of English development to school success and highlights the necessity of developing oral and written *academic* English. Despite being language learners, ELs must use English to learn and to demonstrate their learning of academic content as well as to interact with teachers and other students. Goal 2 also recognizes the importance of learning strategies for effective content learning.

Goal 3 concentrates on the cultural issues associated with language use and recognizes the diverse cultural nature of the United States. It expands on the focus of Goal 1 by noting that ELs need to interact in a variety of social settings with people from a variety of cultural and linguistic backgrounds. Therefore, they need to be able to vary their language for their specific audience, purpose, and setting, and use appropriate forms of nonverbal communication. As with the other two learning goals, Goal 3 includes the use of learning strategies to help students increase their ability to interact in culturally appropriate ways.

The National Standards for Foreign Language Learning

The **National Standards for Foreign Language Learning** includes five broad goals and eleven standards. The five goals—Communication, Cultures, Connections, Comparisons, and Communities—have come to be called the 5 Cs of foreign language education. Since the needs of American foreign language learners differ greatly from the needs of English learners, the goals included in the foreign language standards differ substantially from the goals included in the ESL standards. No distinction is made, for example, between social and academic language because, unlike the case of ELs, the new language is generally not *required* for learning outside of the language class. Interestingly, only the first goal, Communication, specifically addresses the use of the target language. The three standards associated with this goal call for students to engage in conversations and to understand and produce spoken and written language on a variety of topics.

The second goal is labeled Cultures. Many language educators feel that increased cultural understanding is one of the most important reasons for American students to study a foreign language. Accordingly, increased awareness and appreciation of the target culture has a prominent place in the foreign language standards. The two standards associated with the Cultures goal focus on students developing the understanding that cultural practices are not arbitrary.

The third goal in the foreign language standards concerns connections between language study and other content areas. The standards associated with this goal emphasize the contributions of foreign language study to other types of learning such as social studies or English. Standard 3.2 points out the usefulness of a second language in acquiring new information. Goal 4, Comparisons, is related to Goal 3 because it recognizes the advantages students can gain from comparing the new language and culture with their own. The final goal, Communities, anticipates that students will use the new language both in school and in other settings. It also suggests that students need to develop personal affinities for language learning.

VOICES FROM THE CLASSROOM

Standards for Foreign Language Learning

Communication

Communicate in Languages Other than English

> **Standard 1.1:** Students engage in conversations, provide and obtain information, express feelings and emotions, and exchange opinions.
>
> **Standard 1.2:** Students understand and interpret written and spoken language on a variety of topics.
>
> **Standard 1.3:** Students present information, concepts, and ideas to an audience of listeners or readers on a variety of topics.

Cultures

Gain Knowledge and Understanding of Other Cultures

> **Standard 2.1:** Students demonstrate an understanding of the relationship between the practices and perspectives of the culture studied.
>
> **Standard 2.2:** Students demonstrate an understanding of the relationship between the products and perspectives of the culture studied.

Connections

Connect with Other Disciplines and Acquire Information

> **Standard 3.1:** Students reinforce and further their knowledge of other disciplines through the foreign language.
>
> **Standard 3.2:** Students acquire information and recognize the distinctive viewpoints that are only available through the foreign language and its cultures.

Comparisons

Develop Insight into the Nature of Language and Culture

> **Standard 4.1:** Students demonstrate understanding of the nature of language through comparisons of the language studied and their own.

Standard 4.2: Students demonstrate understanding of the concept of culture through comparisons of the cultures studied and their own.

Communities

Participate in Multilingual Communities at Home and Around the World

Standard 5.1: Students use the language both within and beyond the school setting.

Standard 5.2: Students show evidence of becoming lifelong learners by using the language for personal enjoyment and enrichment.

Source: Standards for foreign language learning: Preparing for the 21st century, www.actfl.org/files/public/execsumm.pdf

---

Issues in Language Testing

While both the ESL and foreign language standards make clear statements about what students ought to be able to do in their second language, their implications for testing are less straightforward. How do you test whether a student uses "English to participate in social interaction"? What actually constitutes a social interaction? What if the student can use English successfully in some social interactions but not in others? What if some teachers believe the student to be successful, but others do not? Before discussing ways to test the standards, there are first a number of important testing concepts to be considered.

The Competence-Performance Problem

One of the most important difficulties in language testing is called the **competence-performance problem.** Simply put, it is impossible to directly access a person's internal language system, their "true" ability in the second language. All teachers and researchers can do is to make inferences about how well someone "knows" a language from how well the person speaks or writes in a particular situation. Such performances, however, are fraught with problems. The learner could be anxious, tired, unmotivated, or simply have nothing to say about a particular topic. Think about a time you found yourself unable to talk because of fatigue or confusion or some other discomfort. If you had been observed on that occasion, it is possible that an onlooker would have concluded incorrectly that you did not have very good language competence. This competence-performance problem is the reason that language tests are "compromises" and that we use them to "estimate" a learner's true language ability. Since we cannot reach into the human brain to measure actual second language knowledge, we must use imperfect tests as a rough index of a person's true language ability. At the same time, all language tests, like compromises, are not equal; some are better than others, and this chapter is designed to help you judge the quality of the compromises made by the language tests you will encounter.

Reliability

Reliability is a fundamental concept in language testing that refers to the consistency of a test. Reliability is the first characteristic that must be examined in judging the quality of a test, since without consistency, any test is essentially useless. It is easy to understand that there would be a problem if students took the same test on different days and got different scores each time or if several graders gave the same test paper a different score. Testing professionals refer to reliability as a "necessary but not sufficient" condition for a good test. This means that it must first be determined if a test is consistent before considering other factors such as whether it elicits authentic language or whether it encourages students to concentrate on the right material.

Reliability is generally assessed through a statistical procedure called **correlation.** Roughly put, a correlation determines mathematically the extent to which two sets of scores overlap. To determine the reliability of a test, among other procedures, test developers have groups of people take it on different occasions to assess its **test-retest reliability** and have different graders evaluate learners' responses to assess its **inter-rater reliability.** High correlations between students' scores on the different administrations of the test and among the graders are taken as indications of a test's reliability.

Validity

If a test is found to be reliable, it means that it is measuring *something* consistently, but we do not know yet what it is measuring consistently. The next step then in examining a test is to determine what exactly the test is measuring. As a student, you may sometimes have had the feeling that you were graded unfairly. Perhaps you were downgraded because you missed one class too many or you received a lower grade because the margins on your paper were a sixteenth of an inch off. In each case, your feelings of unfairness probably stemmed from the fact that you believed that your grades should be based on your knowledge of the subject matter and the quality of your work rather than on your attendance or page formatting abilities. Thus, you did not find your final grades in those classes to be **valid** measures of your work in the course. A valid test is one that measures what it is supposed to measure. So if you want to know how well a student can write a social studies essay, a multiple-choice test of verb formation would not be a valid test. A particularly egregious example of poor test validity test stems from the 1950s when non-English–speaking children in the United States were given intelligence tests in English and then judged to be less intelligent than English-speaking children. An intelligence test taken in a foreign language is obviously a test of something other than intelligence!

While it is relatively easy to determine the reliability of a test, establishing validity is much less straightforward. Even so, there are several things that you, as a teacher, can do to make sure a test is as valid *as possible.* First of all, you can look at the test and decide if it looks like it measures what it is supposed to be measuring. This type of validity is called **face validity.** For example, a written pronoun test would not look like a good test of a student's oral ability. You can also check to see if a test makes good predictions about students. This type of validity is called **predictive validity.** If students are having difficulty in mainstream content classes even after they have passed the exit test for ESL, it is likely that the exit test was not a valid measure of the language abilities they need in mainstream classes. It is also important to make sure that the results of one test are reasonably similar to results from other tests of the same ability. This is called **concurrent validity.** Two tests that are supposed to be measuring the same thing should yield reasonably similar scores. For example, if students are doing well in their classes but fail a state-mandated exam, it is likely that either the exam or the class grades are not valid measures of what the students have learned.

It is tempting to label tests as either valid or invalid, but the issue of validity is more complicated. The case of the inappropriate use of an intelligence test written in a foreign language points to the fact that test validity is not absolute. That is, a test cannot be found to be valid for all learners in all circumstances. Tests are only valid for the group and circumstances for which they have been developed. Just as an intelligence test developed for English speakers is not valid for non-English speakers, a language test developed for one type of language learner cannot be used with another type of learner without reestablishing its validity. Factors such as age, cultural background, and learning situation can render a test that has previously been found to be valid to be invalid in a new situation. For example, some oral language tests developed for children use drawings of cartoon figures and ask the test taker to make up a story concerning the characters. While children might find the pictures appealing, adults might find them juvenile and be unable to think of anything to say. It is also important to remember that a test could be generally valid but still be unsuitable for certain students. Oral interviews, for example, may work well with talkative students but not with those who are culturally or personally reserved.

Even if a test has been found to be reliable and generally valid, it is inappropriate to use any *single* measure to make decisions about a student. In fact, the use of multiple tests is seen as an important way to increase validity in the assessment of student ability. At the very least, teachers should pair any testing with careful observation of students' performance on a variety of classroom tasks to make sure that their test results seem to be consistent with their actual ability to use the language.

Since standardized tests can have such serious consequences for students, teachers who work with English learners often have to be advocates for their students with respect to their performance on district- and statewide tests. The results of these kinds of standardized tests may not be valid for this group of learners, either because the students were tested in English rather than their L1 or because they were not familiar with the testing format due to their different cultural backgrounds.

Authenticity and Washback

As discussed in Chapter 5, it can be difficult for teachers to create opportunities for authentic target language use in the classroom. It is, perhaps, even more difficult for teachers or test developers to devise authentic language tests. The issue of authenticity is strongly related to validity in language testing. Ultimately, language tests are supposed to determine whether learners will be able to use the target language effectively *when* and *where* they need to. In order to accomplish this goal, a language test must include the kinds of activities students need to perform in real life. Thus, particularly in the case of language testing, it is difficult to separate authenticity from validity.

Authenticity in testing is also important because of the consequences language tests can have for language learners and teachers. Tests often influence how and what students study as well as what teachers teach. As you know, the term **washback** refers to the impact that tests have on teaching and learning. Teachers may tell students to use language communicatively and creatively, but if grades are based on grammatical accuracy, students quickly learn to spend their time studying grammar. Similarly, teachers often complain that state-mandated or national tests interfere with their ability to teach written expression and higher-order thinking skills.

Testing Approaches

Integrative versus Nonintegrative Testing

Language educators generally talk about two types of language tests: **integrative** and **nonintegrative**—also known as **discrete-point tests** because of their frequent use of fill-in-the-blank formats. Nonintegrative tests focus on one unit of language at a time and are based on the premise that it is useful to know whether or not a student has control of all the basic units of a language. If you have ever taken a language class, you are probably familiar with nonintegrative tests using a discrete-point format. This type of test can be recognized by directions that say something like: "Fill in the blank with the correct form of the verb provided." The strength of nonintegrative tests lies in their ability to determine exactly what students know. If a student fills in "falled" in response to the item

The child _____ down and hurt her toe. (to fall, past tense)

the teacher knows immediately that this student does not know the irregular past tense form of the verb *to fall*. Because of their simple format, nonintegrative tests tend to be highly reliable. Students either know or do not know the particular forms, and scoring is very straightforward. Critics of nonintegrative testing, however, complain that humans do not produce language one unit at a time and that "knowing" the correct verb form for a test has little to do with the ability to use that verb in a conversation. Thus, this type of test lacks face validity for many language educators.

Integrative tests require students to coordinate their knowledge of the language and are meant to tap into their underlying interlanguage; thus, they resemble natural communication more closely. The most common types of integrative tests are oral interviews and written compositions. These types of tests are called integrative since students must "integrate" all aspects of the language when they write a composition or respond to oral questions. Most language educators feel that integrative tests have high face validity because they require students to use language similarly to the way they would use it in the real world. However, reliability can be a problem with integrative tests. Students might have more to say about one topic than another, and different raters may look for different things when they grade students' oral or written responses. Consequently, rater training and specific scoring rubrics like the ones discussed in Chapters 5 and 7 are essential to ensure the reliability of conversation and composition tests.

Fortunately, several types of integrative tests have fewer reliability problems. These are dictations, elicited imitation, grammaticality judgments, cloze tests, and self-assessments. These test types also limit the amount of speaking or writing the student has to do, thus reducing the competence-performance problem.

As noted in Chapter 4, dictation can be a useful method of testing listening comprehension. **Dictations** are considered integrative tests when they are rated according to the specific ideas understood (see Chapter 4 to review Savignon's grading method). **Elicited imitation** functions similarly to dictation except that students do not have to write. A number of studies have found that learners tend to simplify when they repeat and spontaneously form sentences consistent with their stage of interlanguage development. For example, if learners do not yet control pluralization, they would typically change "Solara put her books in her backpack" to "Solara put her book in her backpack." In fact, a learner at that stage of English development would be more likely to produce a sentence like "Solara put book in backpack." **Grammaticality judgments** tap into the learner's internal sense of the language in a similar manner. Learners read or listen to sentences and then indicate whether or not the sentence is grammatical.

Cloze tests were discussed in Chapter 6 because they are primarily associated with second language reading. As you remember, in cloze tests words are deleted from a written passage and students use their expectancy grammar to fill in the blanks. Like dictation and elicited imitation, simple cloze tests (Cloze Passage #1, Chapter 6) are classified as integrative tests, but scholars do not agree whether rational-deletion cloze tests (Cloze Passage #2, Chapter 6), where a specific part of speech such as prepositions or verbs is purposefully deleted, are truly integrative tests. In any case, it is important not to confuse cloze tests with discrete-point tests simply because they use a fill-in-the-blank format.

Direct, Indirect, and Performance Testing

Closely related to integrative and nonintegrative tests are the categories of direct and indirect language tests. **Direct tests** are similar to integrative tests in that learners must perform the actual skill that the teacher is interested in assessing. Writing a composition or explaining the results of a science experiment are examples of direct language tests. **Indirect tests,** in contrast, are more similar to nonintegrative or discrete-point tests and are designed to examine some of the sub-skills involved in a language task. Testing students on specific sounds would be an example of an indirect test of their oral ability.

Performance tests are an even more focused form of direct testing. They are used to assess a learner's ability to use the second language effectively under *authentic* circumstances. Performance tests were originally developed for professional or workplace assessment, and the testing simulations can be very elaborate, with realistic sets and actors playing the role of customers.

Portfolios

To avoid problems associated with basing grades or placement decisions on a single test or type of test, as well as to encourage student involvement in the evaluation process, many language educators have begun to use an alternative form of assessment called a portfolio (see Chapter 7). A portfolio is a *purposeful* selection of student work by both the student and the teacher. Students select examples of their work that they believe best represent their effort and achievement in the class. Teachers may add items to the portfolio to give a fuller picture of the student's work. For example, a portfolio *might* include an assignment that the student is proud of, a formal test, a composition selected by the teacher, and a recording that the student made at home to substitute for an oral exam that the student was not pleased with. Both the student and the teacher are involved in the evaluation of the contents of the portfolio, with student self-assessments and teacher-student conferences integral parts of the process. Proponents of portfolios maintain that they foster learner autonomy since self-assessment makes learners more aware of their progress and teacher conferences help them develop realistic learning plans.

Assessment for Learning

In recent years, many educators across the curriculum have questioned the somewhat arbitrary distinction between testing and teaching. Many educators have also moved from a focus on **summative evaluation** or evaluation at the endpoint of instruction to **formative evaluation** or the *ongoing* collection and use of assessment with the goal of improving instruction. Within the language education community, the focus on **learner autonomy** asks that students have greater control over their language learning. **Assessment for learning (AFL)** is consistent with all these developments.

> Assessment for learning is designed to give teachers information to modify the teaching and learning activities in which students are engaged in order to differentiate and focus on how individual students approach learning. (Hawley, 2007, p. 90)

AFL integrates the choice of learning objectives, teacher assessment, student self-assessment and goal setting, and the possibility of making instructional modifications throughout the instructional sequence. From an AFL perspective, the goal of testing and assessment is not to assign grades but to improve student learning. The first step in AFL is for teachers to choose appropriate instructional objectives and make students aware of these objectives. This clear communication of objectives to students distinguishes AFL from other approaches to assessment. Teachers also give students feedback about their progress, opportunities for self-assessment, and suggestions for improvement *throughout* the learning cycle. Both teachers and students can benefit from AFL. Teachers receive timely information about student learning so that they can offer students different teaching approaches where necessary, and students are given feedback and differentiated instruction to help them achieve as much as possible.

Testing for a Variety of Purposes

Norm-Referenced versus Criterion-Referenced Tests

One important distinction with respect to all types of educational tests—not only language tests—is whether they are **norm-referenced** or **criterion-referenced.** Norm-referenced tests compare a student's performance to other students in the same group. In that way, it is possible to tell how an individual learner or a group of learners is performing in relation to their *peers*. Norm-referenced tests are often used to compare groups of students to all students in a particular school district, state, or country. Scores on norm-referenced tests typically include a **percentile ranking**, which indicates the percentage of test takers who rank at or below a particular score. For example, a student who is ranked at the 85 percentile scored as well or better than 85 percent of the students who took the test.

While it is useful to know how students compare to other students, many educators argue that norm-referenced tests say little about what students actually know or do not know. In contrast to norm-referenced tests, criterion-referenced tests focus on a set of specific learning objectives developed for the course. Scores on this type of test reflect the number of objectives a test taker has successfully completed. Criterion-referenced tests are, therefore, a good choice for **achievement tests** because they can assess the progress a student has made based on the specific objectives of the course. While norm-referenced tests are based on the premise that some students will perform well on a test and others will do poorly, it is possible for all students to achieve a perfect score on a criterion-referenced test. Such a result would indicate that all the students who took the test had achieved all the instructional objectives that the test covered!

Placement, Diagnostic, and Achievement Tests

Placement tests are used to help determine a learner's appropriate level in a sequence of courses. For example, since high schools use different curricula and textbooks, universities commonly use placement tests to determine which language class a student should take. Placement tests typically assess students' knowledge of elements of the school's language curriculum as well as their general level of language proficiency. **Diagnostic tests** are usually more specific than placement tests and are designed to identify specific areas of weakness in a learner's competence that a teacher might want to address. Similarly, **achievement tests** assess the progress a student has made based on the specific objectives of a course or program. Elicited imitation, grammaticality judgments, rational-deletion cloze tests, self-assessments, and discrete-point tests are good choices for diagnostic and achievement testing because they can target specific grammatical structures and vocabulary.

Testing the Standards

The ESL and foreign language standards offer teachers a set of objectives which *could* form the basis for criterion-referenced tests; however, each standard needs to be translated into more precise objectives based on the student's grade level and learning before clear testing procedures can be developed. Testing scholars tell us that learning objectives must be stated clearly and specifically in order to be testable. For example, with respect to Goal 2 (to use English to achieve academically in all content areas), Standard 1 provides that "Students will use English to interact in the classroom"; but the standard does not include the type of interaction, the frequency of the interaction, whether the interaction should be with teachers or other students or both. For younger learners, using English to interact in the classroom might mean singing and calling out answers, while for older learners it might imply participating in class discussions and taking notes. Thus, the standard is too general to be testable in its present form. This is not meant to be a criticism of either the ESL or the foreign language standards. Both documents were written to be flexible so that they could be applied in a variety of learning settings.

Both the ESL and foreign language standards include additional materials to help teachers apply the standards in their teaching setting. They include representative descriptors and sample progress indicators to give teachers an idea of what to look for in their students' language development and learning scenarios with lesson plans that are consistent with the standards. For example, with respect to Goal 2, Standard 1, *The ESL Standards for Pre-K–12 Students* lists "asking and answering questions" as a descriptor and "ask a teacher to restate or simplify directions" as a sample progress indicator. TESOL and ACTFL have published assessment guides for their respective sets of standards. TESOL's *Scenarios for ESL Standards-based Assessment* and ACTFL's *Integrated Performance Assessment (IPA) Manual* illustrate possible testing and assessment approaches for learners of different ages and language proficiency levels. The assessment scenarios resemble **task-based** activities and use both individual and group organizations. Here is an excerpt from an observation guide for participation in science activities for students in grades four through eight. As is often necessary for ELs, the language and content objectives are intertwined.

VOICES FROM THE CLASSROOM

Goal 2: To use English to achieve academically in all content areas.

Standard 2: Students will use English to obtain, process, construct, and provide subject matter information in spoken and written form.

In this activity, the student

- developed relevant inquiry questions _____

- developed an inquiry plan _____

- followed directions _____

- used materials _____

Source: TESOL (2001), *Scenarios for ESL Standards-Based Assessment*, p. 66.

Several of the testing procedures already discussed in this chapter would work well for standards testing. Observations, self-assessments, and the evaluation of student work with rubrics are especially good choices when your purpose is information about whether students have achieved a particular standard or part of a standard without the complication of having to assign a grade. Your choice of test type will depend on many factors such as your students' age, grade level, language proficiency, target language, and learning context. The following list gives some basic considerations for developing tests to assess your students' progress based either on the ESL or foreign language standards.

Appropriate Test Types	*Considerations in Standards Testing*
Criterion-Referenced	■ Students' age
Integrative	■ Proficiency level
Direct	■ Grade level
Performance	■ Language needs
Portfolios	■ Academic needs

To a great extent, the standards are an attempt to increase the authenticity of language teaching. I said earlier in this chapter, that it is impossible to develop a satisfactory language test without having a clear vision of what you want to test. The standards are meant to encourage teachers to base tests on what students ultimately need to be able to *do* with the language, and thus their ultimate aim is to make language teaching and testing more authentic.

Although the Standards give you a general idea about what you should test, it is still up to the individual teacher to develop a specific set of objectives or criteria to test. You will need to think carefully about what each standard means *in your setting for your particular students* in order to develop a list of objectives to serve as a basis for your tests. For example, in the observation framework for science activities "developed relevant inquiry questions, developed an inquiry plan, followed directions, and used materials" are examples of the objectives being assessed.

You must also think about the reliability and validity of your tests. You will want to assess students on more than one occasion and in more than one situation to monitor their progress with respect to the standards. You should also assess each standard in more than one way to ensure concurrent validity. The use of portfolios that include your own observations are ideal for standard testing, and an assessment for learning approach integrates ongoing assessment with your specific instructional goals. Ultimately, the Standards ask teachers to seriously consider the predictive validity of their tests. Will students be able to use the language successfully in the real world for their individual needs and purposes?

The TOEFL, the ACTFL OPI, the TOEIC, and the IELTS

The tests that you develop for your students have the great advantage of being tied to your specific teaching goals and the instruction that your students have received. Thus, they are a result of *your* curriculum and *your* decisions about what your students need to know and be able to do. However, there are a number of important national and international language tests with varying degrees of consistency with the ESL and foreign language standards that will also influence what and how you teach.

The **ACTFL Oral Proficiency Interview (OPI),** developed by the American Council of Teachers of Foreign Languages; the Test of English as a Foreign Language (TOEFL), developed by the Educational Testing Service; the **Test of English for International Communication (TOEIC);** and the British **International English Language Testing System (IELTS)** are four of the most highly influential language tests in the world. Publisher-developed tests such as the OPI, the TOEFL, the IELTS, and the TOEIC have been tested with tens of thousands of learners and are held to higher standards of reliability and validity than are **teacher-made tests.**

The ACTFL OPI

The ACTFL OPI is a structured live (either face-to-face or by telephone) oral interview which uses a ten-level scale to rate learners from "novice low" to "superior" and corresponds to the communication goal of the foreign language standards. It is a criterion-referenced test based on an oral interview procedure originally developed by the U.S. Foreign Service Institute (FSI) to test government employees with job responsibilities that required the use of a second language professionally. ACTFL developed an expanded set of guidelines to gauge students' proficiency levels ranging from novice to superior. Students at the novice low level have only minimal oral skills; they can answer a few questions with formulaic answers and list some L2 vocabulary. At the other end of the scale, superior speakers can use the language comfortably for many professional and academic purposes. According to the ACTFL website, the OPI is available in 37 languages including English. In addition to interview questions, the OPI uses role-play scenarios to put examinees in situations where they have to use grammatical structures and vocabulary that they might not use spontaneously in response to the more conversational interview questions.

The OPI testing process can be complicated. Testers choose interview questions and scenarios that seem to be appropriate for each test taker's level of oral proficiency. When a test taker shows competence with that level of questions, the tester poses questions at a higher level. Testers continue to probe the test taker's proficiency level until they are satisfied that the test taker is unable to answer questions or participate effectively in scenarios at the higher level. The interviewer, then, brings the conversation back down to a level that the examinee is comfortable with so that the test taker does not leave the exam feeling discouraged. The ACTFL OPI has had a great influence on foreign language teaching in the United States by making the development of oral proficiency the accepted goal of language teaching.

Because of the expense of administering the OPI to individuals, there have been several attempts to develop more efficient oral tests. You might be especially interested to know that several states in the United States have begun to use **Simulated Oral Proficiency Interviews (SOPI)** based on the ACTFL OPI as part of the certification process for bilingual teachers and teachers of world languages. Test takers listen to recorded questions and scenarios and record their responses. The recorded responses are later evaluated by raters—usually more than one—to insure inter-rater reliability. So far, SOPIs have only been developed for a limited set of purposes, such as teacher certification, because the format does not easily allow for the testing of a full range of ten proficiency levels. In the case of teacher certification, for example, states set a level of acceptable proficiency usually in the range of intermediate-high or advanced. A certification SOPI, therefore, does not need to probe all possible proficiency levels; it only needs to test the test taker's ability to respond to questions at and around the targeted proficiency level. Candidates with proficiency below intermediate do not have sufficient proficiency to be certified in many states, and any proficiency level above advanced is, of course, acceptable.

The TOEFL

The **Test of English as a Foreign Language,** or **TOEFL,** is very familiar to English learners and teachers across the world. It is the principle English examination required of international students who hope to study in North America. It is designed, therefore, to test whether students have adequate English ability to undertake high school, undergraduate, or graduate study in English in the North American context. Since the TOEFL is used to assess readiness for academic study, it has a greater focus on academic language than the ACTFL OPI or the TOEIC. Historically, the TOEFL has used a written format (either paper and pencil or computer-based) to test the areas of listening comprehension, structure and written expression, reading comprehension, and composition writing; but the new Internet version of the TOEFL (IBT) is more interactive and has a greater focus on oral skills. The IBT includes a test of spoken English that is similar to a SOPI in that students record their answers to previously recorded questions. Students answer questions on familiar topics and discuss texts they have read or listened to. The listening sections on the IBT range beyond American English to include British or Australian speakers.

The IBT reports scores for listening, speaking, reading, and writing. The TOEFL does not set a passing score; rather, individual educational institutions have internal guidelines for the level of scores they expect from applicants. The TOEFL has aspects of both norm-referenced and criterion-referenced tests. It is generally classified as a norm-referenced test because scores indicate a student's ranking in relation to other test takers, but students also receive feedback about the specific areas where they answered correctly and incorrectly. In addition, the scores on the oral and composition parts of the test are based on a specific set of grading criteria.

Since so many people hope to study and gain scholarships to study in North America, there is great pressure on students around the world when they take the

TOEFL. Students often feel that their high school and university English classes do not prepare them adequately to take the test, and many enroll in special TOEFL preparation classes or buy **self-study** materials. Unfortunately, many students do not associate the TOEFL with actually learning English. I have even had students tell me that they did not have time to take an English class because they had to prepare for the TOEFL!

The IELTS

Like the TOEFL, the Academic Version of the **International English Language Testing System (IELTS)** is a four skills (listening, speaking, academic reading, and academic writing) English test used to assess readiness for undergraduate or graduate study in an English-speaking environment. Unlike the TOEFL, however, the speaking section is administered by a trained examiner in person rather than the SOPI-type Internet speaking exam used by the TOEFL. The British Council, IDP: IELTS Australia, and the University of Cambridge ESOL Examination administer the IELTS, which is more closely aligned with the Common European Framework than any of the American language standards. (It is available at numerous sites in the United States.) A second version of the IELTS, the General Training Version, tests "basic survival skills in a broad social and educational context" and is designed to test readiness for secondary school, training, work, or immigration. In fact, the General Training Version is a requirement for immigration to the United Kingdom, Canada, Australia, and New Zealand. It uses the same listening and speaking sections as the Academic Version but replaces the academic reading and writing sections with general reading and writing sections. The Academic Version of the IELTS has been growing in popularity in recent years, and an increasing number of American colleges and universities accept it for admissions purposes in place of the TOEFL. IELTS scores are reported in "bands" ranging from 1 "non user" to 5 "modest user" to 9 "expert user." There are a number of tables available that purport to convert IELTS scores to TOEFL scores and vice versa.

The TOIEC

Like the TOEFL, the **Test of English for International Communication,** or **TOEIC,** is administered by the American Educational Testing Service (ETS) at Internet-based sites, but rather than testing English for use in academic settings, it is designed to test English "for daily life and the global workplace." It is often used by companies around the world to assess whether potential and/or current employees possess adequate English ability to conduct professional activities in English. Although it targets English use in the workplace and uses tasks that simulate workplace interactions, it does not test or require knowledge of business content. Historically, the use of the TOEIC has been particularly widespread in Japan and South Korea. The TOEIC has two separate tests: one for **productive** language skills, the TOEIC Speaking and Writing Test, and a second for **receptive** skills, the TOEIC Listening and Reading Test. The speaking and writing test is evaluated by trained raters and includes tasks at a variety of difficulty levels (i.e., reading a passage aloud, describing a picture orally, writing a sentence about a picture, expressing an opinion orally, and writing an opinion essay). Speaking and writing and listening and reading scores are reported separately.

FINDING YOUR WAY

REFLECTIONS

Have you ever taken an oral proficiency interview in a second language? Do you feel that it was a valid test of your second language ability?

_____

_____

_____

_____

_____

What impact do you think the ESL and foreign language standards will have on second language teaching?

_____

_____

_____

_____

_____

PLANNING FOR YOUR CLASSES

What language and/or content tests do your students have to take?

_____

_____

_____

_____

_____

What advantages would an assessment to learn approach have for you and your students?

_____

_____

_____

_____

_____

PROJECTS

- Obtain a copy of a publisher-made test in your second language. Classify it using as many testing categories listed in this chapter as possible. Do you have any concerns about the test's reliability or validity?
- Working either by yourself or with a small group of other students, review either the ESL or foreign language standards. Do you think they give adequate guidance about your students' language learning needs? What revisions would you make?

IN YOUR JOURNAL

- How did you feel when you took an important test such as the SAT, the GRE, the TOEFL or the ACTFL OPI? Did you feel prepared for these tests? Did you feel that they were a valid test of your ability?
- Have you ever been asked to produce a portfolio or participated in any other type of alternative assessment?

TEACHING CHECKLIST

This checklist will help you develop language tests that are consistent with your students' language needs.

Yes No

☐ ☐ I consider the ESL or foreign language standards when developing or choosing tests.

☐ ☐ I develop clear instructional objectives based on my students' language needs to use as a basis for testing.

☐ ☐ My grading procedures reflect listening, speaking, reading, writing, and culture.

☐ ☐ I use multiple sources of information about my students' language abilities.

☐ ☐ I attempt to make my tests as reliable and valid as possible.

☐ ☐ I limit my use of nonintegrative tests.

☐ ☐ I try to make my tests as authentic as possible.

☐ ☐ I use assessment to help me differentiate instruction.

☐ ☐ I use assessment to help improve my teaching.

REFERENCES AND SUGGESTIONS FOR FURTHER READING

American Council of Teachers of Foreign Languages. (1999). *Oral proficiency guidelines.* Yonkers, NY: ACTFL.

American Council of Teachers of Foreign Languages. (2003). *Integrated Performance Assessment (IPA) Manual.* Yonkers, NY: ACTFL.

American Council of Teachers of Foreign Languages. (2006). *Standards for foreign language learning: Preparing for the 21st century 3rd edition.* Lawrence, KA: Allen Press.

American Language Review. (1998). Computer-based TOEFL test: A complete guide. *American Language Review, 2,* 32–36, 44.

Bachman, L. (2000) Modern language testing at the turn of the century: Assuring that we count what counts. *Language Testing 17,* 1–42.

Chalhoub-Deville, M., & Turner, C. E. (2000). What to look for in ESL admission tests: Cambridge certificate exams, IELTS, and TOEFL. *System, 28,* 523–539.

Chapelle, C., Enright, M., & Jamieson, J. (2008). *Building a validity argument for the Test of English as a Foreign Language.* New York, NY: Routledge.

Chapelle, C., Jamieson, J., & Hegelheimer, V. (2003). Validation of a web-based ESL test. *Language Testing, 20,* 409–439.

Colby-Kelly, C., & Turner, C. (2007). AFL research in the L2 classroom and evidence of usefulness: Taking formative assessment to the next level. *Canadian Modern Language Review, 64,* 9–37.

Council of Europe. (2001). *The Common European Framework of Reference for Languages: Learning, teaching, assessment,* Cambridge, UK: Cambridge University Press.

Davidson, F. & Fulcher, G. (2007). The Common European Framework of Reference and the design of language tests: A matter of effect. *Language Teaching, 40,* 231–241.

Duran, R. (2008). Assessing English-language learners' achievement. *Review of Research in Education 32,* 292–327.

Ellis, R. (1991). Grammaticality judgments and second language acquisition. *Studies in Second Language Acquisition, 13,* 161–186.

Fotos, S. S. (1991). The cloze test as an integrative measure of EFL proficiency: A substitute for essays on college entrance exams? *Language Learning, 41,* 313–336.

Glisan, E. W., & Foltz, D. A. (1998). Assessing students' oral proficiency in an outcome-based curriculum: Student performance and teacher intuitions. *Modern Language Journal, 82,* 1–18.

Gottleib, M. (2006). *Assessing English language learners.* Thousand Oaks, CA: Corwin Press.

Hawley, W. (2007). *The keys to effective schools: Educational reform as continuous improvement.* Thousand Oaks, CA: Corwin.

Hiple, D. V., & Manley, J. H. (1987). Testing how well foreign language teachers speak: A state mandate. *Foreign Language Annals, 20,* 147–153.

Horwitz, E. (1985). Formative evaluation of an experimental foreign language class. *Canadian Modern Language Review/La Revue Canadienne des Langues Vivantes, 42,* 83–90.

Hughes, A., & Swan, M. (2002). *Testing for language teachers.* Cambridge, UK: Cambridge University Press.

Kuo, J., & Jiang, X. (1997). Assessing the assessments: The OPI and the SOPI. *Foreign Language Annals, 30,* 503–512.

Little, D. (2011). The Common European Framework of Reference for Languages: A research agenda. *Language Teaching, 44,* 381–393.

Murray, J. (2002). Creating placement tests. *ESL Magazine, 5,* 22–24.

Peal, E., & Lambert, W. E. (1962). The relation of bilingualism to intelligence. *Psychological Monographs, 76,* 1–23.

Pray, L. (2005). How well do commonly used language instruments measure English oral-language proficiency? *Bilingual Research Journal 29,* 387–410.

Stoynoff, S., & Chapelle, C. (2005). *ESOL tests and testing.* Alexandria, VA: Teachers of English to Speakers of Other Languages.

Tellez, K. (1998). Class placement of elementary school emerging bilingual students. *Bilingual Research Journal, 22,* 279–295.

TESOL. (1997). *The ESL standards for pre-K–12 students.* Alexandria, VA: Teachers of English to Speakers of Other Languages.

TESOL. (2001). *Scenarios for ESL standards-based assessment.* Alexandria, VA: Teachers of English to Speakers of Other Languages.

Thompson, M. (2001). The TOEFL and grammar. *Forum, 39,* 2–9.

Valdés, G., & Figueroa, R. A. (1994). *Bilingualism and testing: A special case of bias.* Norwood, NJ: Ablex.

Vinther, T. (2002). Elicited imitation: A brief overview. *Applied Linguistics, 12,* 54–73.

Wertheimer, C., & Honigsfeld, A. (2000). Preparing ESL students to meet the new standards. *TESOL Journal, 9,* 23–28.

10 How Do I Plan My Classes?

- What makes a class exciting? What makes a class boring?
- How should class time be divided between listening, speaking, reading, writing, and culture?
- What have you liked or disliked about the language textbooks you used as a language learner?
- How can you differentiate instruction for the different learners in each of your classes?

PLANNING FOR SECOND LANGUAGE ACQUISITION IN THE CLASSROOM

Second language acquisition requires sustained contact with the new language. The conversation theories in particular maintain that people learn to speak a second language by participating in conversations and receiving individualized feedback on their conversational attempts. The Output Hypothesis requires that these conversations push students to produce increasingly precise and appropriate language, while the sociocultural theories see students as steering conversations to elicit the kind of feedback they need. One important feature of conversations that encourages second language acquisition is their repetitiveness. Although the actual information exchanged varies from conversation to conversation, conversations can also be formulaic in that many of the same questions, responses, and observations are used over and over. Similarly, task-based and content-based approaches maintain that students benefit from receiving *interrelated* target language input by both listening and reading on multiple occasions as well as by having *multiple opportunities* to express similar ideas in the target language. All of these approaches support the idea that language classes should include a mix of language skills and a *coordinated* set of learning activities.

Language teachers have a wide array of activities and materials to choose from. The problem, of course, is deciding which activities and materials to use and how to organize them for each class session and for each student. The decision of what and how to teach is complicated, since each class needs to be related to the school's or program's curriculum, the course textbook, the learners' needs, and any required tests that students will have to take. Ideally, the curriculum, the textbook, students' needs and background knowledge, and any testing procedures will be in perfect agreement. In reality, teachers have to balance all these sources of teaching goals and somehow figure out what to do in class each day. The process of deciding what and how to teach is called **lesson planning** and is essential to effective language teaching.

Unfortunately, new teachers often have several misconceptions about lesson planning. Many new teachers confuse the course curriculum or textbook with a lesson plan. That is, they take these documents as actual statements of what to do in class day by day. This practice usually leads to lessons that are not clearly thought-out and overly generic; they are neither linked to the needs of the students in a particular class nor to the teacher's special talents. In contrast, some new teachers prepare elaborate written plans but do not recognize the connection of these plans to what they do in class. Some of my student teachers would meticulously record lists of detailed learning goals and classroom activities that did not include plans for what they would actually teach. They had not planned how to explain new material or even looked over the exercises or reading materials they planned to use. When their classes started, they simply did not know what to do. Consider the following two partial lesson plans for the same discussion activity in an advanced high school Japanese class.

VOICES FROM THE CLASSROOM

Excerpt from Lesson Plan 1, John Smith

Conversation Lesson on Economic Conditions in Japan:

Students read textbook reading on the economy in Japan. Lead discussion of the current economic conditions in Japan. 15 minutes.

Excerpt from Lesson Plan 2, Thomas Jones

Conversation Lesson on Economic Conditions in Japan:

Step 1: Assign students to read textbook selection on the Japanese economy as homework. Remind them to use their reading strategies. Give them the following questions to guide their reading:

1. Describe the Japanese economy during the 1980s.
2. What social and population trends occurred in Japan during the 1990s that impacted the economy?
3. What is the current state of the economy and what are its prospects for the future?

Step 2: In-class discussion. Whole-class format because I want to make sure everyone gets the economy material. 20 minutes.

1. Ask if they had any questions about the reading. Check with Joan.
2. Elicit descriptions of the economy in the 1980s. Be sure competition with the U.S. is mentioned.
3. Elicit events of the 1990s. Be sure bank problems and low birth rate are mentioned. Ask students to speculate on the impact of a low birth rate on an economy.
4. Ask about the current economy and if they are optimistic or pessimistic about Japan's economic future.
5. I will mention some economic changes that have occurred in the four years since the textbook was published.
6. If the discussion goes well, assign them to write a one page composition for homework on what they foresee for the Japanese economy in 10 years. If the discussion goes poorly, for homework, have them brainstorm ideas about what might happen in the Japanese economy in the future.

Mr. Smith has produced only the bare beginnings of a lesson plan. He lists a class discussion on current economic conditions in Japan that is tenuously linked to a textbook reading on the Japanese economy. We do not know what questions he is going to ask to start the discussion or even if he is going to use a small-group or whole-class format. Mr. Jones, in contrast, has carefully thought through the steps of his lesson. He has designed prereading questions that will guide his students' reading and prepare them for the next day's discussion. He will start the lesson by asking students if they had any questions about the reading, and he reminds himself to check with a student named Joan whom he knows may have had difficulty. He has chosen a whole-class format for the discussion because he wants to be sure that the students learn several specific points, and he would not be able to monitor the content of several small-group discussions. He will next ask questions about the content of the reading assignment, followed by a question that requires students to hypothesize (*Ask students to speculate on the impact of a low birth rate on an economy*). He then plans to add more current information and assign a related writing assignment asking students to speculate about what might happen to Japan's economy in the coming years. He recognizes, however, that the writing assignment might not be a good idea if the in-class discussion is not successful, so he also has an alternative activity.

A lesson plan is really a script for a lesson. If the teacher unexpectedly became ill or otherwise unable to teach a class, another teacher should be able to conduct a very similar class by relying on the first teacher's lesson plan. By saying that a lesson plan should be a script for a lesson, I do not mean that teachers should not deviate from their plan. Like Mr. Jones's alternative writing assignment, the best lesson plans have contingencies for unforeseen difficulties. Good teachers are also willing to change their plans when students need extra help or an activity is going exceptionally well.

Many new teachers note that the more experienced teachers they work with seldom write out detailed lesson plans and often use lesson plans that look a lot like Mr. Smith's. Experienced teachers are able to teach from sketchy lesson plans because they have already thought through and even taught the same or similar lessons on numerous occasions. Their lesson plans are more like reminders to themselves than true lesson plans. New teachers, on the other hand, need to follow Mr. Jones's example because they need to plan out each lesson step by step to be able to conduct their classes effectively.

The brief plans that we have just looked at are only plans for a small part of a class session; true lesson plans have to detail the instruction for entire class sessions during the duration of a course so that the course goals are achieved. Effective lesson plans take into account all your knowledge about your students, your teaching situation, second language acquisition theories and research, and the teaching approaches available to language teachers.

Planning for *Your* Students

Long-Term Planning

Before you can begin planning for your daily classes, you must first decide on your goals for the course. That is, what do you want *your* students to be able to do at the end of the year or semester you have them. Most of your goals will concern language learning. For example, in terms of the ESL standards, you might include an objective about students being able to ask questions in their math class. Remember to think about the **language domains** that your students will need access to, and what you know about their language abilities and background knowledge. You may also have goals with respect to your students' development as language learners as well as their general personal development. For example, you might hope that your students develop more effective language learning strategies or you might want to encourage the development of more positive **self-concepts** in general. As you begin your **long-term planning,** I hope that you will go back over the notes that you have made to yourself throughout this book. Your instructional goals will also be guided by any formal curriculum that your school, your school district, or your program has adopted, as well as your textbook, any tests that your students will have to take, and your students' individual needs and characteristics. Unfortunately, you may not have much information about your students until instruction starts, and you may need to modify your long-term plans when you actually meet and get to know your students. (Chapter 1 discussed a number of important learner characteristics to keep in mind when planning your lessons.)

In order to begin long-term planning, first list your specific instructional objectives. Since most language curricula are closely tied to the course textbook, you should review your textbook to identify topics and activities. Please remember that language classes are not always organized around grammatical topics nor do they have to be. There are a number of other possibilities including conversational functions, cultural themes, and ongoing written or oral narratives such as soap operas or continuing stories (see Chapter 8). On the other hand, there shouldn't be too many instructional topics. Many teachers and textbook publishers greatly underestimate the amount of time it takes to learn a language and include so much material that teachers must rush students from chapter to chapter.

After identifying and selecting instructional topics, consult a calendar for important dates and start to map out a schedule. Begin by penciling in target dates for important course occurrences such as major tests, trying to choose dates that do not conflict with holidays or important school events. If possible, consult with a more experienced teacher for advice about designing a syllabus that is workable in your setting. Next, fill in the dates with other material and activities you want to include. I call this day-by-day listing of topics and activities a **planning block.** A block is not a lesson plan; rather, it is an outline of the material that you want to include in a lesson plan and is similar to the syllabi you might have used in some of your college courses. In some settings where there are a number of instructors teaching the same course, the block or syllabus is developed by one lead teacher or cooperatively by all the teachers. Try to include the following steps for each new topic or activity in your block:

1. Introduction including student familiarization with lesson objectives
2. Presentation of material
3. Practice
4. Communicative use
5. Evaluation (Evaluation can be formal, such as a test, or a quiz, or informal observation by the teacher to make sure that the material has been learned. The evaluation step could lead you back to any of the previous steps if you are not satisfied with how well your students performed.)

There is an example of a block for a beginning ESL class in the following section. Although blocks will likely be highly related to the textbook, they should be more than a reproduction of the book's table of contents.

Short-Term Planning

Once a block for a unit has been determined, it is time for actual daily and weekly lesson planning. To begin each day's lesson plan, start with the material listed for that day on your block. It is now necessary to translate the goals and topics into a set of activities for the day. This is an opportunity to apply all your creativity, as well as your knowledge of your students, of your target language, of second language acquisition theories, and of language teaching methodologies to decide what content and activities to include in each class session. This is also a good time to review the *Teaching Checklists* and any thoughts about language teaching that you recorded in response to the *Finding Your Way* and *Journal* reflection questions in each chapter. When faced with the seemingly monumental task of lesson planning, it is easy to forget what you originally hoped to accomplish with respect to the various aspects of language learning and teaching.

Here is some simple advice to help you organize each day's lesson:

1. Begin with a warm-up activity.
2. Include at least one listening, speaking, reading, and writing activity in each class session and include appropriate strategy instruction.
3. Have students use any new grammar communicatively.
4. Recycle vocabulary and grammar.
5. Integrate culture into your lessons.
6. Provide periodic opportunities for self-assessment.

With this advice in mind, you should take your block for the first week of the unit and preview any textbook or other materials that you listed on the block for each day. Try to map out a set of activities for each day that will engage your students while accomplishing your instructional objectives. When you have decided on activities, reconsider the plan from the perspective of a student. That is, think about what a student will be doing throughout the class session to make sure that there will be a variety of types of activities. Look at the following daily block.

VOICES FROM THE CLASSROOM

Block 1, Thursday, October 18, Beginning ESOL, Period 1:

Introduce and present new dialogue.

Poem about the changing seasons.

Grammar presentation: Question Formation.

Structure Drills: Questions.

From the teacher's perspective, this lesson block might seem like a balanced group of activities. It includes a new dialogue, some grammar, and some reading (the poem). From the students' perspective, however, this sequence of activities does not provide very much variety. Students will be asked to listen to and probably repeat the dialogue, listen to the poem, and listen to a grammar presentation. All the activities are whole-class activities, and students will spend most of their time listening to the teacher. This block could be improved by including some small-group work and true conversational tasks. Maybe students could divide into groups to write their own poems about the seasons.

It is a good idea to keep classroom management considerations in mind when planning lessons. It is helpful to review lesson plans in terms of **pacing,** amount of **structure,** and amount of teacher control. Activities such as quizzes engender high teacher control while other activities, such as small-group work, afford less control. Intensive reading activities tend to be slow-paced while many structure drills are rapid and energetic. Role-plays and many of the task-based activities are low-structure activities since students do not have clear steps to follow in order to complete them, while quizzes and grammar worksheets are high-structure activities. I generally advise new teachers to follow a low-structure or high-energy activity, such as a game, with an activity that allows for more teacher control, such as a grammar presentation. I would anticipate that a lesson that started with a quiz, followed by a game, a small-group conversation activity, and individual personalized questions might lead to classroom management problems, since the highest level of teacher control comes at the beginning of the class with the quiz, and the energetic game is followed by the low-structure small-group activity. It would be better to start the lesson with the individual question-answer activity followed by the quiz, the small-group conversation activity, and finally, the game. This second sequence begins with a medium-structure activity followed by the quiz, which is a high-structure, high-control activity to help the teacher reassert control of the class before the small-group conversation activity.

You may want to ask a more experienced teacher look at your final lesson plan. New teachers have a difficult time estimating how much time activities will take. It is not unusual to think that students will be able to read through a new text in a few minutes or that they will be attentive to conversational role-plays for 20 or 30 minutes. An experienced teacher can help you make more realistic judgments about timing. In any case, it is a good idea to have extra activities planned so that any extra time at the end of a class will not be wasted.

At this point, your lesson is almost ready, but you cannot expect to "perform" smoothly without practice. During these rehearsals, you will likely make additional changes to your plan. Finally, after you have used the lesson plan in class, you should make notes to yourself about any changes you might want to make to the plan before you teach the lesson again.

Giving Directions

Good lesson plans include specific, well-thought-out directions. You may have planned an interesting and well-balanced class session, but if students do not understand what they are supposed to do, your lesson will not be successful. In my experience, many new teachers often have difficulty giving clear classroom directions because they have not actually thought through their directions prior to the lesson. In addition to carefully planning your directions, it is important to make sure that your students pay attention to them. I suggest the following set of steps for helping students understand your directions:

1. Get students' attention.
2. Focus students' attention.
3. Give a motivation for the activity.

4. Give the directions *step by step.*
5. Give concrete examples wherever possible.
6. Take questions.
7. Monitor students.

This set of steps asks teachers to get and focus their students' attention before they start to give directions for an activity. Many times students miss directions because they are not paying attention or do not know which assignment the teacher is talking about. Getting and focusing the class's attention can be as simple as saying, "Class, turn to page 50 and look at the reading passage." When you have your students' attention, you need to give students a reason for the activity. Giving a motivation can be as simple as saying, "To practice direct objects, we are going to . . .," or as elaborate as dressing up as an old lady and announcing to the class that she is going to tell them about her childhood as an introduction to a lesson on past tense formation. Examples (Step 5) give students a concrete model of what they are supposed to do and are especially important when directions are given in the target language. New teachers often complain that they carefully prepare directions but that their students ask so many questions that they never get a chance to give the directions; Step 6 addresses this concern. In my experience, students should not be allowed to ask questions before the teacher has explained the activity completely. Allowing the students to break in with questions whenever they want interrupts the process and prevents the teacher (you) from giving directions in a logical order. If the directions are complicated, you should break them into steps and invite questions after each step.

Finally, monitoring student participation (Step 7) after starting an activity is essential. While giving the directions, you should watch the students' faces for signs of confusion and modify the directions accordingly. After you have given the directions, you should watch to make sure that your students actually begin the activity. If not, you should elicit questions or ask the students what they do not understand. If you know that certain students avoid starting activities or have difficulty understanding a task on their own, you should observe whether those students are doing what you have told them to do, and if not, be ready to step in and help them get started.

Choosing a Textbook

Few new teachers will have the opportunity to choose their own textbook, but many teachers are involved with textbook selection at some time during their teaching career. Fortunately or unfortunately, the array of textbooks can be overwhelming. Some textbooks have a very specific position on SLA issues and are written to be almost "teacher-proof," while others are very flexible and can be used by teachers with different philosophies of language teaching. Textbooks also vary with respect to their graphics and illustrations. ESL textbooks and books for the more commonly taught languages in the United States tend to have high production values with many pictures and expensive multicolored printing. Such artistic features are possible because of the high profit potential for textbooks for these languages. Books for the **less commonly taught languages** (LCT) such as Chinese, Japanese, Russian, and Arabic are usually less elaborate because there are fewer students who study these languages. Textbooks also differ with respect to the variety of the target language they emphasize. EFL teachers abroad must decide whether to focus on American or British English, and American teachers of Spanish have to decide how they are going to balance instruction in the various varieties of Spanish.

For most of my language teaching career, I believed that a good language teacher could use almost any textbook successfully and that a poor language teacher would still be poor no matter the textbook. I still believe this to some extent, but I have also come to recognize the importance of the textbook to students. The textbook *is* the language class for many students. They depend on the book to help them prepare for whatever the class asks of them. Moreover, since many new teachers use the textbook by itself to determine what they should do in class each day, it is important that the book be consistent with your beliefs about second language learning and teaching. Thus, textbooks, like language tests, can have a washback effect. If teachers believe that students should have the opportunity to listen to interesting and comprehensible target language input, then the textbook should offer excellent listening tasks or at least leave enough time for the teacher to provide those listening experiences in some other way. It is also true that there are no "perfect" textbooks. You are not likely to find one that is consistent with all your beliefs about language learning and teaching. Most teachers supplement their textbook in some way or other. You may remember that the SIOP Model includes the identification and incorporation of appropriate supplementary materials as a regular part of the lesson planning process.

Common Language Teaching Activities

Many textbooks include a number of common language teaching activities that are used by teachers regardless of their language teaching philosophy or teaching setting.

Dialogue Presentations

Language textbooks have long used dialogues to present examples of spoken language. The best dialogues present a *plausible* conversation with a twist of humor, and the poorer ones resemble the Shy-Date conversation from Chapter 5. Dialogues typically include new vocabulary and grammatical structures that are being introduced in the textbook chapter. Many textbooks follow the dialogue with a set of comprehension questions or a type of exercise called **directed dialogue** where students are told to say things to each other that were said in the dialogue. For example, if a character in the dialogue says, "I'm going home to study," the teacher would say to a student, "Amanda, tell Patricia that you are going home to study," and Amanda is supposed to say, "Patricia, I'm going home to study." (Frankly, I always found this kind of exercise to be display-like and too complicated for students. My students would get confused by the pronouns and usually say something like, "Patricia, *you* are going home to study.") Language texts often follow dialogues with presentations of the new vocabulary words and grammatical structures.

Personalized Questions

Personalized questions are common in language classes and are an excellent way to make classes more communicative. It is important, however, that the questions are true questions rather than display questions. Personalized questions have many uses. They can utilize grammatical structures in a communicative context, stimulate a writing assignment, or be the basis of small-group activities. Remember, however, to use sensitivity and discretion when asking personal questions. For example, not all students live in traditional families, and homeless students have difficulty when asked to describe their house or apartment. Your knowledge of your students should guide you in your selection of personalized questions so that you choose questions that will stimulate conversation rather than draw attention to delicate differences among students.

Oral Presentations

Language teachers often ask individual students or groups of students to prepare and make presentations on a variety of topics. Although students deliver these presentations orally, they are usually more similar to written rather than spoken varieties of language. Students usually write out their presentations in advance and then either practice them so that they can speak from notes or memorize them entirely. Students also have the opportunity to revise and proofread their presentation scripts, so it is likely that they will be using *monitored* rather than *unmonitored* language.

Grammar Presentations

Even though the first language, cognitive learning, experience, and social SLA theories all insist that language learners spend the majority of their time *using* the language, grammar presentations—either in the L1 or in the target language—followed by structure drills have been the core of many second language classes for generations. Most scholars and language teachers agree, however, that students should not be taught the sophisticated grammars used by linguists but rather simplified and concrete **pedagogic grammars.** Pedagogic grammars emphasize the grammatical structures that are most useful in terms of day-to-day conversations and explain grammar as nontechnically as possible. Many scholars agree, however, that it is probably not possible to write a complete pedagogic grammar that includes all the structures that language learners will need to speak and/or write. Many structures will need to be learned through negotiation of meaning and acquisition as the conversation theories and the Input Hypothesis suggest.

Structure Drills

Structure drills, also called pattern drills, can be used orally or in writing. They are exercises focused on specific grammatical structures that give students practice with new grammatical forms. Structure drills are often used for practice with new verb forms, but they can also be used for negation and question formation, word order, pronoun usage, and so forth. Structure drills should be followed with truly communicative usage of the forms so that students can begin to see the communicative value of the particular structure. For example, after learning the forms of regular verbs in the past tense, many language teachers ask students questions about how they spent their weekend or the previous summer.

Minimal Pairs

Minimal pairs are used to help students learn to differentiate sounds in the second language. The ability to distinguish sounds helps in the development of both pronunciation and listening comprehension. The English words "pin" and "pen" are considered a minimal pair in most varieties of English because they only differ by the **phonemes** *e* and *i*. Students usually are first given listening exercises where they are asked to distinguish the minimal pairs and later they are asked to practice pronouncing the words. Most textbooks go on to use the minimal pairs in sentences or paragraphs so that students learn to use context clues to help them distinguish the targeted sounds.

Although the term minimal pair refers to phoneme differences, many textbooks contain exercises that contrast pairs of sentences that differ with respect to other aspects of language. These activities may, for example, ask students to listen to sentences or paragraphs and then indicate whether the actions are taking place in the present (present tense) or if they took place in the past (past tense).

Vocabulary

Most language textbooks present a large number of vocabulary words. Some books use pictures to illustrate the new words and others use **glosses** in the L1. Since the number of words that textbooks include can be overwhelming to the student, it is important to distinguish between words that students should be able to use when they are speaking or writing and those words that just need to be recognized, especially when reading. These two categories of vocabulary words are often referred to by language teachers as **active** and **passive** vocabulary. Some language teachers also choose to teach less common or very formal grammatical structures for passive recognition only.

Cultural Vignettes

Many textbooks contain passages that describe the target country (or countries) and its culture and customs. These passages are meant to give students some explicit understanding of the lives of the people who speak their language. Some teachers distinguish between **big "C" culture** and **small "c" culture.** Big "C" (or capital C) culture refers to the great accomplishments of a culture and typically includes topics like literature, philosophy, architecture, important historical events and figures, and the arts. Some language teachers use the term *civilization* instead. Small "c" culture, on the other hand, corresponds more to an anthropological definition of culture and refers to the life ways and worldview of a people, or all the things that people do and know because they are members of a particular group.

Small-Group Activities and Pair Work

As second language classes have focused on communication, teachers have increasingly used small-group activities to give students a greater number of opportunities to talk during each class session. Current language textbooks include many conversational activities where classes are divided into small groups or pairs of students. Small-group activities can decrease the anxiety associated with speaking and are particularly well-suited to task-based activities. Small-group activities are also commonly used in content classes. Structuring activities in ESL classes similarly to those in content classes can help prepare ELs for the demands of their other classes.

Information-Gap Activities

Information-gap activities are usually pair but sometimes small-group activities that are arranged so that each of the participants receives only part of the necessary information. In order to accomplish the task, the students need to exchange the information they have. The task can be language-based or academic. In fact, this activity type is also commonly used in mainstream content classes. At the simplest level it is a matching activity: one student has a list of vocabulary words and the second student has definitions which have to be paired up with the words. A more complex information-gap activity asks students to decide which movie to go to. One student would have a list of movies and times, a second student would have the list of movies and the location of the theatres, and a third student could have the list of movies with different ticket prices. Many information-gap activities can also be classified as task-based activities.

Task-Based Activities

Task-based activities make classroom language more authentic by giving a genuine purpose to target language use. They also integrate listening, speaking, reading, writing, and culture. By providing opportunities for both spontaneous and prepared speech, tasks can give students more time to think before they have to talk (remember Judith Shrum's discussion of teacher wait-time in Chapter 5). Imagine that you are at a lecture and the speaker calls on you unexpectedly to explain your views on energy conservation. You would probably be able to say something on the topic, but at home that evening you would probably think of many others things you could have said or could have said better ("gee, I wish I had remembered to mention hybrid cars"). Thinking time is especially necessary when students discuss the more abstract CALP–type topics associated with content learning. Since task-based activities require several steps, students have the opportunity to offer their ideas at a later stage of the task even if they were not prepared to speak earlier.

Whole-Class Activities

Although there is a trend for language teachers to use a greater proportion of small-group activities, much language instruction still utilizes a whole-class format. Whole-class activities are appropriate for presenting information that everyone needs to know and for activities where you want to have the opportunity to scaffold or correct students' responses. Whole-class activities also afford the possibility of greater amounts of structure and teacher control.

Strategy Instruction

As recommended by the SIOP Model and the CALLA approach, explicit instruction in language learning and even content learning strategies is becoming more frequent in language classes. This instruction can be conducted in the L2 or in the L1 when learners have a common first language. Strategy instruction is often embedded in class activities so that students will know how best to approach any new type of learning.

Differentiating Instruction and Supporting Learner Autonomy

Current approaches to language teaching stress the development of higher-level academic language as well as cultural appropriateness and understanding. In addition, our understanding of second language acquisition has advanced greatly in the past few decades. For these reasons, your lessons will probably be very different than the ones you experienced as a language learner. This chapter has discussed the general process of lesson planning, but as you know from the rest of this book, language learners differ in many important ways and the same lesson plan will not be equally suited to the needs of all the students in the same class. Lessons will even need to be modified for classes with the same title since every group of students is different. It is important to **differentiate instruction,** particularly with respect to previous educational experiences, differing learning styles, and proficiency levels. In the case of content-based language teaching, background knowledge is an especially crucial variable. **Assessment to learn** allows teachers to modify their short- and long-term plans with ongoing feedback about how students are progressing.

It is important to remember that only a limited amount of language learning can happen during any class session, and it is essential for language teachers to foster learner **autonomy** so that language development is more likely to continue outside of the classroom. Students should be engaged in planning, problem solving, and eliciting language feedback both in and outside of the classroom. Accordingly, language (and content) teachers are increasingly incorporating strategy training, self-assessment, and other metacognitive approaches in their lesson plans to help students think about and control their language learning.

FINDING YOUR WAY

REFLECTIONS

What kinds of events have you had experience planning? For example, have you ever planned a party or an afternoon of activities for children? In what way was this kind of planning similar to lesson planning?

_____

_____

_____

_____

How can you incorporate the ESL or foreign language standards into your lesson planning?

_____

_____

_____

_____

_____

What would you look for in choosing a textbook?

_____

_____

_____

_____

PLANNING FOR YOUR CLASSES

What are some of the particular lesson planning considerations for your target student group? For example, younger learners have shorter attention spans and have difficulty concentrating during long activities.

_____

_____

_____

_____

Although most language teachers learn to use communicative language teaching approaches in their methods classes, they often find grammar-based teaching in the schools where they teach. As you plan your daily lessons, what can you do to ensure that there are substantial amounts of authentic communication and comprehensible input in your classes?

_____

_____

_____

_____

_____

PROJECTS

- With the help of your methods instructor, locate a copy of any curriculum documents you will be using in your teaching setting. Do you think they represent a good set of goals for language teaching?
- Review the first ten chapters of this book. Make a list of statements that _you_ believe to be true about second language learning and teaching. "More motivated students are more successful as language learners" and "It is important for teachers to encourage their students' motivation" would be examples of such statements. Share your lists of beliefs with a small group of other people in your methods class.
- Select a textbook in your target language. Plot out a block for the third chapter of the book. (The first chapter, and often the second chapter, of many language textbooks are not typical.) Write a lesson plan for the first day of the unit. Share your lesson plan with another person in your methods class to see if you have included enough detail so that your partner would be able to teach your lesson.

IN YOUR JOURNAL

- What were your favorite and least favorite classroom activities as a language learner?
- How carefully do you think your language teachers prepared their lessons?
- Did any of your language teachers have classroom management problems? Do you think that they or their lessons caused any of these problems?

TEACHING CHECKLIST

This checklist will help you develop lesson plans that are consistent with your teaching goals.

Yes   *No*

☐   ☐   I review the course textbook and program curriculum before I begin my long-term lesson planning.

☐   ☐   I consider the ESL or foreign language standards when developing lesson plans.

☐   ☐   I identify goals for my class guided by my language teaching philosophy, school, school district, textbook, and students' needs.

☐   ☐   I develop long-term plans for my classes so that my students have adequate time to learn all the material on the syllabus.

☐   ☐   I consult my notes and the Teaching Checklists when I am doing my daily lesson plans.

☐   ☐   I consider my students' particular learning needs when I plan my lessons.

☐   ☐   The textbook does not control my lesson plans.

☐   ☐   I include listening, speaking, reading, writing, and culture in my lessons.

☐   ☐   I include learning strategy instruction.

☐   ☐   I provide for differentiation in my lesson plans.

☐   ☐   I include opportunities for assessment for learning and student self-assessment in my lesson plans.

☐   ☐   I practice my lessons before each class.

☐   ☐   I review and revise my lesson plans for pacing and other classroom management considerations.

☐   ☐   I review and revise my lesson plans so that there will be a variety of activities from the students' perspective.

☐   ☐   I have extra activities planned in case my students finish the lesson early.

☐   ☐   After I have taught a lesson, I make changes to the plan or notes to myself about how I want to change the lesson the next time I teach it.

REFERENCES AND SUGGESTIONS FOR FURTHER READING

Allen, L. Q. (2002). Teachers' pedagogical beliefs and the standards for foreign language learning. *Foreign Language Annals, 35,* 518–529.

Arens, K., & Swaffar, J. (2000). Reading goals and the standards for foreign language learning. *Foreign Language Annals, 33,* 104–122.

Baily, K. (1996), The best laid plans: Teachers' in-class decisions to depart from their lesson plans. In K. Bailey & D. Nunan (Eds.), *Voices from the language classroom* (pp. 15–40). Cambridge, UK: Cambridge University Press.

Borg, S. (2003). Teacher cognition in language teaching: A review of research on what language teachers think, know, believe, and do. *Language Teaching, 36,* 81–109.

Chamot, A. U. (2009). *The CALLA handbook: Implementing the cognitive academic language learning approach* (2nd ed.). White Plains, NY: Pearson.

Echevarría, J., Vogt, M. E., & Short, K. (2008). *Making content comprehensible for English learners: The SIOP R Model* (3rd ed.). Boston, MA: Pearson.

Gearing, K. (1999). Helping less-experienced teachers of English to evaluate teachers' guides. *ELT Journal, 53,* 122–127.

Govani, J. M., & Feyton, C. M. (1999). Effects of the ACTFL-OPI–type training on student performance, instructional methods, and classroom materials in the secondary foreign language classroom. *Foreign Language Annals, 32,* 189–204.

Haley, M. (2004). Learner-centered instruction and the theory of multiple intelligences with second language learners. *Teachers College Record, 106,* 163–180.

Horwitz, E. K. (2005). Classroom management for teachers of Japanese and other foreign languages. *Foreign Language Annals, 38,* 56–68.

McKinley, K. K. (2002). National board certification available for teachers of world languages other than English. *Learning Languages, 7,* 10–15.

Poynor, L. (1998). ESL standards for pre-K–12 students: What they mean for primary teachers. *TESOL Journal, 7,* 4–5.

Rifkin, B. (2003). Guidelines for foreign language lesson planning. *Foreign Language Annals, 36,* 167–179.

Scebold, C. E., & Wallinger, L. M. (2000). An update on the status of foreign language education in the United States. *NASSP Bulletin, 84,* 1–9.

Seelye, H. N. (1974, 1976). *Teaching culture: Strategies for foreign language educators.* Skokie, IL: National Textbook Co.

Swaffar, J. (1998). Major changes: The standards project and the new foreign language curriculum. *ADFL Bulletin, 30,* 34–37.

Swender, E., & Duncan, G. (1998). ACTFL performance guidelines for K–12 learners. *Foreign Language Annals, 31,* 479–491.

Teachers of English to Speakers of Other Languages. (1997). *The ESL standards for pre-K–12 Students.* Alexandria, VA: TESOL.

Tucker, H. (2000). The place of the personal: The changing face of foreign language literature in a standards-based curriculum. *ADFL Bulletin, 31,* 53–58.

Yamada, Y., & Moeller, A. J. (2001). Weaving curricular standards into the language classroom: An action research study. *Foreign Language Annals, 34,* 26–34.

Young, D. J., & Oxford, R. (1993). Attending to learner reactions to introductory Spanish textbooks. *Hispania, 76,* 593–605.

PART FOUR

Where Do I Go from Here?

11 So, Am I Now a Language Teacher?

- What does it mean to be successful as a language teacher?
- What does it mean to be successful as a teacher?

Thinking of Yourself as a Language Teacher

As you read this book, I hope that you began to see yourself as a capable language teacher, confident in your abilities to guide and support students through the second language acquisition process. You may still recognize some areas in need of improvement, but I hope that you have discovered or rediscovered some unique talents that will make you a very special language teacher.

Not surprisingly, I still have several additional pieces of advice. First of all, do not worry *too* much about whether your students like you. This may sound like a very strange recommendation. After all, liking students and wanting to help them were probably important reasons why you decided to become a language teacher in the first place. Moreover, I have stressed the importance of understanding and caring for your students throughout this book. Why, then, should I now advise you not to worry about what the students think of you? The answer is simple. New teachers are often overly sensitive to their students' reactions, which is, of course, understandable. New teachers have chosen a profession where positive student regard is one of the primary benefits. In addition, new teachers are conscientious and work very hard to prepare their first year's lessons. It is only natural to expect that students will appreciate their work. Unfortunately, it is not always natural for students to show their gratitude. Students can often sense when their teachers are too worried about gaining their approval. Remember that it is the teacher's (your!) responsibility to decide what will go on in the language classroom and then to work to ensure that those plans come to pass. Sometimes your students will not immediately like your decisions, but it is your job to make those decisions. If you are overly focused on your students' reactions, you are more likely to be perceived by students as asking for their approval. Too often, new teachers put tag phrases at the end of their directions ("Take out your books, OK?") or phrase their directions as questions ("Do you want to take out your homework?"). This type of announcement makes teachers seem tentative, as if they are unsure whether the students will actually follow their directions. And ironically, students do not tend to like teachers who seem unsure of themselves. Although I am suggesting that you face your students with confidence, I am *not* suggesting that you should never change your mind when faced with reasonable proposals from your students or that you should try to hide any mistakes you make.

I have two other important pieces of advice for you. They are: talk to your students and listen to your students. Sometimes, students do not do what their teachers want them to do because the teachers did not clearly communicate their expectations. During my first year of teaching, my last period class was a Spanish class. As I had taken only two years of high school Spanish, I felt very uncomfortable teaching the class, and I am sure my students sensed my tentativeness. Every day was a struggle to keep the students on task until one day, in frustration, I threw my book on the floor. My class was astonished, and I believed them when they said that they had not realized how unhappy I was with their behavior. I had been so busy "understanding their behavior" and worrying about my own competency in Spanish that I never actually told them that I was unhappy about the way they were acting. After that day, if the class was starting to become uncooperative, I would pretend to drop my book, and the class would *usually* get back on task relatively quickly. If I had not "told" them that their behavior was unacceptable by dropping my book, their behavior would probably have never improved and would have likely gotten worse.

My final piece of advice is to listen to your students. This advice refers to your work both as a language teacher and as a teacher. As a *language teacher*, it is essential for you to listen to your students to understand what they are trying to say, so that you can help them say it. You already know that the technical term for this is *scaffolding*. If students do not believe that you are listening to them, they will not be motivated to try to talk to you in the target language. As a *teacher*, being aware of your students' welfare is fundamental to your job. Sometimes students will talk to you directly, but you also need to keep a careful watch on your students because they will not always tell you what you need to know. Second language teachers, especially, have the responsibility of helping their students cope with their entire academic experience.

Becoming Open to New Ideas About Language and Language Teaching

In the preface to this book, I asked you to accept my challenge to examine your preexisting assumptions about language learning and teaching. You might remember my anecdote about the student who told me that my methods course had reinforced everything that she believed about language learning and teaching. I hope that as you read this book you questioned your assumptions about language learning and arrived at a new, more informed set of working beliefs. I use the term "working beliefs" because I strongly hope that you will continue to learn more about second language acquisition and language teaching methodologies and that you remain open to new perspectives throughout your career as a language teacher. At the end of this chapter, I will ask you to compare your current beliefs about language learning and teaching with the ones you had when you started reading this book and the ones you expect your students to have. I recommend that you do this again from time to time during your teaching career.

Becoming a Better Language Teacher

I sincerely believe that you will be a wonderful beginning language teacher, but teachers improve with experience, and you will not be as good a language teacher in your first years of teaching as you will be later on. There are three areas that are especially important for your continued development as a language teacher: maintenance and improvement of second language competence, observation of your teaching, and participation in professional communities. By engaging in these three activities, you will go a long way toward achieving your full potential as a language teacher.

Improving Your Second Language Competence

If you are a learner of your second language, you are going to need to pay close attention to maintaining your second language competence throughout your teaching career. If English is your L1, you should make a special effort to learn more about your students' languages and cultures. If you are teaching your heritage language, you may need to concentrate on your academic language proficiency. It is especially difficult to maintain your ability to speak a second language when you only speak it with language learners. The only oral input you get is from speakers who speak an interlanguage, and you do not have more competent speakers to scaffold your own conversational attempts. You should, therefore, develop a plan to improve and maintain your language competency. Just as musicians must practice to keep up their musical skills, second language speakers must continue to use their receptive and productive language skills to keep up their second language competence. People who live outside their L1 environment even find that over time they begin to lose some of their language facility.

Now that you are familiar with many SLA theories and language teaching methodologies, you are in an excellent position to design a language learning program for yourself. You could be your own student and choose a set of experiences and tasks that are perfectly coordinated with your needs and interests. In addition to the personal benefits, you will also be a positive role model as a language learner for your students.

Action Research

Although most teachers do not do formal research in their classes, most do do informal research whether they recognize it or not. When teachers try new teaching methods or activities and then observe the results to decide whether or not their students benefited from the new approach, they are doing informal research. One type of formal research is based on the idea that the best educational research is done in real classrooms with the teachers who are most familiar with the students and the instructional setting taking an active role. This type of research is called **action research**, and it is similar in many ways to the informal research that many teachers do. According to Geoffrey Mills (2000), "Action research is any systematic inquiry conducted by teacher researchers, principals, school counselors or other stakeholders in the teaching/learning environment to gather information about the ways their particular school operates, how they teach, and how well students learn" (p. 6). In fact, action research is often carried out by individual classroom teachers.

You may not feel ready to undertake something with as grand a label as "action research," but you should be prepared to begin the systematic observation of your teaching. In systematic observation you observe the results of your own instruction over time, from multiple perspectives, and with as little bias as possible. It is very easy to notice pronunciation difficulties in your class one day and conclude that your students have pronunciation problems, but not all your students might be having problems or they might only have difficulty during certain activities. Therefore, before you decide to change the way you are teaching, it is important to ask yourself some questions:

- Do my students always make these pronunciation errors, or did they just make them today?
- Do the students consistently make those errors, or did the students only make them during specific activities?
- Did all students make the errors, or was it only a few students?
- If only a few students made the errors, were they all from the same first language background?
- Do other teachers notice these errors, or is it just me?

These questions ask you to consider whether the errors are made consistently (over time), whether they are made on different language learning tasks (multiple sources), and whether the errors are noticed by people who are not looking for pronunciation errors (with as little bias as possible).

You actually are not very far from doing true action research if you can answer the questions. Action research involves a similar set of steps:

1. Ask questions.
2. Collect data from multiple sources. (Do systematic observation.)
3. Analyze the data.
4. Report the results.
5. Design an action plan.

You might be wondering how action research differs from any other kind of educational research, since all educational research asks questions, collects data, analyzes data, and draws conclusions. One important difference is the requirement in action research to report the research results to the individuals who are in the best position to make any indicated changes. So in the case of teachers doing action research in their own classrooms, they would report the results to themselves! In addition, action research requires the development of an actual plan to implement the suggested changes. In other words, action research is not simply focused on understanding why or why not students learn, but on how to make *changes* that will actually *improve* student learning. Action research requires the involvement of an individual—usually the teacher—who is closely *connected to the learning setting*, the selection of *practical questions* that are important to the people involved, the examination of real *classrooms or schools*, the reporting of the results to the people involved, and the *application of the results to improve instruction* in the particular setting. Action research is initiated by the people who are closest to the research questions with the intention of improving instruction in *their* setting.

In the preface to this book, I said that I considered language learning and language teaching to be dynamic processes and that language teachers should pay attention to how our students learn languages and how we as teachers make decisions about how we teach. I hope that you can see how closely action research is related to the idea that learning and teaching should be viewed as processes rather than products. Since after reading this book you understand the importance of teachers observing the processes of language learning and teaching, it is not a very large jump to true action research. Either action research, or less formal observation of your teaching, will make you aware of the effectiveness of your teaching so you can correct problems and build on strengths. You will become a better language teacher so that your students can be better learners. The concepts of **assessment for learning** and learner **autonomy** call for you to communicate your teaching objectives directly to your students and give them feedback about their progress so that they can plan how they can go forward **(metacognition).**

Professional Development

Self-study is an excellent option among the many sources of professional development for language teachers. The Finding Your Way sections in this book were designed for self-study, and I hope that you read back over your thoughts from time to time throughout your language teaching career. I also hope that you will read at least some of the books and articles listed in the References and Suggestions for Further Reading sections of this book. I have chosen both practical and theory-oriented materials to give you suggestions for new activities and teaching approaches as well as a fuller understanding of the nature of language learning. I specifically chose articles that are appropriate for teachers with different amounts of experience. Some of the articles will be more interesting to you as a beginning teacher, and some will become more interesting to you later in your teaching career.

As a teacher, you should also plan to regularly read at least one of the many excellent journals related to language teaching. The References and Suggestions for Further Reading sections include a number of good choices, and your methods instructor can give you more specific recommendations for your particular target language and learner group. The Teaching Checklist in Chapter 3 also lists a number of language teaching journals related to some of the less commonly taught foreign languages. Browse through some recent issues of language teaching journals to see which ones are the most interesting to you. There will be new SLA theories, research studies, and language teaching methodologies for you to consider throughout your career; sometimes it can be overwhelming to keep up with new trends in your teaching field and your professional responsibilities at the same time. If you find it difficult to interpret research articles in professional journals, you may find it helpful to ask yourself the same questions that I did about SLA theories in Chapter 2: Do children and adults learn second languages differently? Why are some learners more successful than others? and How should learner errors be handled? Then, use your common sense, your teaching experience, and your knowledge of second language acquisition to decide if it is a theory that can help you in your teaching.

As you look at the professional journals, you will notice that several of them are published by professional organizations for language teachers, such as the International Association of Teachers of English as a Second Language (TESOL), the National Association of Bilingual Education (NABE), the International Association of Teachers of English as a Foreign Language (IATEFL), and the American Council of Teachers of Foreign Languages (ACTFL). There also are organizations related to the teaching of specific languages (see list of journals in Chapter 3). By joining one or more professional organizations, you will be able to network with other language teachers and keep up-to-date on the latest trends through online communities, e-mail groups, webcasts, meetings, and other resources. Before long, you may develop a new teaching approach or an action research project of your own that you might want to share with other language teachers. Your methods instructor can tell you about language teaching groups and meetings in your area. Many cities, states, and provinces across the world have their own associations and meetings for language teachers. The TESOL association has affiliates in every state in the US and across the world. If there are not already organizations for language teachers in your area, maybe you will be the person to start one!

I also strongly encourage you to find a mentor teacher and other beginning teachers to talk with, especially during your first years of teaching. Many new teachers are surprised to find that teaching can sometimes be a lonely profession. Certainly, you see and talk to many students during the day, but contact with other adults can be less frequent. Teaching can be especially lonely when you have a problem and no one to ask for help. I have always found the language teachers I have worked with to be compassionate and truly helpful people, and I urge you to ask a colleague teacher for help whenever you need it. I am certain that if one of your colleagues were having a problem, you would try to help. I also want to personally invite all teachers who have read this book to become members of the unofficial BLT (Becoming a Language Teacher) Club. I sincerely hope that all club members will support each other through teaching successes and teaching challenges.

Your Future as a Language Teacher

In the course of my career as a language teacher I have seen many trends and quite a few fads in language teaching. In the 1970s, language teachers were told that language teaching would soon be revolutionized by the new language laboratories where students could listen to target language materials and record and listen to their own speech. Language teachers could listen to individual students repeating material from prepared tapes and responding to structure drills. But while many language learners and teachers found the laboratories to be useful, the labs did not prove to be the panacea that they were advertised to be. I mention language laboratories because today's language teachers are also hearing about the great possibilities that new electronic media are bringing to language teaching, and I expect that you will also hear many claims and see many changes during your career.

It is important to remember that technology cannot change the way humans learn second languages. Technology can only provide assistance to the language learning process. Therefore, when you think about using new technology in your teaching, you should ask yourself the same kinds of questions that you would ask when choosing a language textbook or other curriculum material. You should think about your understanding of how second languages are learned and consider whether the medium in question is consistent with those understandings. If you believe, for example, that second language vocabulary is learned through reading or listening to new words in an authentic language context, you should not adopt materials that have students clicking on isolated words to see translations. It is also important to choose technological resources that are compatible with your students' specific learning needs and learning styles.

It is, of course, difficult to predict exactly how technology will change language teaching in the future. Many language educators in the 1970s were sure that language laboratories would be an integral part of language programs from that time on, but that prediction did not come true. Students soon owned their own audiocassette recorders so that they did not have to come to the language lab to listen to recorded tapes. In addition, students did not always use the technology in the ways they were supposed to use it. Instead of listening to the tapes and carefully repeating after them, many students made noises and only pretended to mimic the model sentences. I am hesitant to speculate how technology will change language teaching in the coming years. But I will offer you a few suggestions for integrating technologies that are already available to language teachers. (You should also look back over Chapters 4 through 9 for suggestions about how to use technology in various aspects of a second language curriculum.) Most importantly, use the authentic language materials that are now readily available. Students have many sources for language materials in addition to their course textbooks, and these materials make it possible for individuals and groups of learners to pursue a great variety of realistic tasks in the second language. Frankly, I am disappointed that these materials are not used more frequently in language classes. Digital approaches also have the potential for making authentic language testing more available and less burdensome to teachers.

Today's language learners have greater access to members of the target language community and to the target culture than any previous generation of language learners. With digital media, it is relatively easy for students to communicate with each other in writing, and more and more websites are offering opportunities for real-time conversations. I am hopeful that these technologies will help reduce the amount of social distance that currently exists between many learning and target groups as well as the amount of anxiety that students experience when using their new language. They should certainly contribute to greater learner autonomy. However, it is unlikely that untrained conversational partners will supply the kind of careful scaffolding and conversational feedback that SLA theories see as most advantageous for language learning; thus, classroom interactions will still have an important role in helping students develop full language competence.

In addition to technological changes, various economic, social, and political trends will also influence how languages are learned and taught in the future. You are probably aware that many economists and political scientists are forecasting increased economic interdependence among the countries of the world in the coming decades. Such factors will likely mean changes in which languages are commonly and less commonly taught and who will study and teach these languages. It will be especially interesting to see how the distinction between second and foreign language context changes in the coming years in light of our increasingly interconnected world. For example, are English learners in China second or foreign language learners when they interact regularly with English speakers through social media? Economic influences are also causing the growth of more specialized language classes, and classes for learners who want to use a language for a specific career purpose are a growing trend (LSP). Increased digital resources will allow greater numbers of students to pursue language learning without enrolling in formal classes.

My best advice is to start your career as a language teacher with the expectation that your work will be different in the years and decades to come. You will not be able to develop a detailed set of lesson plans during your first year of teaching and teach from those plans for the rest of your time as a language teacher. But you probably would not want to! In my experience, language teachers are creative and flexible people who thrive on new challenges.

Beginning Your Journey as a Language Teacher

It is now time to begin your journey as a language teacher. I hope that this book has helped you "find your way" and that you will look back over the thoughts you recorded here from time to time. I recommend recording some of your thoughts that you would like to remember later in your teaching career, and if you took my suggestion and recorded your answers to the Reflections and In Your Journal questions in this book, look over those responses now and periodically during your teaching career. I also suggest that you review the Teaching Checklists, especially when planning new lessons. Try not to be too hard on yourself if the demands of teaching have pulled you away from some of your original goals. Teaching is a demanding career, and no one is perfect. I sincerely believe that you are well on your way to becoming the teacher *you* want to be. I wish you a fascinating and fulfilling journey. May I be the first to welcome you to the language teaching profession. I am proud to have you as a colleague!

FINDING YOUR WAY

REFLECTIONS

How can language teachers help each other? What would you like to do at a BLT Club meeting?

_____

_____

_____

_____

_____

How will your teaching situation be different from the ones you experienced as a student?

_____

_____

_____

_____

_____

PLANNING FOR YOUR CLASSES

What do you want to remember about your own learning experiences when you become a language teacher?

_____

_____

_____

_____

_____

What do you want to remember from your language teaching methods course when you become a language teacher?

_____

_____

_____

_____

What do you want to remember from this book when you become a language teacher?

_____

_____

_____

_____

Now that you have read this book, what goals do you have for your students in learning a second language? How are they different from the goals that you listed in Chapter 1?

_____

_____

_____

_____

PROJECTS

- Observe several language classes at different levels. Do the classes seem different to you now that you have more knowledge and experience as a language teacher? What language teaching methods and activities do you recognize? What would you do differently than the teachers that you observed?
- Complete the Beliefs about Language Learning Inventory and the Teacher Foreign Language Anxiety Inventory (see Appendixes A and C) again and compare the results to the answers you gave after reading Chapter 1.
- Review the list of statements about language learning and teaching that you made after Chapter 10. Make any changes based on your current beliefs. Compare your lists of beliefs with a small group of other people in your methods class.
- Make a plan to improve or maintain your language competence. Give a rationale for each step in your plan from the perspective of SLA theory and research. Compare your plan with other students' in your methods class.
- Browse through some recent issues of language teaching journals. What are some of the important topics that the authors are discussing? What do the authors see as future trends in language teaching? Do you agree with their forecasts?

IN YOUR JOURNAL

- Do you feel prepared to start your work as a language teacher?
- Do you still want to be a language teacher?
- What can you do to overcome the inevitable stresses that come with being a new teacher?

TEACHING CHECKLIST

This checklist will help guide you during your journey as a language teacher.

Yes   *No*

☐   ☐   I demonstrate confidence in my language abilities.

☐   ☐   I communicate to my students confidence in my ability to manage the learning in my classroom.

☐   ☐   I present myself as a good model as a language learner.

☐   ☐   I reflect on my beliefs about language learning.

☐   ☐   I observe the results of my teaching and make appropriate changes.

☐   ☐   I maintain my language ability.

☐   ☐   I have people with whom I can talk when I have teaching difficulties and successes.

☐   ☐   I keep up with new approaches in language teaching.

☐   ☐   I keep up with new technological approaches that can be applied to language teaching.

☐   ☐   I use digital media in my teaching.

☐   ☐   I am happy that I am a language teacher.

REFERENCES AND SUGGESTIONS FOR FURTHER READING

Allen, H., & Negueruela-Azarola, E. (2010), The professional development of future professors of foreign languages: Looking back, looking forward. *Modern Language Journal, 94*, 377–395.

Árva, V. , &. Medgyes, P. (2000). Native and non-native teachers in the classroom. *System, 28*, 355–372.

Bartels, N. (2002). Professional preparation and action research: Only for language teachers? *TESOL Quarterly, 36*, 71–79.

Chapelle, C. (2007). Technology and second language acquisition. *Annual Review of Applied Linguistics, 27*, 98–114.

Crookes, G., & Chandler, P. M. (2001). Introducing action research into the education of post-secondary foreign language teachers. *Foreign Language Annals, 34*, 131–140.

Dhonau, S., & McAlpine, D. (2002). "Streaming" best practices: Using digital video-teaching segments in the FL/ESL methods course. *Foreign Language Annals, 35*, 632–636.

Dove, M., & Honigsfeld, A. (2010). ESL Co-teaching and collaboration: Opportunities to develop teacher leadership and enhance student learning. *TESOL Journal, 1*, 3–22.

García, P. (2010). What every beginning language teacher needs to know . . . and begins to learn. In G. C. Lipton (Ed.), *Practical handbook to elementary FLES programs.* (5th ed.) (pp. 425–430). Kensington, MD: National FLES Institute.

Hayward, N. M., & Tuzi, F. (2003). Confessions of a technophobe and a technophile: The changing perspective of technology in ESL. *TESOL Journal, 12*, 3–8.

Keyes, R. (1976). *Is there life after high school?* Boston, MA: Little, Brown.

Lacorte, M., & Krastel, T. C. (2002). "Zapatero a tus zapatos"? Action research in the Spanish language classroom. *Hispania, 85*, 907–917.

Levy, M. (2009). Technologies in use for second language learning. *Modern Language Journal, 93,* 769–782

Liu, M., Moore, Z., Graham, L., & Lee, S. (2002). A look at the research on computer-based technology use in second language learning: Review of literature from 1990–2000. *Journal of Research on Technology in Education. 34,* 250–273.

Liu, M., Traphagan, T., Huh, J., Koh, Y., Choi, G., & McGregor, A. (2008). Designing websites for ESL learners: A usability testing study. *CALICO Journal, 25,* 207–240.

Lord, G., & Lomicka, L. L. (2004). Developing collaborative cyber communities to prepare tomorrow's teachers. *Foreign Language Annals, 37,* 401–408.

Luton, L. (2003). If the computer did my homework, how come I didn't get an "A"? *French Review, 76,* 766–770.

Mills, G. E. (2000). *Action research: A guide for the teacher researcher.* Upper Saddle River, NJ: Prentice-Hall.

Morrison, S. (2002). *Interactive language learning on the Web.* (Report No. ED472851). Washington, DC: ERIC Clearinghouse on Languages and Linguistics.

O'Dowd, R. (2011). Online foreign language interaction: Moving from the periphery to the core of foreign language education? *Language Teaching, 44,* 368–380.

Payne, B., & Manning, B. (1990). The effect of cognitive self-instructions on pre-service teachers' anxiety about teaching. *Contemporary Education Psychology, 15,* 261–267.

Pope, S. (2002). Journal reflections of a first-year teacher. *Learning Languages, 7,* 8–10.

Roever, C. (2001). Web-based language testing. *Language Learning and Technology, 5,* 84–94.

Ryan, K. (Ed.). (1992). *The roller coaster year: Essays by and for beginning teachers.* New York, NY: Harper Collins.

Salaberry, M. R. (2001). The use of technology in second language learning and teaching: A retrospective. *Modern Language Journal, 85,* 39–56.

Swanson, P. (2010). Efficacy and language teacher attrition: A case for mentorship beyond the classroom. *NECTFL Review, 66,* 48–72.

Yamada, Y., & Moeller, A. J. (2001). Weaving curricular standards into the language classroom: An action research study. *Foreign Language Annals, 34,* 26–34.

APPENDIX A

The Beliefs About Language Learning Inventory (BALLI): ESL Version 2.0*

Each item on the BALLI asks about a specific belief that a person might have about language learning. The BALLI is not a single scale so the items should not be added together or averaged. Students who respond with a "1" or a "5" usually have a stronger belief than students who respond with a "2" or a "4" to that same question, but it is important to remember that some people tend to avoid the extreme points on a scale when responding to a questionnaire of this type. "Threes" should be considered a neutral response indicating either that the person is not sure or that he or she has not previously thought about the issue. Items 4 and 14 use a multiple choice format. If there are particular topics you want to learn your students' opinions of, you could include additional items on the questionnaire when you use it with your students. You should choose either 44a or 44b or simply modify item 44 to include the specific test(s) your students will have to take.

It is likely that your students will have a range of responses on most questions. Although there are no right or wrong answers to the BALLI, some responses will be more consistent with what scholars know about how people learn second languages than others. When students demonstrate a limited view of language learning (i.e., they strongly agree that "learning English is mainly a matter of learning a lot of new vocabulary words"), you may want to address those beliefs directly in strategy training.

This version of the BALLI uses English as the language the learner is trying to learn. It is also written in simple language so that you can use it with English learners from a number of first language backgrounds. If you are teaching a different language, you can change English to any other language, or you could replace it with the phrase, "the language I am trying to learn." To think about your own beliefs, substitute the phrase, "the language I teach."

Directions: For each item, indicate whether you (1) strongly disagree, (2) disagree, (3) neither agree nor disagree, (4) agree, or (5) strongly agree. For questions 4 and 14, select the number that most closely corresponds to your opinion.

1. It is easier for children than adults to learn a foreign language.
2. Some people have a special ability for learning foreign languages.

*To use the BALLI for research purposes, please contact Elaine Horwitz at horwitz@mail.utexas.edu.

3. Some languages are easier to learn than others.
4. English is:
    1. a very difficult language.
    2. a difficult language.
    3. a language of medium difficulty.
    4. an easy language.
    5. a very easy language.
5. People from my country are good at learning foreign languages.
6. I believe that I will learn to speak English very well.
7. It is important to speak English with an excellent accent.
8. It is necessary to know about English-speaking cultures in order to speak English.
9. You shouldn't say anything in English until you can say it correctly.
10. It is easier for someone who already speaks a foreign language to learn another one.
11. It is best to learn English in an English-speaking country.
12. I enjoy practicing English with the people I meet.
13. In order to speak English, you have to think in English.
14. It's ok to guess if you don't know a word in English.
15. If someone spent one hour a day learning a language how long would it take for them to learn that language very well?
    1. less than a year.
    2. 1–2 years.
    3. 3–5 years.
    4. 5–10 years.
    5. You can't learn a language in one hour a day.
16. I have a special ability for learning foreign languages.
17. The most important part of learning English is learning vocabulary words.
18. It is a good idea to practice speaking with other people who are learning English.
19. It is better to have teachers who are native-speakers of English.
20. If I learn to speak English very well, I will have better opportunities for a good job.
21. If beginning students are permitted to make errors in English, it will be difficult for them to speak correctly later on.
22. The most important part of learning English is learning the grammar.
23. It is important to practice with multi-media.
24. Women are better than men at learning foreign languages.
25. I want to speak English well.
26. I can learn a lot of from group activities with other students in my English class.
27. It is easier to speak than understand English.
28. I would like to learn English so that I can get to know English speakers.
29. I can learn a lot from non-native English teachers.
30. Learning a foreign language is different from learning other academic subjects.

31. It is possible to learn English on your own without a teacher or a class.
32. The most important part of learning English is learning how to translate from my native language.
33. Students and teachers should only speak English during English classes.
34. I can find a lot of useful materials to practice English on the Internet.
35. It is easier to read and write English than to speak and understand it.
36. I have to spend so much time preparing for big English tests, that I don't have time to actually learn English.
37. It is important to speak English like a native speaker.
38. People who are good at mathematics or science are not good at learning foreign languages.
39. People in my country feel that it is important to speak English.
40. I would like to have English-speaking friends.
41. People who speak more than one language are very intelligent.
42. Everyone can learn to speak a foreign language.
43. I feel timid speaking English with other people.
44. a. State exit tests are good tests of my English ability.
    b. Tests like the TOEFL, the IELTS, or the TOIEC are good tests of my English ability.

APPENDIX B

Foreign Language Classroom Anxiety Scale (FLCAS)*

The FLCAS has 33 questions which are scored on a 5-point scale ranging from 1 (strongly disagree) to 5 (strongly agree). This version uses the phrase "foreign language," but English or any other language can be substituted in the items.

The FLCAS can be tricky to score because some of the questions reflect anxiety and some of them reflect a lack of anxiety, but if you read each item carefully, you should not be confused. You should always score a "5" for the highest level of anxiety and a "1" for the least anxiety.

For example, for item 3 (I tremble when I know that I'm going to be called on in language class), "5" (strongly agree) indicates a high level of anxiety while "1" (strongly disagree) indicates a low level of anxiety. Items 1, 3, 4, 6, 7, 9, 10, 12, 13, 15, 16, 17, 19, 20, 21, 23, 24, 25, 26, 27, 29, 30, 31, and 33 should be scored in this straightforward way. However some of the items like, item 2 (I don't worry about making mistakes in language class), reflect a lack of anxiety. For these items, a "5" (strongly agree) would indicate a low level of anxiety while a "1" (strongly disagree) would indicate a high level of anxiety.

Items 2, 5, 8, 11, 14, 18, 22, 28, and 32 are called reverse-scored items. For these items, you will need to switch your students' responses. "Fives" should be reverse-scored to "1s," "4s" to "2s," "1s" to "5s," and "2s" to "4s." Of course, "3s" will not have to be switched. By paying attention to the regular and the reverse-scored items, higher total scores on the FLCAS will represent higher levels of anxiety.

To determine a student's anxiety level, add up their responses to all the questions, remembering to first reverse-score the items that need reverse-scoring, then divide the total by 33 (the total number of questions). Students with averages around 3 should be considered slightly anxious, while students with averages below 3 are probably not very anxious. Students who average near 4 and above are probably fairly anxious, and you should begin to work with them to find a way to reduce their anxiety.

Directions: For each item, indicate whether you (1) strongly disagree, (2) disagree, (3) neither agree nor disagree, (4) agree, or (5) strongly agree.

1. I never feel quite sure of myself when I am speaking in my foreign language class.
2. I don't worry about making mistakes in language class.

*To use the FLCAS for research purposes, please contact Elaine Horwitz at horwitz@mail.utexas.edu.

3. I tremble when I know that I'm going to be called on in language class.
4. It frightens me when I don't understand what the teacher is saying in the foreign language.
5. It wouldn't bother me at all to take more foreign language classes.
6. During language class, I find myself thinking about things that have nothing to do with the course.
7. I keep thinking that the other students are better at languages than I am.
8. I am usually at ease during tests in my language class.
9. I start to panic when I have to speak without preparation in language class.
10. I worry about the consequences of failing my foreign language class.
11. I don't understand why some people get so upset over foreign language classes.
12. In language class, I can get so nervous I forget things I know.
13. It embarrasses me to volunteer answers in my language class.
14. I would not be nervous speaking the foreign language with native speakers.
15. I get upset when I don't understand what the teacher is correcting.
16. Even if I am well-prepared for language class, I feel anxious about it.
17. I often feel like not going to my language class.
18. I feel confident when I speak in foreign language class.
19. I am afraid that my language teacher is ready to correct every mistake I make.
20. I can feel my heart pounding when I'm going to be called on in language class.
21. The more I study for a language test, the more confused I get.
22. I don't feel pressure to prepare very well for language class.
23. I always feel that the other students speak the foreign language better than I do.
24. I feel very self-conscious about speaking the foreign language in front of other students.
25. Language class moves so quickly I worry about getting left behind.
26. I feel more tense and nervous in my language class than in my other classes.
27. I get nervous and confused when I am speaking in my language class.
28. When I'm on my way to language class, I feel very sure and relaxed.
29. I get nervous when I don't understand every word the language teacher says.
30. I feel overwhelmed by the number of rules you have to learn to speak a foreign language.
31. I am afraid that the other students will laugh at me when I speak the foreign language.
32. I would probably feel comfortable around native speakers of the foreign language.
33. I get nervous when the language teacher asks questions I haven't prepared for in advance.

APPENDIX C

Teacher Foreign Language Anxiety Scale (TFLAS)*

The TFLAS has 18 questions, and like the FLCAS, it is scored on a 5-point scale ranging from 1 (strongly disagree) to 5 (strongly agree). Also like the FLCAS, it has reverse-scored items (items 2, 4, 8, 10, 11, 12, 14, 16, 17, and 18). (See the FLCAS directions for a full description of reverse-scoring.) This version of the TFLAS uses the phrase "foreign language," but English or any other language can be substituted in the items.

To determine your anxiety level, add up your responses to all the questions, remembering to first reverse-score the items that need reverse-scoring, then divide the total by 18 (the total number of questions). If your average is around 3, it is possible that you are slightly anxious about your language proficiency. An average near or above 4 implies at least some amount of anxiety. Whatever your score on the TFLAS indicates, however, you are really the best judge of your own anxiety. Simply use the questionnaire as a resource to help you begin to examine your language confidence.

Directions: For each item, indicate whether you (1) strongly disagree, (2) disagree, (3) neither agree nor disagree, (4) agree, or (5) strongly agree.

1. It frightens me when I don't understand what someone is saying in my foreign language.
2. I would not worry about taking a course conducted entirely in my foreign language.
3. I am afraid that native speakers will notice every mistake I make.
4. I am pleased with the level of foreign language proficiency I have achieved.
5. I feel self-conscious speaking my foreign language in front of teachers of my foreign language.
6. When speaking my foreign language, I can get so nervous I forget things I know.
7. I feel overwhelmed by the number of rules you have to learn in order to speak a foreign language.
8. I feel comfortable around native speakers of my foreign language.
9. I never feel quite sure of myself when I am speaking my foreign language in front of native speakers.

*To use the TFLAS for research purposes, please contact Elaine Horwitz at horwitz@mail.utexas.edu.

10. I am not nervous speaking my foreign language with students.
11. I don't worry about making mistakes in my foreign language.
12. I speak my language well enough to be a good foreign language teacher.
13. I get nervous when I don't understand every word a native speaker says.
14. I feel confident when I speak my foreign language.
15. I always feel that other teachers speak the language better than I do.
16. I don't understand why some people think learning a foreign language is so hard.
17. I try to speak my foreign language with native speakers whenever I can.
18. I feel that my foreign language preparation was adequate to become a foreign language teacher.

GLOSSARY

abstract language   A variety of language used to discuss objects or people who are not present in the "here and now," as well as concepts or ideas. *See also* concrete language.

academic language   A somewhat formal variety of language used for academic purposes in school settings to discuss abstract topics. It uses precise vocabulary terms.

academic literacy   Emphasizes the development of reading and writing abilities in academic varieties of the language. Also refers to the development of content and cultural knowledge necessary to school success and the ability to function in the school environment.

academic writing   The type of writing that students must do in content classes and other academic environments. Academic writing is purposeful and analytic and includes *genres* such as essays, compositions, outlines, and tests. It requires reflection and problem solving.

acculturation   The process of adjusting to and becoming part of a new cultural group.

Acculturation Theory   Also called the *Social Distance Hypothesis*. This theory of *SLA* views language learning from the multiple perspectives of the learner, the learner's L1 group, and the target language group. It stresses the importance of the relationship of the learning group and the target group in successful language learning. If there is low social distance between the two groups, it is believed that learning will be more successful. In addition, more successful learners are believed to be emotionally receptive to language learning and to the target language speakers and culture. *See also* psychological distance.

achievement tests   Assesses the progress a student has made based on the specific objectives of a course or program.

ACTFL OPI   *See* American Council of Teachers of Foreign Language Teachers Oral Proficiency Interview (ACTFL OPI).

acquisition   *See* language acquisition.

action research   A type of educational research done in real classrooms with the teachers who are most familiar with the students and the instructional setting taking an active role. According to Geoffrey Mills*, "Action research is any systematic inquiry conducted by teacher researchers, principals, school counselors or other stakeholders in the teaching/learning environment to gather information about the ways their particular school operates, how they teach, and how well students learn" (p. 6). Action research allows teachers to better understand their own practices and to monitor the impact of instructional decisions.

active vocabulary   Refers to vocabulary words that students should be able to use when they are speaking or writing.

advance organizer   David Ausubel's term. An advance organizer is used to help integrate new information into the student's preexisting knowledge. Before teaching new material, the teacher provides an oral or written statement or outline of the new information which links the content to learners' background knowledge.

affective factors   Also known as emotional factors. These learner characteristics include students' feelings about language learning and toward their particular target language and culture.

affective filter   According to Stephen Krashen, this filter determines learners' receptivity to second language input. It is made up of emotional factors connected to language learning, such as motivation to learn the language, anxiety, and feelings toward target language speakers and the target culture. The affective filter determines whether target language *input* becomes *in-take*.

alternative assessment   Assessment produced from portfolios and other procedures that emphasize authentic, holistic, and integrative language measures and are typically tailored to the specific educational context. *See also* portfolios.

American Council of Teachers of Foreign Language Oral Proficiency Interview (ACTFL OPI)   A structured live (either face-to-face or by telephone) oral interview which uses a ten-level scale to rate learners from "novice low" to "superior." Students at the novice low level have only minimal oral skills, while superior speakers can use the language comfortably for many professional and academic purposes. The ACTFL

---

*Mills, G. E. (2000). *Action research: A guide for the teacher researcher*. Upper Saddle River, NJ: Prentice-Hall.

OPI and adaptations of it are used for language proficiency testing in many American colleges and universities as well as secondary schools. *See also* Simulated Oral Proficiency Interview (SOPI).

anxiety Uncomfortable feelings that some people have when they have to use a second language.

assessment for learning (AFL) An approach to testing and assessment that is designed to give teachers information to modify the teaching and learning activities in which students are engaged, to differentiate instruction, and to focus on how individual students learn. Assessment for learning allows teachers to modify instruction with ongoing feedback about how students are progressing.

assimilative motivation Refers to the extremely strong desire of a language learner to become part of the target language group.

attention theories *See* cognitive learning theories.

Audiolingual Method (ALM) Language teaching methodology that isolates patterns in the target language, sequences them from simple to complex, and presents drills designed to make these patterns automatic to the learner.

authentic communication Classroom conversation that is as lifelike and meaningful as possible.

authentic materials Materials used in the language classroom that are also used by L2 speakers. Advertisements, food containers, and train schedules are examples of authentic materials.

authentic self-presentation My personal image of what it means to "know" a language: People must be able to be themselves when using the second language and be perceived consistently with their true selves when participating in the target language community.

automatic processing Spontaneously using language without the conscious manipulation of rules.

autonomous A term used to refer to learners who manage their own learning. Also called *self-directed.*

background knowledge Refers to a student's pre-existing knowledge of a particular topic.

basic interpersonal communication skills (BICS) One of two types of second language proficiency described by James Cummins. This term refers to a type of everyday language commonly used for social interaction. Also referred to as *social language* or *playground language.*

behavioral psychology (behaviorism) Theory of learning associated with B. F. Skinner that maintains learning is achieved through reinforcement.

big "C" culture Refers to the great accomplishments of a culture and typically includes literature, philosophy, architecture, important historical events and figures, and the arts. Also commonly referred to as *civilization.*

bilingual education An educational program where students receive instruction in both their first and second languages to keep them from falling behind in their content learning and to encourage the development of their first language while they are learning English.

bottom-up processing Learners read by sounding out individual words and attempting to understand a text by processing every sound and word. Bottom-up processing is associated with a phonics approach to reading. When applied to listening, learners attempt to understand text by understanding or translating each word individually. *See also* top-down processing.

brain lateralization Refers to the theory that the human brain becomes less flexible and less able to learn languages after puberty.

chunks Processing language input in pieces rather than word by word. *See also* formulaic language.

cloze tests Type of assessment used to test reading or grammatical knowledge. Cloze tests are written passages in the target language that have had words deleted; the students are expected to read the passage and fill in each blank.

cognates Words that are related in form and in meaning to ones in another language.

Cognitive Academic Language Learning Approach (CALLA) Anna Chamot's widely used method for teaching language through content.

cognitive academic language proficiency (CALP) One of the two types of second language proficiency described by James Cummins and also referred to as *academic language.* This term refers to a more abstract variety of language commonly used in academic classes.

Cognitive-Code A language teaching methodology which evolved as a reaction to the Audiolingual Method (ALM). It required grammatical explanations before language drills.

cognitive development Refers to children's growth of understanding as they continue to learn and hypothesize about the world around them. The Swiss developmental psychologist Jean Piaget found that children go through a predictable set of cognitive stages.

cognitive factors Learner characteristics centered around the different ways that language learners process information.

cognitive learning theory of SLA Theory that views language learning as similar to other types of human learning and emphasizes the development of automatic behaviors through practice and meaningful learning. This theory was referred to as attention theory in the first edition of this book.

coherence Refers to both the logical sequence of a text and to the way a writer links ideas together within a text.

collocation The tendency for certain words and phrases to go together in a language. For example, in American English the noun *role* tends to go with the verb *play*. Language *corpora* are useful for finding collocations.

Common European Framework Statements about second language learning outcomes at various levels adopted by the Council of Europe in 2001 to guide curriculum development and language testing among member states.

communication strategies Steps that learners take to be as successful as possible when communicating in the new language. They include such actions as asking a conversational partner to repeat or talk more slowly, using gestures and pantomime, and repeating important words or phrases.

communicative competence Sandra Savignon's term referring to a language learner's ability to communicate in the target language. A learner is considered communicatively competent if she can participate in a spontaneous interchange with a L2 speaker.

Communicative Language Teaching (CLT) Methodology that emphasizes authentic communication in the target language from the first day of class. Typical CLT activities include whole- and small-group discussions, problem solving, and role-play activities.

communicative writing Similar to authentic oral communication and free expression writing, these kinds of writing activities focus on meaning and students are not limited to the vocabulary and structures they have already studied.

competence-performance problem Inability to directly access a person's internal language system making it necessary for teachers and researchers to make inferences about how well someone knows a language from how well the person uses the language on a particular occasion.

computer-mediated communication (CMC) Refers to communication via in-class or out-of-class computer networks. CMC exchanges can be either synchronous (immediate like texting) or asynchronous (with a time lag like e-mail).

concrete language Refers to the use of language that is connected to objects or people in the immediate environment. *See also* abstract language.

concurrent validity Yielding of reasonably similar scores on tests that are supposed to measure the same ability. Thus, the scores on two tests of listening ability should be more similar than the scores on a listening test and a writing test.

consciousness-raising *See* grammatical consciousness-raising.

constructed materials Listening or reading materials that are created specifically for language classrooms.

constructivist Learning theory that views new knowledge as constructed and linked to prior knowledge through the learner's observations and experiences. Constructions are individual and result from the learner's attempts to understand the world.

contact stance Refers to the desire of a cultural group to preserve its own culture entirely, or to adapt to the new culture to some extent, or to assimilate entirely.

Content-Based Instruction (CBI) Type of instruction focusing on teaching content, while tailoring the instruction to meet the needs of second language learners.

context 1) The setting where language learning takes place; particularly the difference between a foreign language setting and a second language setting. 2) Background information about material that students are about to read or listen to in the target language (contextualized).

Contrastive Analysis Hypothesis An early second language acquisition theory that maintained that the structure of the learner's first language either helped or hindered the learning of a second language.

controlled processing   Using language in a limited and conscious way before the learner is able to use it automatically.

conversation theories   These theories maintain that people learn to speak in a new language by participating in conversations.

corpora   *See* language corpora.

correlation   Mathematical determination of the extent to which two sets of scores overlap.

criterion-referenced tests   Measures the number of specifically developed learning objectives a test taker has successfully completed. *See also* norm-referenced tests.

critical period   A biological concept referring to the idea that there is a specific moment in an animal's lifespan when a particular ability must be learned.

cultural vignettes   Textbook passages either in the native language or in the target language or both that describe the target country (or countries) and its culture and customs.

culture   Refers both to the sociological and psychological characteristics of groups as well as the arts, beliefs, institutions, and other products of each group. *See also* big "C" culture *and* small "c" culture.

culture shock   A state of anxiety, tension, and/or disorientation resulting from being exposed to or living within a different culture.

declarative knowledge   Consists of facts and information already known by the learner. *See also* controlled processing.

diagnostic tests   Identify specific areas of strengths and weaknesses in a learner's language ability.

dialogue   A written presentation of a plausible conversation between two or more people, typically used to introduce new vocabulary and grammatical structures in a textbook chapter.

dialogue journal   An extended written conversation, usually between a teacher and a student, similar to letter writing.

dialogue presentations   Teacher-planned activities to help students learn dialogue. A presentation could include having students listen to and read the dialogue, repeat the lines after the teacher, or orally perform the parts of the dialogue.

dictation   Students write down a target language passage read by the teacher. Dictations can be *integrative tests* if the grade is based on the number of ideas that the student has understood.

Differentiated Instruction   The idea that instruction should be modified to the needs and background knowledge of each individual learner. Since language learners differ in many important ways, the same lesson plan will not be equally suited to the needs of all the students in the same class.

digital storytelling (DS)   Software programs, available in a number of languages, with varying capabilities that allow students to create their own animated storybooks.

Direct Method   Language teaching methodology that focuses on conversational speech and conducts lessons almost entirely in the target language. Common features of a Direct Method classroom include target language–only production from the teacher and students, and dramatic and artistic teachers acting out what they are saying or employing elaborate props and pictures to help students understand.

direct strategies   Language learning strategies that use the target language. They include memory strategies (word associations and use of imagery), cognitive strategies (practicing and analyzing), and compensation strategies (guessing words and directing the conversation to a familiar topic). *See also* indirect strategies.

direct tests   Assessments where learners must perform the actual skill being assessed, such as writing a composition or explaining the results of a science experiment. *See also* integrative (language) tests.

directed dialogue   A type of exercise where students are told to say things to each other that were said in a dialogue.

directed listening   An activity in which students are given a specific purpose for listening. The purpose may be different each time they listen to the same passage.

directed reading   An activity in which students are given a specific purpose for reading. The purpose may be different each time they read the same passage.

discrete-point tests   *See* nonintegrative (language) tests.

display questions   The teacher already knows the answer to these questions and only asks them to find out if the students know the answers and if they did their assignment.

domains *See* language domains.

dominant language Term used to describe the language in which a bilingual person is most proficient.

dual-language programs Involve teaching a new language and content simultaneously to groups of language learners with two different first languages.

eclectic language teaching Approach using a combination of language teaching methods.

elicited imitation A language test similar to dictation where students are asked to repeat language that is presented to them. A number of studies have found that learners tend to simplify when they repeat and spontaneously form sentences consistent with their stage of interlanguage development. *See also* implicit linguistic knowledge.

emergent bilingual Refers to language learners who maintain their first language as they develop second language competence. This term emphasizes the importance of maintaining learners' first languages.

English as a foreign language (EFL) Refers to learning or teaching English in an overseas context where English is not spoken.

English as a second language (ESL) Refers to learning or teaching English within an area where English is spoken. *See* English language development (ELD).

English language development (ELD) A recent term to replace English as a Second Language (ESL).

English language learner (ELL) *See* English learner.

English learner (EL) A student from another language background who is learning English. Also referred to as English language learner (ELL).

English-only An educational policy that forbids the use of students' first languages and requires that all instruction be done in English.

error A consistent inaccuracy in the way the learner produces the target language. This type of inconsistency represents gaps in the learner's L2 competence.

expectancy grammar Refers to a learner's internalized L2 knowledge of the sentence structure, vocabulary, and grammar of the target language.

experience theories Second language acquisition theories maintaining that languages are learned through direct experiences (listening, speaking, reading, or writing) with the target language.

explicit linguistic knowledge Knowledge about the language; being able to talk about the language. Associated with the research of Ellen Bialystok. *See also* monitor.

extensive reading When students read longer texts with the goal of achieving a general rather than a close understanding of the material.

extracts Refers to a part of a text (oftentimes a work of literature) that has been purposefully selected by a teacher or a textbook author for student reading.

extrinsic motivation Refers to motivation that comes from outside an individual.

face validity A superficial way to examine the validity of a test and decide if it looks like it measures what it is supposed to be measuring. For example, a written test would not seem to be a good test of oral proficiency.

feedback A response that gives a conversational partner information about whether a previous comment has been understood and possibly offers suggestions for improvement.

field dependence–field independence (FD–FI) A widely studied learning style variable associated with language learning. FD learners tend to be influenced by the overall setting (called a field), while FI are better able to ignore the overall field and focus in on details.

first language Usually the learner's home language and the learner's strongest language.

focal attention Concerted attention; when a behavior needs so much attention that it is difficult to do anything else at the same time.

foreign language Refers to language learning or teaching in an overseas context.

foreigner talk Refers to a variety of simplified speech used by proficient speakers to talk to nonnative speakers.

formal operations The highest stage of Piaget's hierarchy of cognitive development. Formal operations refers to the ability to think abstractly, including scientific and logical thought, inductive and deductive reasoning, and the ability to use and manipulate mental symbols.

formative evaluation The ongoing collection and use of assessment with the goal of improving instruction.

formulaic expressions Unanalyzed phrases that learners use strategically in conversations. *See also* chunks.

fossilization Refers to the theory that errors in the target language can become permanent or at the very least extremely resistant to change.

fossilized error An error that has become permanent or resistant to change.

free-expression writing Type of writing activity in which the student typically self-selects the theme. Activities associated with free-expression writing include weekly free-writing assignments, diaries and journals, and dialogue journals.

generalization Refers to an assumption that a language learner makes about the structure or usage of the language based on observed patterns in the language. It can also refer to simple summaries of grammatical topics presented by the teacher or a textbook.

Generation 1.5 Generation 1.5 learners are long-time immigrants to the United States who are not literate in their first language and also have language problems in English. They are called Generation 1.5 because they have characteristics of both first- and second-generation immigrants. Like second-generation immigrants, they can seem very acculturated to American society; but like first-generation immigrants, they may not be literate in English.

glosses Explanations in the L1 of selected words or terms in a textbook or reading passage.

graded readers Books written expressly for second language learners which target vocabulary and grammatical structures for various levels of language proficiency. They are often simplified versions of well-known stories or books and may include only a limited number of common words and structures.

Grammar Translation Method Language teaching methodology that emphasizes understanding the target language and how it is put together. Grammar Translation classroom activities include reading and translating authentic texts and completing written grammatical exercises focusing on the grammatical features that appeared in the text.

grammatical consciousness-raising An instructional practice in which teachers try to make learners aware of a grammatical structure before they listen to it or are asked to use it in conversation.

grammaticality judgments Opinions given by learners after having read or listened to sentences about whether or not the sentences are grammatical in the L2. This type of test is meant to tap into the learner's internal sense of the language and is designed to avoid the competence-performance problem. *See also* competence-performance problem and implicit linguistic knowledge.

habit formation In behavioral psychology, reinforced behaviors that become habits.

heritage A person's cultural background including language.

heritage learners Refers to learners studying a target language that is also their heritage language. This person may speak or only understand the heritage language.

hypothesis testing Language output used by learners to test their emerging ideas about how the target language functions.

i + 1 Phrase offered by Stephen Krashen to describe input that is neither too complex nor too simple for a particular learner. If "i" is the learner's current level of listening ability, i + 1 input is language that is just a bit beyond the learner's existing ability.

identity negotiation Modification of self-concepts in the course of language learning, because of limitations in language ability and expectations from the new culture.

imitation From a sociocultural perspective, a modeling strategy that may be combined with private speech so that the learner can think about how the new language functions.

immersion Instructional practice where language learners are put into a target language environment and are given additional assistance because they are not yet competent in the new language. *See also* submersion.

implicit linguistic knowledge Linguistic knowledge that is automatically used when speaking or writing. *See also* language acquisition and explicit linguistic knowledge.

indirect strategies Strategies that support language learning without using the language directly. These include metacognitive strategies, which help learners organize and plan their learning; affective strategies, which help learners manage language learning emotions; and social strategies, which involve interaction with other people. *See also* direct strategies.

indirect tests   Similar to *nonintegrative and discrete-point* language *tests*, indirect tests examine some of the subskills involved in a language task. Testing students on specific sounds would be an example of an indirect test of their oral ability.

inference question   A question that cannot be answered by simply repeating the words in an oral or written text. The student must understand the material in order to answer the question correctly.

information gap activities   Pair or small-group activities that are arranged so that each of the participants has only some of the information necessary to accomplish a particular task.

information processing   How the human brain sorts and deals with the incoming information it receives at any given moment.

input   Material to listen to or read in the target language.

Input Hypothesis   Stephen Krashen's theory that views second language acquisition rather than learning as the basis of all true language development.

instrumental motivation   Learners' pragmatic reasons for learning a language.

in-take   The amount of input learners actually absorb. The amount of in-take depends on learners' receptivity to the input (the *affective filter*) and the comprehensibility and interest level of the input.

integrative motivation   Learners' desire to learn the target language in order to get to know target language speakers and the target culture.

integrative (language) tests   Assessments of students' coordinated ability to use the language, including their underlying *interlanguage*. The most common types of integrative tests are oral interviews and written compositions.

intensive reading   The reading of a relatively short text for a thorough understanding of the content, grammar, vocabulary, and organization.

interference   The negative influences or intrusion of the native language on second language learning. Also called *negative transfer*.

interlanguage   The way learners produce the target language. Learners' interlanguages are systematic and reflect learners' *implicit linguistic knowledge*.

internalization   *See* L2 internalization.

International English Language Testing System (IELTS)   Like the TOEFL, the academic version of this test is a four skills English test used to assess readiness for undergraduate or graduate study in an English-speaking environment.

inter-rater reliability   High *correlations* among the scores given by a test's graders are indications of a test's reliability.

intonation   The rising and falling of the tone of voice when speaking.

intrinsic motivation   Motivation that comes from within the individual.

L2 internalization   Automatic use and control of the second language by the learner.

language acquisition   The unconscious development of a language through exposure to the target language.

language acquisition device (LAD)   The human capacity for learning a first language. According to this view, all babies are born with the same language universals in their brains. Scholars differ as to whether and to what extent the LAD is available to second language learners.

language aptitude tests   Assessments originally developed by the American military to identify personnel who would be able to develop second language skills relatively quickly.

language corpora (corpus)   Large amounts of text which have been scanned into searchable databases. By searching one of these databases, a student can find words and phrases that tend to go together (*collocation*).

language domains   Different types of language required for the discussion of different topics. This term recognizes that some topics require specific vocabulary and sometimes even specific grammatical structures.

language learning   The learning of a language through conscious effort such as study and practice.

language learning self-access centers   Places where learners can go to access a variety of language learning materials and advice about language learning.

language learning strategies (LLS)   Activities or techniques that learners can use to improve or enhance their target language ability.

language for specific purposes (LSP) The study and teaching of languages for learners who have specific professional, academic, or work-related reasons to use the target language. Also referred to as *language for special purposes*.

language universals Basic patterns or principles shared by all languages.

languages other than English (LOTE) Refers to the languages spoken in the United States by non-English speakers whose increasing population numbers make the distinction between foreign and second languages less clear. *See also* World Languages.

learner autonomy A perspective that students should have control over their own language learning. *See* autonomous.

learning styles A learner's natural and preferred orientation to learning. Learning style is considered a cognitive characteristic.

less commonly taught languages (LCT) Languages, such as Chinese, Japanese, Russian, and Arabic, that are not widely taught in the United States. Recently the term *strategic languages* has begun to be used for many of these same languages in the United States.

lesson planning The process of deciding what to teach (objectives) and how to teach and assess your objectives.

limited-English proficient (LEP) Students who are second language speakers of English who do not have sufficient English ability to function in English-speaking classrooms. The term LEP is currently generally considered to be outdated and somewhat pejorative.

linguistics The study or understanding of the nature of language.

locally made Tests and materials that are developed by an individual teacher, school, or program for their specific needs and purposes.

logographic A writing system that is based on characters, such as Chinese. Logographic writing systems are not phonetic.

long-term planning Refers to establishing a plan for an entire semester or year of instruction. Steps include identifying specific instructional objectives, scheduling important events, such as test dates, and identifying materials and activities.

mainstream school program The regular school program which is not specifically organized for language learners.

manipulatives Concrete objects that a student can use in a hands-on way during an instructional activity.

marked features (markedness) Language features that differ from the universal. *Unmarked* features are more consistent with language universals.

meaning support The instructional practice of providing pictures, sound effects, and other extralinguistic material to make target language input more understandable.

meaningful learning Learning that involves the connection of new material to the learner's existing knowledge or schema.

mediation In sociocultural theory, language learning is said to be mediated. The human brain does not learn language directly by being exposed to language. Rather, humans use cultural tools such as books, computers, institutions, and other people to learn language (and content).

metacognition (metacognitive factors) How learners think about and control their language learning. Includes learners' beliefs about language learning and use of different language learning strategies.

metatalk Vygotskian concept referring to the learner's use of self-talk to think about the language. Self-talk may be silent or spoken.

minimal pairs Pairs of words that differ by only one phoneme, such as *fit* and *fat*. They are used to help students learn to differentiate sounds in their target language.

mistake Unlike an error, this phenomenon is similar to the slips of the tongue that native speakers make when speaking their L1.

monitor The learner's knowledge *about* the target language. According to the *Input Hypothesis,* the monitor is the result of language learning rather than language acquisition. *See also* explicit linguistic knowledge.

morpheme The smallest unit of language that indicates a difference in meaning.

narrow listening Listening approach that involves purposeful listening and relistening to the same authentic texts or to a number of texts on a similar topic.

National Standards for Foreign Language Learning A general second language curriculum designed by the American Council of Teachers of Foreign Languages to guide foreign language instruction in the United States.

nativism   The perspective that the human brain contains language universals which direct the acquisition of language. This position contrasts with the behavioral view that all aspects of language are learned through practice and reinforcement.

Natural Approach (NA)   Language teaching methodology emphasizing the development of listening comprehension, especially at early stages of language learning. Typical features of the Natural Approach include oral target language instruction, Total Physical Response, and a focus on everyday conversations. NA classes allow students to respond in any way that shows that they understand the language that is directed at them.

negative feedback   *See* feedback.

negative transfer   The negative influences of the learner's L1 on the production of the L2 due to differences in the two languages. Also called *interference.*

negotiation of meaning   The process of collaboration and negotiation in communication between conversational partners. Conversational partners must come to a joint understanding of what a conversation is about. *Conversation theories* maintain that negotiation can assist the learner's linguistic development by pointing out connections between words and phrases and their meanings.

newcomer centers   Programs for newly arrived language learners. These programs offer both English and content instruction and other services in a single place. They are often directed at learners with gaps in their schooling and/or low levels of literacy in their native language.

nonintegrative (language) tests   Also known as *discrete-point tests* because of their frequent use of fill-in-the-blank formats. Nonintegrative tests focus on one unit of language at a time and are based on the premise that it is useful to know whether or not a student has control of all the basic units of a language.

nonverbal behaviors   The gestures, facial expressions, and body postures used by speakers that contribute to the message they are trying to communicate.

norm-referenced tests   Assessments comparing a student's performance to other students in the same group. This type of test is often used to compare groups of students to all students in a particular school district, state, or country.

noticing   An important concept in the *Output Hypothesis.* Learners may become aware, by speaking or writing, that they do not know how to communicate ideas or concepts that they want to communicate or that there are differences between how they produce the language and how the language is produced by proficient users of the language.

novice   The lowest level of language proficiency according to the ACTFL Proficiency Guidelines. Superior is the highest level.

output   The language produced by the learner either orally or in written form.

Output Hypothesis   Merrill Swain's theory that input alone is insufficient to develop high-level language competence. Emphasizes pushed or forced output so that learners are encouraged to produce increasingly complex and native-like language.

overgeneralization   The language learner's tendency to use either a language rule or a word for many different situations, often inappropriately.

pacing   Refers to the timing and level of energy required by a particular class activity. For example, if students are given five minutes to do a short group activity they will do it more quickly and with more energy than if they are given fifteen minutes to complete the same activity.

parameter setting   When children are born into an L1 community, their brains select the value of the universal feature that corresponds to the specific language they are being exposed to. The brain selects the appropriate setting or parameter for the child's particular language.

passive vocabulary   Words that students should be able to recognize when reading but do not necessarily need to be able to use when they are speaking or writing.

pattern drills   An Audiolingual activity that involves teaching isolated patterns in the target language, sequencing them from simple to complex, and presenting drills designed to make these patterns automatic to the learner. Also called *structure drills.*

pedagogic grammars   A type of grammar used for instructional purposes. Pedagogic grammars emphasize grammatical structures that are most useful in terms of day-to-day conversations and explain them as simply as possible.

percentile ranking   Percentage of test takers who rank at or below a particular score on a norm-referenced test. A student who is ranked at the 85th percentile has scored as well as or better than 85 percent of the students who have taken the test.

performance test A more intense form of *direct testing*. This type of test is used to assess a learner's ability to use the second language effectively under *authentic* circumstances. Performance tests were originally developed for professional or workplace assessment. Testing simulations can be very elaborate, with realistic sets and actors playing the role of customers.

peripheral attention Background attention. When a behavior is sufficiently automatic that the individual can focus on something else simultaneously.

personalized questions Asking students to provide personal information in order to give them practice with grammatical structures in a communicative context, to stimulate a writing assignment, or as the basis of small-group activities, among other possibilities.

phoneme The smallest unit of sound that results in a difference in meaning.

phonetic Refers to the sounds of a language.

phonics-based A teaching approach to reading that emphasizes *correspondences between sounds and symbols* (letters) and encourages students to sound out words as the basis of reading. Related to *bottom-up processing*.

phonology The sound system of a language.

placement test Assessment used to help determine a learner's appropriate level in a sequence of courses. For example, since high schools use different curricula and textbooks, universities commonly use placement tests to determine which language class a student should take. Placement tests typically assess elements of the school's language curriculum as well as general levels of language proficiency.

planning block An outline of the material to be included over a certain time period or unit. Similar to a syllabus.

portfolios A *purposeful* selection of student work representing the student's perceived best effort and achievement. Teachers sometimes add items to the portfolio to give a fuller picture of the student's work. Both the student and the teacher are involved in the evaluation of the contents of the portfolio, and student self-assessments and teacher-student conferences are integral parts of the process. Portfolios are a less traditional or alternative form of assessment in language classes.

positive transfer The positive influences of the learner's L1 on the production of the L2 resulting from similarities in the two languages.

predictive validity Whether a test makes good predictions about students. For example, if students are having difficulty in mainstream content classes even after they have passed the exit test for ESL, it is likely that the exit test was not a valid measure of the language abilities they need in *mainstream* classes.

preview Used especially in listening and reading comprehension activities to develop students' expectations about the content that is about to be read or listened to.

prewriting strategies Practices like brainstorming and outlining which help students generate ideas and organization for writing.

private speech Also known as inner speech, self-talk, or Metatalk. L1 or L2 speech, either spoken or internal, that learners direct to themselves for the purpose of understanding the world and to solve problems. Private speech is an important concept in Vygotskian theory and sociocultural theories of SLA. *See also* Metatalk.

procedural memory Similar to automatic processing, procedural memory refers to things we know how to do without thinking about them. According to the Cognitive Academic Language Learning Approach (CALLA), it is the basis for our ability to understand and generate language automatically.

productive Refers to the language skills of speaking and writing because learners must create language.

proficiency A language learner's overall ability in the target language.

Proficiency-Oriented Instruction A language teaching method that attempts to maintain the communicative focus of Communicative Language Teaching (CLT) while at the same time fostering greater grammatical accuracy. In addition to communicative activities, it typically includes grammatical consciousness-raising and explicit correction of grammatical and phonological errors.

psychological distance Refers to a learner's motivation, anxiety, feelings toward the target language speakers, and other emotional traits. Similar to Stephen Krashen's *affective filter*.

publisher-made   Tests or materials developed by a company (usually for profit) or organization outside of the school or educational program.

pull-out program   An ESL program where students leave their regular mainstream classes for special language instruction.

rational deletion cloze passage   A type of cloze passage in which words are deleted intentionally in order to assess the student's knowledge of a specific grammatical structure or set of vocabulary words.

reading for pleasure   Reading for enjoyment or recreational purposes; self-directed reading.

reading to learn   Using reading to learn content material. Reading is secondary to learning the content.

realia   Authentic, "real-world" target language materials that are used in the language classroom, such as advertisements or food packagings.

recall   An activity used by teachers to determine what students have understood from a listening or reading passage. Students write down all of the ideas that they remember from an oral or written text, often in the students' native language so they will not have difficulty expressing their ideas.

recall question   A question that calls for the retelling of a specific piece of information from an oral or written text. Recall questions can often be answered by simply repeating words or phrases from the text.

recasts   Refers to the restatement of a learner's unclear or poorly formed utterance in more accurate language.

receptive   Refers to the language skills of reading and listening because learners must process language.

recombinations   Written or oral materials constructed to include vocabulary and grammatical structures that students have already learned.

recycling   Including previously taught materials at various times throughout a course.

redundancy   The amount of repeated information contained in an oral or written text.

registers   The levels of formality of a language.

reinforcement   A reward or other positive response to an action.

reliability   Applied to testing, it refers to the consistency of scores a specific test produces.

scaffolding   A term used to describe the act of a more proficient target language speaker supporting a conversation so that less proficient speakers with limited linguistic resources can participate.

scan   A reading strategy where learners quickly look over a written text to find a specific piece of information.

schema (schemata)   Mental representations of knowledge.

second language   Refers to language learning or teaching within an area where the target language is spoken.

second language acquisition   The academic field of second language acquisition seeks to understand how humans learn new languages. Second language acquisition theories are descriptions of how people learn second languages and the factors that help or hinder their learning.

self-assessments   Reflections by students on their academic strengths and weaknesses. With respect to language testing, self-assessments are usually groups of statements that describe various ways a person might use the target language. Learners rate their ability to accomplish the specific task included in each statement.

self-concepts   Refers to someone's sense of self, or self-image.

self-directed   Refers to learners who manage their own learning. Also called *autonomous*.

self-regulation   Central to sociocultural SLA theories, refers to the ways learners reflect on, plan, and use various tools and strategies to control their learning.

self-study   Refers to learners who choose to study a language without attending a formal class. Some learners might utilize a self-access center for language learning.

sensory mode preference   Natural preferences that students have to learn in a particular way. Some learners prefer to learn visually, some by listening, some by touch and feeling, and some by moving.

sheltered English   Refers to an approach where English learners are grouped together so that they do not have to compete with English speakers while they are supported in their development of academic skills and competence in academic English.

Sheltered Instruction (SI)   Instruction focusing on teaching content, but tailored to the needs of second language learners. Typically, all of the students are second language learners from the same L1 background.

Sheltered Instruction Observation Protocol (SIOP) Approach to language teaching developed by Echevarría, Vogt, and Short (2008)*. It offers teachers advice in the areas of lesson planning, building learner background, offering comprehensible input, incorporating strategy instruction, classroom interaction, practice/application, lesson delivery, and review and assessment. Its hallmark is making language and content comprehensible to learners.

short-term planning Refers to daily and weekly lesson planning.

sight vocabulary words Words that learners recognize as meaningful based on their recognition of the entire word, in contrast to sounding out the word to gain its meaning.

silent period A time when learners develop their language ability by listening in the target language. A silent period is consistent with the fact that babies listen to language long before they actually talk.

Simulated Oral Proficiency Interviews (SOPI) An oral proficiency test in which test takers listen to audio-recorded questions and record their responses. Often required as part of the certification process for teachers of LOTE.

skim A reading strategy where learners quickly look over a written text to get a general idea of its contents.

small "c" culture Refers to the life ways and worldview of a people—all the things that people do and know because they are members of a particular group.

social distance Refers to the relative dominance (economic, political, and social power) of the learning and target groups. The *contact stance*, degree of enclosure, degree of cohesiveness, size of the learning group, ethnic stereotypes, and amount of time the learning group intends to remain in the target language area all make up the social distance between the learning and target groups. It is believed that high social distance between the learning and target groups is an impediment to language learning.

Social Distance Hypothesis SLA theory that views language learning from the multiple perspectives of the learner, the learner's L1 group, and the target language group. It stresses the importance of the relationship of the learning group and the target group in successful language learning. If there is low social distance between the two groups, it is believed that learning will be more successful. In addition, more successful learners are believed to be emotionally receptive to language learning and to the target language speakers and culture (*see* psychological distance). Also called *Acculturation Theory*.

social theories Explain second language learning from the multiple perspectives of the learner, the learner's first language group, and the target language group.

Socio-Cognitive Theory An SLA theory associated with CALLA, combining cognitive learning and sociocultural theories of SLA. It maintains that language learning is a cognitive process that is influenced by social and cultural factors.

socio-constructivist Perspective generally associated with Lev Vygotsky that knowledge is socially constructed and learning occurs through social interactions.

sociocultural theories Approach(es) to understanding second language acquisition that apply the development theories of the Russian psychologist Lev Vygotsky . These theories emphasize the role of social and cultural factors in second language acquisition.

sociolinguistic competence Language production that is socially and culturally appropriate as well as grammatically accurate. Learners must follow cultural conventions for verbal and nonverbal behavior within interpersonal communication in areas such as suitability of topics, politeness, and turn-taking. Learners must also understand the cultural content of language and vary their productions according to the social context and their conversational partners.

sound-symbol correspondences Refers to associations between the sounds of a language and its writing system.

stand-alone language classes Separate classes focusing on language instruction that students attend for at least part of the school day.

standardized test A type of test created by an agency or organization and tested on large groups of people to determine how well people usually perform on the test.

---

*Echevarría, J., Vogt, M. E., & Short, K. (2008). *Making content comprehensible for English learners: The SIOP Model* (3rd ed.). Boston: Pearson Education.

standards General statements of goals for teaching English as a second language and languages other than English to help teachers establish appropriate learning goals for their students.

strategy training A component of language instruction where teachers help students develop useful language learning strategies.

structural linguistics A linguistic theory that conceives of languages as made up of a finite set of units or structures.

structure Refers to the information load and amount of choices the student is expected to make. High-structure classroom activities include demonstrations and drilling. Spontaneous small-group discussions are low-structure activities.

structured oral communication activity An oral activity in which either the grammatical structure or the content, or both, of questions and responses is dictated in advance by the language teacher or the textbook.

structured writing activity A writing activity that requires specific grammatical structures or content. Corresponds to *structured oral communication activity.*

submersion An educational practice where language learners are put into regular mainstream classes with native-speaking peers and are given no extra support while they are learning the new language. Also referred to as "sink or swim." *See also* immersion.

summative evaluation Waiting until the end of an instructional sequence to gather and consider evaluation and assessment information.

syntax The grammar or structure of a language.

target language The second or foreign language of instruction.

targeted input The instructional practice of tying listening or reading materials to the structures and vocabulary students are learning to use in speaking or writing.

task A learning activity with a specific purpose. Tasks could include devising and preparing a meal for a class event or the development of a pamphlet to help new students adjust to high school.

Task-Based Language Instruction Instructional practice that sets specific goals for a task to be accomplished by a group of learners and encourages learners to strategize as to how best to complete the task.

teacher-made tests Assessments developed by teachers for use in their own classrooms. One type of *locally-made tests.*

Test of English as a Foreign Language (TOEFL) The principle English examination required of international students who hope to study in North America. It is designed to test whether students have adequate English ability to undertake high school, undergraduate, or graduate study in English in the North American context.

Test of English for International Communication (TOEIC) Administered by the Educational Testing Service (ETS) at Internet-based sites to assess the test taker's ability to use English in everyday situations, including at work.

test-retest reliability High correlations between students' scores on different administrations of the same test are taken as indications of a test's reliability.

threshold Applied to second language reading. Refers to the minimal level of second language competence necessary for learners to be able to begin to read in the second language.

top-down processing Application of background knowledge by learners to focus on understanding a target language utterance, text, or anecdote as a whole. Learners use the predictability of the text's content and grammatical patterns in their target language to guess the meaning of unfamiliar words or phrases. *See also* bottom-up processing.

Total Physical Response (TPR) Language teaching methodology that assumes listening comprehension is the basis of all language ability and focuses on the development of students' listening abilities. TPR classroom activities involve the teacher giving commands in the target language and modeling the actions required by the commands. Students are supposed to follow the commands with their "whole" bodies.

Total Physical Response Storytelling (TPRS) An approach to TPR for more advanced learners. Typically, students are first introduced to new vocabulary words and expressions in the target language via pictures, actions, or gestures. Once the students have learned the actions, the teacher reads a short story in the target language containing the learned vocabulary and expressions. Students are encouraged to act out the story as the teacher tells it. As students progress in language acquisition, they offer their own versions of the story, combining the gestures they have learned with oral narration.

transnationals Students from families who move back and forth between the United States and their countries of origin. These learners may have gaps in their literacy development in both their L1 and in English due to interruptions in their schooling in both countries.

true communication activities Oral activities where the students choose their conversational partners and what they want to talk about. Also called *authentic communication*.

Universal Grammar Theory A second language acquisition theory based on Chomsky's theory of *language universals* and *marked features*. In learning a new language students must reset the *parameters* of their L1 to achieve the features of the new language.

validity Applied to testing, refers to whether a test actually tests what it is supposed to test. Test makers usually consider different types of validity, such as *face validity, predictive validity,* and *concurrent validity.*

wait-time The amount of time that teachers wait for student responses. It is important to give students enough time before they must answer.

warm-up activity An activity conducted at the beginning of a class period to get the class ready for instruction, to remind learners of materials studied the day before, or to introduce them to a new topic.

washback effect The effect of tests on language instruction and the language curriculum. The ACTFL OPI, for example, has caused foreign language classes in the United States to focus more on oral communication.

whole language approach A teaching approach to reading that allows readers to get a general sense of the meaning of a reading passage and use their general knowledge of the world and the predictability of the grammatical patterns in their target language to guess the meaning of unfamiliar words or phrases. Related to *top-down processing.*

willingness to communicate (WTC) The readiness of learners to use their second language when they have the opportunity. It reminds language teachers that anxiety and motivation should be considered together.

world languages Refers to languages other than English that are taught in the United States. A term that is increasingly replacing the term foreign languages.

writing genre Refers to the variety of types of writing such as essays or poems.

zone of proximal development (ZPD) Refers to the distance between the kind of language learners are able to produce on their own and the language they can construct with the support of others through scaffolding. It implies that as the learners' interlanguage develops, it will be ready to integrate the next appropriate language structure(s). This term is associated with sociocultural theories of SLA and comes from the work of Lev Vygotsky.

INDEX

Abstract language, 180–81
Academic language. *See also*
 Cognitive Academic
 Language Proficiency
 (CALP); Content-Based
 Instruction (CBI)
 assessment of, 212
 defined, 179
 development of, 181–83
Academic literacy
 Content-Based Instruction
  and, 179, 183
 definition of, 181
 development of, 188–92
 evaluation of, 183
Academic reading
 assessment of, 189–90, 224–25
 development of, 188–90
Academic writing, 157–58, 160
 activities for, 172–73
 assessment of, 188–90, 224–25
 development of, 190–92
 guidelines for teaching of,
  167–68
 skills required for, 190
Acculturation, 40, 42, 43, 52–53
Acculturation Theory. *See* Social
 Distance Hypothesis
Achievement tests, 220
Acquisition of language.
 See Second language
 acquisition
Acronyms, common, 7
ACTFL. *See* American Council
 of Teachers of Foreign
 Languages
Action research, 251–53
Active vocabulary, 239
Advance organizers, 86, 96, 139,
 143, 189
Affective (emotional) factors in
 language learning, 7, 8–12.
 See also Anxiety
 affective filter, 33, 34–35, 50, 51

and listening, 96
and writing, 169
AFL (assessment for learning),
 210, 241, 253
ALM. *See* Audiolingual Method
Alphabets
 new, reading and, 137–38
 types of, 138
Alternative assessment, 198, 210
American Council of Teachers
 of Foreign Languages
 (ACTFL), 70
 assessment guide of, 221
 journal of, 254
 Oral Proficiency Interview
  (OPI), 128, 223–24
American Education Testing
 Service (ETS), 225
Anxiety, 10–12
 about speaking, 116
 assessment of, 12, 264–67
 culture shock and, 11
 and listening comprehension,
  90
 reducing, 11–12, 256
 speaking instruction and, 122,
  123
 of teacher, 116, 266–67
 writer's block, 169
 in writing, 161–62, 169
Applbaum, R., 10, 11
Applbaum, S., 10, 11
Asher, James, 65, 66
Assessment. *See also* Rubrics;
 Standards of evaluation;
 Testing
 alternative, 198, 210
 of anxiety, 12, 264–67
 competence, definition
  of, 210
 in Content-Based Instruction,
  199–201
 dominant language
  determination, 210

of expectations about
 language learning, 16,
 261–63
importance of, 209
for learning (AFL), 210, 241,
 253
of listening comprehension,
 103–5, 218
portfolios in, 174–75, 219, 222
purposes of, 209
of reading comprehension,
 149–51, 189–90, 224–25
self-, 129–30, 174–75, 201, 218,
 219, 222, 234, 242
of speaking, 116, 128–30
standards for, 210–14
washback effect in, 116, 128,
 217, 237
of writing, 173–75
Assimilative motivation, 8
Attention
 focal, 31, 32
 peripheral, 31, 32
Attitude, in language learning,
 8–10. *See also* Affective
 (emotional) factors in
 language learning
Audiolingual Method (ALM),
 27, 62–64
 on errors, 112
 on listening comprehension,
 93
 and structured *vs.* authentic
  communication, 110
 uses of, 72
Ausubel, David, 31, 86
Authentic communication, 69
 activities to encourage,
  120–23
 in Content-Based Instruction,
  179, 180
 in content classes, 185
 vs. display speaking,
  112–15

282

vs. structured communication, 109–10, 110–12, 119, 120
Authentic materials
availability of, 255–56
for reading, 138–39, 144
teaching methods using, 61, 65, 73
Authenticity
task-based activities and, 240
and testing, 216–17, 218–19, 222
Automatic processing, 31, 32, 198
Autonomy. *See* Learner autonomy

Background knowledge
activation of, 139–40, 142, 143, 149, 189
for content classes, 189
defined, 86
in lesson planning, 241
in listening, 86, 90, 92
for reading, 135, 137, 139–40, 142, 143, 149, 189
BALLI (Beliefs About Language Learning Inventory), 16, 261–63
Basic Interpersonal Communication Skills (BICS), 180, 181–82
activities for, 195–96
assessment of, 212
teaching students about, 189
Behavioral learning theory, teaching methods based on, 27, 62–63
Behavioral psychology, 26
Beliefs about language learning. *See* Expectations
Beliefs About Language Learning Inventory (BALLI), 16, 261–63
Bialystok, Ellen, 32, 33, 157
BICS. *See* Basic interpersonal communication skills
Bilingual education, 3, 6
Birdsong, David, 48
Blyth, Carl, 110

Bottom-up processing, 90, 135, 137
Brain lateralization, 48
Brainstorming, 157, 158, 163, 168, 169
Bygate, M., 77

CALLA. *See* Cognitive Academic Language Learning Approach
CALP. *See* Cognitive Academic Language Proficiency
Chamot, Anna Uhl, 197–98
Children
cognitive development stages in, 18–19
and culture shock, 11
language acquisition theories on, 48–54
language learning in, 30, 34
and listening comprehension, 90–91, 93, 96
and natural communication, 115
Chomsky, Noam, 28, 29
Chunks, processing listening material in, 92
Classroom
discussions, in content classes, 188
display speaking in, 112–15
Classroom management
directions, clarity of, 235–36
lesson planning for, 234–35
wait time, 75, 116, 240–41
Cloze tests, 150–51, 218
CLT. *See* Communicative Language Teaching
CMC (Computer-Mediated Communication), 160–62
Co-construction of meaning, 35, 36–37, 54, 87
Cognates, 91
Cognitive Academic Language Learning Approach (CALLA), 187, 197–99, 241
Cognitive Academic Language Proficiency (CALP), 180–82. *See also* Academic language

and academic writing, 192
activities for, 195–96
development of, 193–94
teaching students about, 189
Cognitive-Code Method, 63
Cognitive development stages, Piaget's model of, 18–19
Cognitive factors in language learning, 7–8, 12–14, 18–19
Cognitive learning theories, 31–33
concepts in, 31
on listening, 85, 93
positions on key issues, 49–50
on repetition and learning, 192
on speaking, 109
teaching methods based on, 61, 70
on writing, 156, 159
Coherence, in writing, 192
Collocation, 165
Common European Framework standards, 210–11, 225
Communication
authentic *vs.* structured, 109–10, 110–12
computer-mediated, 160–62
Communication strategies, 16–17
and communicative competence, 112
teaching of, 122
Communicative competence
and communication strategies, 112
definition of, 110
as goal, 109–10
teaching methods emphasizing, 69
Communicative Language Teaching (CLT), 69
limitations of, 77
on listening comprehension, 85
Communicative writing, 158–59
activities for, 170
guidelines for teaching of, 167–68

Competence, definition of, 210
Competence-performance problem, 214
Comprehensible Output Hypothesis. *See* Output Hypothesis
Computer-Mediated Communication (CMC), 160–62
Concrete language, in content classes, 184
Concurrent validity, 216, 222
Consciousness-raising, grammatical, 33, 63, 70–71, 85, 93
Constructed materials, for reading, 138–39
Constructivism, 31
Contact stance, 42
Content-based approaches, 72–76. *See also entries for* Content-Based Instruction; Sheltered Instruction Observation Protocol (SIOP)
  Cognitive Academic Language Learning Approach (CALLA), 187, 197–99, 241
  Content-Based Instruction (CBI), 72–74
  Sheltered Instruction (SI), 6, 73–76
  Sheltered Instruction Observation Protocol (SIOP), 73–76, 74f
  uses of, 77
Content-Based Instruction (CBI), 72–74
  academic language development in, 181–83
  academic literacy development in, 188–92
  activities for, 195–96
  assessment in, 199–201
  benefits of, 179, 180
  concept in, 180–81
  contextualized input in, 184–85

Generation 1.5 students and, 183–84
  guidelines for, 193–94
  language learning objectives in, 186–87
  on lesson planning, 229
  listening and reading input, appropriate, 187–88
  models in, 194
  projects for, 203
  reading skills, development of, 188–90
  SLA promotion in, 185–88
  SLA theories on, 179–80
  task-based instruction in, 192–93
  teaching checklist for, 203–4
  variety of modalities in, 194
  vs. content classes, 185–86
  writing skills, development of, 190–92
Content classes
  academic literacy development in, 188–92
  activities in, 240
  contextualized input in, 184–85
  coordinating readings with, 144
  coordinating with writing instruction, 168
  ESL teachers' help with, 96, 141–42
  scaffolding in, 184–85
  vs. Content-Based Instruction, 185–86
Content reading
  ESL teachers' help with, 96, 141–42
  strategies for, 143
Content writing. *See* Academic writing
Context
  in authentic communication, 109
  in Content-Based Instruction, 179, 180
  in content classes, 184–85
  and listening comprehension, 88–90, 96, 104

Contrastive Analysis Hypothesis, 26–28, 49
  on errors, 112, 115
  teaching methods based on, 62–63
  use of, 72
Controlled processing, 31, 32, 198
Conversation, repetitiveness of, 229
Conversation theories, 35–37
  concepts of, 35
  on errors, 115
  on grammar learning, 238
  on lesson planning, 229
  on listening comprehension, 85
  positions on key issues, 50–52
  on repetition and learning, 192
  on speaking, 109
  teaching methods based on, 64, 67, 69, 70, 72, 73
  on writing, 156
Correlation, of testing instruments, 215
Criterion-referenced testing, 220, 222
Critical period, 29, 30, 47–48
Critical period hypothesis, 47–48
Cultural appropriateness, teaching methods emphasizing, 69–70
Cultural competence, teaching methods emphasizing, 65
Cultural differences, and listening comprehension, 96, 104
Cultural vignettes, 239–40
Culture
  assessment standards for, 212, 213–14
  big "C" *vs.* small "c," 240
  in lesson planning, 234
  and reading, 137, 139, 143
  and writing, 158, 166–67
Culture shock, 11, 40
Cummins, James, 180, 181, 182–83

Declarative knowledge, 198

Diagnostic tests, 220

Dialogue(s)
directed, 237–38
memorized, teaching
methods using, 62–64

Dialogue journals, 156, 157, 159

Dialogue presentations, 237–38

Diaries, 159

Dictation, 105, 218

Dictionary
in content classes, 188, 189
impossibility of banning, 165
strategies, teaching of, 143,
165, 169

Differentiated instruction, 5,
72, 241

Digital storytelling (DS), 162

Direct learning strategies, 16

Direct method, 64–65

Direct testing, 218, 222

Directed dialogue, 237–38

Directed listening, 96–97

Directions, giving in classroom,
235–36

Discrete-point testing, 217–18

Display questions, 113

Display speaking, *vs.* authentic
communication, 112–15

Dominant language, assessing,
210

Drills, structure, 238, 239

Dual language programs, 6

EAP (English for academic
purposes), 7

Eclectic methods, 55, 71–72

Economic trends, and future of
language teaching, 256

Educational Testing Service, 223

EFL (English as a foreign
language), 7, 181

ELD (English language
development), 7

Electronic writing, 168

Elicited imitation, 218

ELLs (English language
learners), 7. *See also* English
learners (ELs)

ELs. *See* English learners

Emergent bilingual learner, 7

Emotional factors. *See* Affective
(emotional) factors in
language learning

English as a foreign language
(EFL), 7, 181

English as a second language
(ESL), 5
teachers, helping with work
from other classes, 5, 96,
141–42
training for all teachers in, 6
vs. EFL, 7

English for academic purposes
(EAP), 7

English for specific purposes
(ESP), 7, 163

English language development
(ELD), 7

English language learners
(ELLs), 7. *See also* English
learners (ELs)

English learners (ELs), 6, 7
including in conversations
with native speakers, 162
success, components of, 180

English-only instruction, 6

Environment, and learner
attitudes, 8–9

Errors
correction, language learning
theories on, 48–54, 112
definition of, 110
fossilization of, 26, 28, 49,
112, 115
language development
process and, 119
overgeneralization, 119
in speaking, 112, 121
student beliefs about, 115
teacher beliefs about, 115
vs. mistakes, 110, 119
in writing, 159–60, 167, 168, 169

ESL. *See* English as a second
language

*ESL Standards for Pre-K–12
Students* (TESOL), 210,
211–12, 220–21

ESP (English for specific
purposes), 7, 163

ETS (American Education
Testing Service), 225

Everyday language. *See*
Basic interpersonal
communication skills
(BICS)

Expectancy grammar, 150–51

Expectations about language
learning
assessment of, 16, 261–63
realistic, development of in
students, 15–16, 90–91,
95–96, 123, 140–41, 143,
166–67, 168
of teachers, 95, 143, 167, 230

Experience theories, 33–40
conversation theories, 35–37,
50–52
Input Hypothesis, 33–35,
50–51
Output Hypothesis, 38–40,
50–52
positions on key issues, 50–52

Explicit linguistic knowledge,
31, 32, 34, 50

Expressive writing
activities for, 171–72
free-expression writing, 157,
159–60
guidelines for teaching of,
167–68

Extensive reading, 134, 136
activities for, 147–48

Extracts, for reading, 136

Extrinsic motivation, 9

Face validity, of test, 215

Fact-recall questions, in reading
instruction, 144

FD-FI. *See* Field dependence-
field independence

Feedback, 35, 37
negative, 54

Field dependence (FD), 13–14

Field dependence-field
independence (FD-FI),
13–14

Field independence (FI), 13–14

Field sensitivity, 13

First language (L1), 26

First language theories
Contrastive Analysis Hypothesis, 26–28, 49, 62–63, 72, 112, 115
positions on key issues, 48–49
teaching methods based on, 61, 70
Universal Grammar Theory, 28–30, 49

Five Cs of foreign language education, 212

FLCAS (Foreign Language Classroom Anxiety Scale), 12, 264–65

Focal attention, 31, 32

Forced Output Hypothesis. *See* Output Hypothesis

Foreign Language Classroom Anxiety Scale (FLCAS), 12, 264–65

Foreign language learning. *See* Second language acquisition

Foreign language setting, 3, 4

Foreign Service Institute, U.S. (FSI), 223

Foreigner talk, 96, 187

Formal operations stage, 18

Formality of language, levels of, 115

Formulaic expressions
in speaking, 117–18, 120
in writing, 159

Fossilization of errors, 26, 28, 49, 112, 115

Free-expression writing, 157, 159–60

Gardner, Robert C., 8–9

Generalization, teaching methods using, 63

Generation 1.5 students, 183–84

Genres, and writing conventions, 157–58, 162–63, 168

Gist, listening for
activities for, 92, 93, 95, 100–102
as phase of listening comprehension, 92

Gist, reading for, 136

Goals
communicating to students, 253
communicative competence as, 109–10
helping students set, 9
in lesson planning, 232, 233
tailoring instruction to, 163

Graded readers, 138

Grading. *See also* Assessment
and motivation, 116, 128
of speaking, 116, 128
washback effect in, 116, 128

Graham, C. R., 8

Grammar
for academic English, 180
expectancy, 150–51
and language learning, 18–19
and language learning objectives, 186–87
monitor and, 157, 158
pedagogic, 238
presentations, 238–39
and top-down processing, 135

Grammar Translation (GT) Method, 61–62, 134

Grammatical consciousness-raising, 33, 63, 70–71, 85, 93

Grammaticality judgments, 218

Group activities
group writing, 168
in speaking instruction, 122
as teaching method, 240

GT. *See* Grammar Translation (GT) Method

Guide questions, in writing, 169

Habit-formation, 26, 27, 63

Hadley, Alice Omaggio, 70

Heritage learners, 7, 72, 184

Hypothesis testing, 38

I+1 theory on input levels, 94

IATEFL (International Association of Teachers of English as a Foreign Language), 254

Identity, and language learning, 20, 43

IELTS (International English Language Testing System), 225

Imitation, 45
elicited, 218

Immersion, 7

Implicit linguistic knowledge, 31, 32

In-take, contrasted with input, 35

Indirect learning strategies, 16

Indirect testing, 218

Inference questions
in evaluation of listening comprehension, 104
in listening, 86
in reading instruction, 144, 149–50

Information gap activities, 122, 240

Information processing, 31, 32

Inner speech. *See* Private speech

Input, 33, 34, 35

Input Hypothesis, 33–35
concepts of, 33–34
emphasis on listening comprehension, 85
on grammar learning, 238
on listening comprehension, 86–87, 94
positions on key issues, 50–51
on reading, 134, 136
on speaking, 109
teaching methods based on, 64, 65–66, 67, 70, 72, 73, 75
on writing, 156

Input methods, 65–68. *See also* Natural Approach; Total Physical Response method

Instrumental motivation, 8

Integrated Performance Assessment (IPA) Manual (ACTFL), 221

Integrative motivation, 8

Integrative testing, 217–18, 222

Intensive reading, 134, 136, 146–47

Inter-rater reliability, 215, 224

Interference, 26, 27–28, 49, 159

Interlanguage
  assessment of, 217
  defined, 110
  developmental stages in, 117–19

Internalization of L2, 45, 46–47, 54

International Association of Teachers of English as a Foreign Language (IATEFL), 254

International English Language Testing System (IELTS), 225

Internet
  reading materials on, 137, 144
  and Social Distance, 43
  TOEFL on, 224
  TOEIC on, 225

Intonation, and listening, 86, 93

Intrinsic motivation, 9

Journals, 159
  dialogue, 156, 157, 159
  professional, 253–54

Knowledge, declarative, 198

Krashen, Stephen, 33–35, 48, 51, 87, 94, 118, 157, 158

L2 internalization, 45, 46–47, 54

LAD (Language Acquisition Device), 29–30

Lambert, Wallace, 8

Language(s), registers of, 115

Language Acquisition Device (LAD), 29–30

Language aptitude, 7, 12

Language aptitude tests, 12

Language corpora, 165

Language domains, 180, 181, 232

Language for specific purposes (LSP), 7, 77, 256

Language labs, 255

Language learners. *See also* Anxiety
  beliefs about second-language speaking, 115
  characteristics of, 7–18
  children as. *See* Children
  communicating with, 250, 253
  emotions of, 8–12
  expectations, realistic, development of, 15–16, 90–91, 95–96, 123, 140–41, 143, 166–67, 168
  identity, and language learning, 20
  learning styles, 12–14
  motivating, 9–10, 116, 128
  seeking approval of, 249–50
  showing personal interest in, 120–22, 159
  strategies of, 15–18
  variety of, and teaching method, 71–72

Language learning. *See also* Expectations about language learning; Second language acquisition
  affective factors in, 7, 8–12, 33, 34–35, 50, 51
  cognitive factors in, 7–8, 12–14, 18–19
  as dynamic process, 253
  metacognitive factors in, 7–8, 14–18
  settings for, 4–7
  vs. acquisition of language, 4, 34, 50

Language learning self-access centers, 9

Language learning strategies (LLS), 16–18
  CALLA emphasis on, 197
  effective, development of, 17–18

Language teachers
  anxieties of, 116, 266–67
  beliefs about speaking, 115
  expectations, realistic, importance of, 95

Language teaching. *See also* Lesson planning
  action research in, 251–53
  activities in, 237–41
  checklist for, 259
  common acronyms, 7
  communicating with students, 250, 253
  confidence, importance of, 249–50
  differentiated instruction, 5, 72, 241
  as dynamic process, 253
  future of, 255–56
  improvement, opportunities for, 251–54
  new ideas, openness to, 250–51
  professional development, 253–54
  projects for, 258
  review of training in, 256
  second language competence and, 251
  settings of, 4–7
  student approval, attitude toward, 249–50
  support, sources of, 254
  teacher anxiety, 116, 266–67
  teaching tips, 249–50

Language teaching methods, 60–71. *See also specific methods*
  choice of, 71–72
  current methods, 65–71
  definition of, 60–61
  early methods, 61–65
  new, action research on, 251–53
  teacher- *vs.* learner-centered methods, 76–77

Language test, defined, 210. *See also* Assessment; Testing

Language universals, 28, 29

Languages other than English
  (LOTE), 7
Lantolf, James, 44, 45–46, 47,
  118–19
Lateralization, brain, 48
LCT (less commonly taught)
  languages, textbooks for, 237
Learner autonomy, 9
  encouraging, 241–42, 253
  misconceptions and, 15
  teaching methods
    emphasizing, 75, 77
  technology and, 256
Learning. *See also* Language
    learning; Language
    learning strategies; Second
    language acquisition
  assessment for (AFL), 219,
    241, 253
  behavioral theories of, 27, 62–63
  meaningful, 31
  reading for, 134, 136, 149, 188
  styles of, 12–14
Lenneberg, Eric, 48
LEP (limited-English
  proficiency), 7
Less commonly taught (LCT)
  languages, textbooks for,
  237
Lesson planning
  activities, common, 237–41
  checklist for, 244
  classroom management
    considerations, 234–35
  differentiated instruction in,
    241
  directions in, 235–36
  factors in, 229–30
  flexibility of plan, 231–32
  goals, setting of, 232, 233
  learner autonomy,
    supporting, 241–42
  level of detail in, 230–32
  misconceptions about, 230
  pacing of, 234–35
  planning, long-term, 232–33
  planning, short-term, 233–35
  projects in, 243
  structure of, 234–35

Limited-English proficiency
  (LEP), 7
Linguistic knowledge, explicit
    and implicit, 31, 32, 33, 34,
    50
Linguistics, 28, 29
Listening
  as active co-construction of
    meaning, 87
  in content classes, 187–88
  directed, 96–97
  for gist, 92, 93, 95, 100–102
  narrow, 94–95, 187
  true, activities for, 92, 95,
    102–3
Listening comprehension
  assessment of, 103–5, 218
  checklist for, 107
  children and, 90–91, 93, 96
  in classroom, *vs.* natural
    speech, 87–90, 96
  concepts in, 86
  context and, 88–90
  importance of, 86–87
  minimal pairs and, 239
  obstacles to teaching of,
    87–90
  projects for, 106
  stages of development in,
    91–92
  student feedback on, 104–5
  teaching methods
    emphasizing, 85
Listening comprehension
    activities
  examples and ideas for,
    97–103
  guidelines for development
    of, 95–97
  tailoring to listening ability
    level, 91–96
Locally-made language tests,
  210
Logographic writing systems,
  138
LOTE (languages other than
  English), 7
LSP (language for specific
  purposes), 7, 77, 256

MacIntyre, Peter, 10
Mainstream school program,
  5, 187
Manipulatives, 75
Marked features, 28, 29
Markedness, 28, 29
McLaughlin, Barry, 32
Meaning, negotiation of, 35,
    36–37, 54
  in Content-Based Instruction,
    179, 180
  in content classes, 184–85
  in speaking, 111–12
Meaning support, 75
  in listening, 86
  and listening comprehension,
    92, 96
  in reading, 142
Meaningful learning, 31
Mediation, 45, 46
Mejias, H., 10, 11
Memorization of dialogs,
    teaching methods using,
    62–64
Memory, procedural, 198
Mentors, value of, 254
Metacognition, 14–15, 45, 46, 253
Metacognitive factors
  in language learning, 7–8, 14–18
  in lesson planning, 242
Metatalk, 38. *See also* Private
    speech
Mills, Geoffrey, 252
Minimal pairs, 239
Mistakes. *See also* Errors
  in speech, 119
  vs. errors, 110, 119
Models
  in Content-Based Instruction,
    194
  providing students with, 236
  for writing, 168
Modern Language Aptitude
  Test, 12
Monitor, 33, 34, 157, 158
Morphemes
  acquisition sequence for, 118,
    120
  definition of, 118

Morphological complexity, reduction of, 117
Motivation, 8–10
  encouraging, 9–10
  grades and, 116, 128
  types of, 8–9

NA. *See* Natural Approach
NABE (National Association of Bilingual Education), 254
Narrow listening, 94–95, 187
National Association of Bilingual Education (NABE), 254
National Standards for Foreign Language Learning, 212–14, 220–21
Nativism, 29, 30
Natural Approach (NA), 66–68
  emphasis on listening comprehension, 85
  limitations of, 77
  on listening comprehension, 93
Natural speech
  listening to, *vs.* classroom listening, 87–90, 96
  redundancies in, 88
Negative feedback, 54
Negative transfer, 26
Negotiation of meaning, 35, 36–37, 54
  in Content-Based Instruction, 179, 180
  in content classes, 184–85
  in speaking, 111–12
Newcomer center programs, 6, 276
Non-integrative testing, 217–18
Norm-referenced testing, 220
Norton, Bonny, 20, 43
Note taking, for academic reading, 189
Noticing, 38, 39

Objectives for language learning, in Content-Based Instruction, 185–86

Oller, John, 150
OPI. *See* Oral Proficiency Interview
Oral presentations, 238
Oral Proficiency Interview (OPI) [ACTFL], 128, 223–24
Organizations for language teachers, 254
Ortega, Lourdes, 46
Outlining, 157, 163–65, 168
Output, in Output Hypothesis, 38
Output Hypothesis, 38–40
  on academic writing, 190
  concepts in, 38
  on Content-Based Instruction, 180
  on errors, 112
  on lesson planning, 229
  on listening comprehension, 93
  positions on key issues, 50–52
  on speaking, 109
  and task-based instruction, 193
  teaching methods based on, 64–65, 65–66, 69, 70, 72, 73
  on writing, 156, 158
Overgeneralization, 119
Oxford, Rebecca, 16

Pacing, of lesson, 234–35
Pair work, 240
Pappamihiel, Nancy, 11–12, 123
Parameter setting, 29, 30, 48
Passive vocabulary, 239
Pattern drills, 62–63
Pedagogic grammar, 238
Penfield, W., 48
Percentile rankings, 220
Performance tests, 218–19, 222
Peripheral attention, 31, 32
Phonemes, 239
Phonetic alphabets, 138
Phonics-based approaches to reading, 135, 137
Phonology, 58
Phrase boundaries, recognition of
  activities for, 92, 93, 94, 99–100
  as listening ability stage, 92

Piaget, Jean, 18–19
Placement tests, 220
Planning blocks, 233
Playground language. *See* Basic Interpersonal Communication Skills (BICS)
Portfolios, 174–75, 200, 219, 222
Positive transfer, 26, 28
Pre-reading, 140, 149, 189
Pre-writing strategies, 157, 163, 168
Predictive validity, of test, 215–16, 222
Prereading questions, 230, 231
Presentations, oral, 238
Previewing
  in listening, 86, 92
  in reading, 139, 143
Private speech, 44, 46–47
Procedural memory, 198
Process view
  of listening comprehension, 91–95
  of speaking, 117–20
Processing, controlled and automatic, 31, 32
Productive skills, 156, 225
Professional development, 253–54
Professional journals, 253–54
Professional organizations, 254
Proficiency-Oriented instruction, 70–71
Psychological distance, 40, 41–42, 44, 52
Puberty, and language learning ability, 48
Publisher-made language tests, 210
Pull-out programs, 5–6
Pushed Output Hypothesis. *See* Output Hypothesis

Questions
  display, 113
  guide, 169
  inference, 86, 104, 144, 149–50
  personalization of, 238

in reading instruction, 144, 149–50

for writing assignments, 169

Rational deletion cloze passages, 150–51, 218

Readers, graded, 138

Reading in first language
approaches to, 137
assessment of, 188–90

Reading in second language
assessment of, 149–51, 189–90, 224–25
in content classes, 187
cultural issues in, 137, 139, 143
extensive, 134, 136, 147–48
for gist, 136
importance of, 134, 135
intensive, 134, 136, 146–47
to learn, 134, 136, 149, 188
for pleasure, 136
process of, 135–36
as receptive skill, 87
strategies, teaching of, 189
types of, 136
vs. translation, 140, 143

Reading instruction
academic reading, development of, 188–90
activities for, 144–49
approaches to, 137–38
checklist for, 153–54
concepts in, 134–35
in content classes, 188–90
guidelines for, 142–44
individualization of, 144
materials for, 137, 138–39, 142, 149
multimedia approach to, 144
projects for, 153
reading strategies, teaching of, 139–41, 142, 143–44, 189
student expectations, 140–41, 143
teacher expectations, 143

Realia, 138

Recall, in listening, 86

Recall questions, 86, 104

Recasts, 35, 37

Receptive skills, 87, 104, 225

Recognition of isolated words
activities for, 91, 93, 94, 98–99
as listening ability stage, 91

Recognition of phrase boundaries
activities for, 92, 93, 94, 99–100
as listening ability stage, 92

Recognition of target language
activities for, 91, 93, 94, 97–98
as listening ability stage, 91

Recombinations, for listening, 91

Recycling, of language objective, 187

Redundancy
in reading materials, 139
reduced, in speaking, 117

Registers, of language, 115

Reinforcement, 26, 27

Reliability, of testing, 215, 222

Relistening, 92, 96–97, 104

Rereading, 140, 142, 143–44, 149, 189

Revision, of writing, 158, 165, 168, 169

Rivers, Wilga, 136

Roberts, L., 48

Rubrics
in assessment of Content-Based Instruction, 199–200, 201
in assessment of speaking skill, 128–29
in assessment of writing, 173–74, 175
in assessment testing, 222
in integrative testing, 217

Savignon, Sandra, 69, 105, 109, 112

Scaffolding, 35, 36–37
in CLT classroom, 69, 70
in Content-Based Instruction, 180
in content class, 184–85
in SIOP classroom, 73, 75
in sociocultural theories, 46

Scanning, 136, 140, 189
activities for, 144–45

Scenarios for ESL Standards-Based Assessment (TESOL), 221

Schema (schemata), 31

Schumann, John, 41–44, 52

Schwarzer, David, 189–90

Second language acquisition (SLA), 4. See also Language learning; specific topics
in content classes, promotion of, 185–88
eclectic methods of, 55
Five Cs of, 212
listening and, 87
stages in, 118–19
vs. second language learning, 4, 34, 50

Second Language Acquisition (SLA) theories. See also entries for specific theories
cognitive learning theories, 31–33, 40–50
conversation theories, 35–37, 50–52
critical period hypothesis, 47–48
differences on key points, 48–54
experience theories, 33–40, 50–52
first language theories, 26–30, 48–49
Input Hypothesis, 33–35, 50–51
Output Hypothesis, 38–40, 50–52
social theories, 40–44, 52–53
sociocultural theories, 44–47, 53–54

Second language setting, 3, 4

Self-assessment
of content-based learning, 201
as integrative testing, 218
planning to include, 234, 242
with portfolios, 174–75, 219
of speaking skill, 129–30
in standards testing, 222
of writing, 174–75

Self-concepts, development of, 232
Self-direction. *See* Learner autonomy
Self-presentation, authentic, 210
Self-regulation, 45, 46
Self-study
 for professional development, 253
 for TOEFL, 225
Self-talk. *See* Private speech
Sensory mode preference, 12–13
Sheltered English programs, 6
Sheltered Instruction (SI), 6, 73–76
Sheltered Instruction Observation Protocol (SIOP), 73–76, 74f
 and Content-Based Instruction, 185, 186, 187, 194
 on integration of content, 179
 on learning strategies, 197, 241
 on listening, 85
 on reading, 139
 on speaking, 116
Shrum, Judith, 116
SI (Sheltered Instruction), 6, 73–76
Sight vocabulary words, 137
Silent period, 66, 68, 93
Simplified language, in speech instruction, 117, 119–20
Simulated Oral Proficiency Interviews (SOPI), 224
SIOP. *See* Sheltered Instruction Observation Protocol
Skehan, P., 77
Skimming, 136, 140, 189
 activities for, 145–46
Skinner, B. F., 26, 27
Social distance, 41–44
 reading and, 134
 technology and, 256
Social Distance Hypothesis, 41–44, 52–53
Social language. *See* Basic interpersonal communication skills (BICS)

Social theories, 40–44, 52–53
Socio-cognitive theory, 197
Socio-constructivism, 31
Sociocultural theories, 44–47
 concepts in, 44–45
 on Content-Based Instruction, 180
 on errors, 112
 on lesson planning, 229
 on listening comprehension, 85, 93
 positions on key issues, 53–54
 on speaking, 109
 teaching methods based on, 67, 69, 73, 75
 on writing, 156, 158
Sociolinguistic competence, 38, 39
Sound-symbol correspondence, 135
Speaking
 acquisition sequences in, 118–19
 authentic *vs.* display, 112–15
 development, stages of, 117–19
 formulaic expressions in, 117–18, 120
 importance of, 109
 proficiency, as goal, 224
 reduced redundancy in, 117
 simplification of target language, 117
 student anxiety in, 116
Speaking instruction
 for advanced speakers, 127–28
 and anxiety, 116, 122, 123
 assessment in, 116, 128–30
 for beginning speakers, 123–26
 checklist for, 132
 communicative competence as goal of, 109
 concepts in, 110
 errors in, 112, 121
 for intermediate speakers, 126–27
 language learning theories on, 109, 112

 neglect of, 109
 obstacles to, 112–16
 process view, implications of, 119–20
 projects for, 131
 structured *vs.* authentic communication in, 109–10, 110–12
 student beliefs about, 115
 teacher anxiety in, 116
 teacher beliefs about, 115
 true communication, importance of, 110–12
Speaking instruction activities
 examples and ideas for, 123–28
 guidelines for, 120–23
Stand-alone classes, 5
Standardized tests, 210, 216, 223–25
Standards of evaluation, 210–14
 CALLA and, 198
 translating into objectives, 220–22
Strategic learning, 16
Strategy training, 18, 241, 242
Structure drills, 62–63, 238, 239
Structured communication
 definition of, 112
 exercises, 187
 vs. authentic communication, 109–10, 110–12, 119, 120
Structured writing, 158–59
 activities for, 169–70
 guidelines for teaching of, 167–68
Submersion, 6–7
Swain, Merrill, 38–39, 77
Syllabus, design of, 233. *See also* Lesson planning
Syntax, 58

Target language (L2), 7, 26
Target language recognition
 activities for, 91, 93, 94, 97–98
 as listening ability stage, 91
Targeted input, 93
Task(s), in language learning, 77
Task-based activities, 240–41

in assessment, 221
in content classes, 192–93
in lesson planning, 240
Task-Based Language
Instruction, 77, 229
Taylor, Harvey, 91
Teacher Foreign Language
Anxiety Scale (TFLAS),
266–67
Teacher-made tests, 223
Teacher wait time. *See* Wait time
Teachers. *See* Language teachers
Teachers of English to Speakers
of Other Languages
(TESOL), 7, 254
assessment guide of, 221
ESL standards, 210, 211–12,
220–21
Teaching English as a foreign
language (TEFL), 7
Teaching English as a second
language (TESL), 7
Technology
electronic dictionaries, 165
electronic writing, 168
and future of language
teaching, 255–56
language corpora, 165
and reading instruction, 144
and writing instruction,
160–62, 168
TEFL (teaching English as a
foreign language), 7
TESL (teaching English as a
second language), 7
TESOL. *See* Teachers of English
to Speakers of Other
Languages
Test of English as a Foreign
Language (TOEFL), 128,
224–25
Test of English for International
Communication (TOEIC),
225
Test-retest reliability, 215
Testing. *See also* Assessment
achievement, 220
authenticity of, 216–17,
218–19, 222

checklist for, 227
choice of test type, 220
competence-performance
problem in, 214
development of,
considerations for, 220
diagnostic, 220
direct *vs.* indirect, 218
as estimation of ability, 214
fill-in-the blank formats, 218
integrative *vs.* nonintegrative,
217–18
issues in, 214–17
multiple measures, benefits
of, 216
national and international
standardized tests,
223–25
norm- and criterion-
referenced, 220
objectives, development of,
220–22
performance, 218–19
placement, 220
projects, 227
publisher- *vs.* locally-made
tests, 210
purposes of, 220
reliability of, 215, 222
standardized, 210, 216, 223–25
standards for, 210–14, 220–22
teacher-made, 223
validity of, 215–16, 222
washback effect in, 217
Textbook(s)
choice of, 236–37
cultural vignettes in, 239–40
in lesson planning, 232–33
washback effect of, 237
TFLAS (Teacher Foreign
Language Anxiety Scale),
266–67
Thematic units, in content
classes, 192–93
Threshold of language ability,
for reading, 136
TOEFL (Test of English as a
Foreign Language), 128,
224–25

TOEIC (Test of English
for International
Communication), 225
Top-down processing, 90, 135, 137
Total Physical Response (TPR)
method, 65, 66–67
and listening comprehension,
85, 92, 93, 94, 99
TPR Storytelling (TPRS)
method, 65, 66–67, 120
Transfer, negative *vs.* positive,
26, 28
Transition words, and
coherence in writing, 192
Translation
vs. composition, 159, 166, 168
vs. reading, 140, 143
Transnational students, 184
Trotter, R., 10, 11
True communication,
importance of, 110–12
True listening
activities for, 92, 95, 102–3
as stage in listening
comprehension, 92

Universal Grammar Theory,
28–30, 49
Unmarked features, 28, 29

Validity, of test, 215–16, 222
Visual supports, and listening
comprehension, 96
Vocabulary
for academic English, 180
active *vs.* passive, 239
reading and, 136
sight, 137
Vygotsky, Lev, 46

Wait time, 75, 116, 240–41
Warm-up activities, 234
Washback effect, 116, 128, 217,
237
Whole-class activities, 241
Whole-language approaches to
reading, 137
Willingness to communicate
(WTC), 10–11

Willingness to Communicate
Model, 11
Words, isolated, recognition of
activities for, 91, 93, 94, 98–99
as listening ability stage, 91
World languages, 7
Writer's block, 169
Writing. *See also* Academic
writing
coherence of, 192
communicative, 158–59,
167–68, 170
electronic, 168
errors in, 159–60, 167, 168, 169
expressive, 167–68, 171–72
free-expression, 157, 159–60
genres, conventions of, 157–
58, 162–63, 168
group, 168

importance of, 156
process of, 157–58
as productive skill, 156
and revision, 158, 165, 168,
169
structured, 158–59, 167,
169–70
translation *vs.* composition in,
159, 166, 168
types of, 158–63
Writing for specific purposes, 163
Writing instruction
activities for, 169–73
assessment, 173–75, 190–91
checklist for, 177
concepts in, 157
in content class, 190–92
coordinating with content
material, 168

cultural factors in, 158, 166–67
guidelines for, 167–69
language acquisition theories
on, 156
models in, 168
projects for, 176
strategies, teaching of, 163–67
student expectations, 166–67,
168
tailoring to learner goals, 163
teacher expectations, 167
types of writing, 158–63
variety in, 167
WTC (willingness to
communicate), 10–11

Zone of Proximal Development
(ZPD), 44, 46, 47, 54, 110,
118–19